Schopenhauer

'This is a comprehensive, sensible and lucidly presented account
of Schopenhauer's philosophy. The author succeeds in showing
why Schopenhauer still deserves to be studied, but at the same time
he is appropriately critical when discussing Schopenhauer's
doctrines and arguments.'

Severin Schroeder, University of Oxford, UK

Routledge Philosophers

Edited by Brian Leiter
University of Texas, Austin

Routledge Philosophers is a major series of introductions to the great Western philosophers. Each book places a major philosopher or thinker in historical context, explains and assesses their key arguments, and considers their legacy. Additional features include a chronology of major dates and events, chapter summaries, annotated suggestions for further reading and a glossary of technical terms.

An ideal starting-point for those new to philosophy, they are also essential reading for those interested in the subject at any level.

Hobbes	A. P. Martinich
Leibniz	Nicholas Jolley
Locke	E. J. Lowe
Hegel	Frederick Beiser
Rousseau	Nicholas Dent
Schopenhauer	Julian Young
Freud	Jonathan Lear

Forthcoming:

Spinoza	Michael Della Rocca
Hume	Don Garrett
Kant	Paul Guyer
Fichte and Schelling	Sebastian Gardner
Husserl	David Woodruff Smith
Rawls	Samuel Freeman

Julian Young

Schopenhauer

Routledge
Taylor & Francis Group

LONDON AND NEW YORK

First published 2005
2 Park Square, Milton Park, Abingdon, Oxon OX14 4RN

Simultaneously published in the USA and Canada
by Routledge
270 Madison Ave, New York, NY 10016

Routledge is an imprint of the Taylor & Francis Group

Typeset in Joanna MT and Din by
RefineCatch Ltd, Bungay, Suffolk
Printed and bound in Great Britain by
TJ International Ltd, Padstow, Cornwall

British Library Cataloguing in Publication Data
A catalogue record for this book is available from the British Library

Library of Congress Cataloging in Publication Data
Young, Julian.
 Schopenhauer / Julian Young.—1st ed.
  p. cm.—(The Routledge philosophers)
  1. Schopenhauer, Arthur, 1788–1860.   I. Title.   II. Series
 B3148.Y67 2005
 193—dc22   2004017644

ISBN 0-415-33346-6 (hbk)
ISBN 0-415-33347-4 (pbk)

For
Mary Montgomery

Acknowledgements	**xi**
List of abbreviations	**xii**
Chronology	**xiii**
Introduction	**xvi**

Life and Works **One**	**1**
Hamburg	1
Göttingen	3
Berlin	8
Weimar	9
Dresden and Berlin Again	10
Wander-years	12
Frankfurt	13
Summary	16
Further Reading	16

Metaphysics: The World as Representation **Two**	**17**
Partial Versus Radical Idealism	17
Read Kant!	21
Realism as Self-Contradictory	25
Evolutionary Idealism	28
Reason	32
Practical Reason	34
Perception	36
Concepts	39
Intuitive Versus Conceptual Knowledge	42
Criticism of Schopenhauer on Reason and Perception	44
Meaningfulness	46
Observations on Schopenhauer's Criterion of Meaningfulness	48
Summary	52
Further Reading	52

Metaphysics: The World as Will Three 53

Completing the Scientific Image 54
Natural Forces 56
The Nature of Matter 58
The Subjective Versus the Objective Standpoint 60
The Black Box Problem 61
Will as Character 66
Extending the Will 68
Bypassing Solipsism 69
Organic Nature and Teleology 71
Inanimate Nature 74
The World-Will 76
The Platonic Ideas 77
The Influence of Spinoza 78
Nature-Pessimism 79
Can the Will be 'Blind'? 82
Schopenhauer and Darwin 85
Summary 87
Further Reading 88

Metaphysics: Ultimate Reality Four 89

The Early View 89
Qualifications 92
Metaphysics as 'Deciphering' 94
The Possibility of 'Salvation' 98
Summary 101
Further Reading 102

Art Five 103

Schopenhauer Versus Hegel 103
The Question: What is Art? 105

Everyday Consciousness   108
The Aesthetic State   111
Aesthetic Pleasure   113
The Sublime   115
The Lyrical   120
Criticism of Schopenhauer on the Sublime and the Lyrical   124
The Possibility of Genius   125
Summary   127
Further Reading   128

Art (continued)   Six   129

The Platonic Ideas   129
Art and Knowledge   133
The Beautiful   135
Art and Philosophy   136
Tragedy and the Value of Art   142
A Criticism of Schopenhauer's Philosophy of Art   145
Music   150
The Problem of Opera   153
Summary   156
Further Reading   157

Ethics   Seven   158

Can Philosophy Change Your Life?   158
Freedom and Character   160
Is Philosophy 'Dead'?   165
Death and Immortality   168
Egoism   173
Malice   175
Altruism   178
The Metaphysics of Virtue   180

Criticism of Schopenhauer's Moral Philosophy 181
Summary 187
Further Reading 187

Salvation Eight **188**

Denial of the Will 188
Denial of the Will and the Unalterability of Character 192
Suicide 194
Salvation 195
Pessimism 206
Summary 219
Further Reading 220

Schopenhauer's Influence and Legacy Nine **221**

Schopenhauer and the Philosophers 221
Schopenhauer and the Artists 234
Schopenhauer and Freud 238
Schopenhauer and Evolutionary Views of Man 241
Schopenhauer and Us 245
Summary 245
Further Reading 246

Notes 247
Bibliography 265
Index 268

Acknowledgements

I should like to thank those who took part in my Auckland graduate seminar in the first semester of 2003 for a stimulating discussion of the substance of this book: in particular, Brignal Woods, Melanie Dougan, Tim MacKenzie and Mathias Mickl. Thanks are also due to my editor, Tony Bruce, and to the Routledge Philosophers series editor, Brian Leiter, for useful suggestions as to the structure of the work. The two (anonymous) readers of the manuscript saved me from various errors.

I am grateful, too, to the Deutscher Akademischer Austausch-dienst and to the University of Auckland for research grants which enabled me to visit the Schopenhauer Archive in Frankfurt am Main and to benefit from discussions with German colleagues in Bonn and Lüneburg.

Finally I should like to thank Günter Seubold and Christoph Jamme for those helpful and enjoyable discussions.

Abbreviations

The *World as Will and Representation*, vols I and II — WR I, WR II
The *Fourfold Root of the Principle of Sufficient Reason* — FR
On the *Will in Nature* — WN
On the *Basis of Morality* — BM
On the *Freedom of the Will* — FW
Parerga and Paralipomena — vols I and II — PP I, PP II
Manuscript Remains vols I–IV — MR 1–4

1632	Spinoza born (dies 1677)
	Locke born (dies 1704)
1685	Berkeley born (dies 1753)
1717	Hume born (dies 1776)
1724	Kant born (dies 1804)
1749	Goethe born (dies 1832)
1762	Fichte born (dies 1814)
1770	Hegel born (dies 1831)
1775	Schelling born (dies 1854)
1781	Kant's *Critique of Pure Reason* appears.
1788	Arthur Schopenhauer is born.
1793	The Schopenhauer family move to Hamburg.
1797	Schopenhauer travels to Paris and Le Havre with his father.
	Stays two years in Le Havre with family of business associate of his father.
1803–4	Grand tour of Holland, England, France, Switzerland, Austria.
1804	Apprenticed to merchant Kabrun in Danzig.
1805	Apprenticed to merchant Jenisch in Hamburg.
	Apparent suicide of his father.
1806	Mother moves to Weimar. Goethe starts to visit her tea parties.
1807	Studies at grammar school in Gotha to obtain university entrance.

1809–11	University studies at Göttingen: natural science, Plato, Kant.
1811–13	University studies in Berlin. Attends lectures by Fichte, Schleiermacher, Wolf.
1813	Flees Berlin on account of war. Short stay in Weimar. Quarrels with mother, moves to nearby Rudolstadt where he writes his Ph. D. dissertation *On the Fourfold Root of the Principle of Sufficient Reason*. Conversation with Goethe in mother's house concerning theory of colours. Richard Wagner born (dies 1883).
1814	Schopenhauer's final break with mother. Leaves Weimar for Dresden.
1815	*On Seeing and Colours*. Draft of first version of *World as Will and Representation*.
1818	*World as Will and Representation* published (though with '1819' on title page). Leaves Dresden for Italy.
1820	Lectures in Berlin. Hardly anyone turns up.
1821	Falls in love with singer Caroline Médon. Beginning of the 'Marquet affair' (assault on seamstress and suit for damages).
1823–33	Lives in Italy, Munich, Frankfurt, Mannheim, Dresden, Bad Gastein and Berlin. Tries and fails to establish himself as a translator. Illness, depression.
1833	Settles in Frankfurt, where he remains until the end of his life.
1835	*On the Will in Nature*
1839	Competition essay 'On the Freedom of the Will' wins first prize.
1840	Competition essay 'On the Basis of Morality' not awarded the prize even though only entry. Rude remarks about Hegel upset Hegelian judges.
1844	Second edition of *World as Will and Representation* appears, amplified by a second volume. Nietzsche born (dies 1900)

1851   *Parerga and Paralipomena* appears.

1853   Beginning of Schopenhauer's fame.

1856   Sigmund Freud born (dies 1939).

1859   Third edition of *World as Will and Representation*. Darwin's
        On the Origin of Species by means of Natural Selection appears.

1860   Schopenhauer dies.

1872   Nietzsche's first book *The Birth of Tragedy* appears.

1889   Nietzsche goes mad. Wittgenstein born (dies 1951).
        Heidegger born (dies 1976).

1895   Max Horkheimer born (dies 1973).

Introduction

This is a book written primarily, though not exclusively, for those coming to Schopenhauer for the first time. It aims to introduce the reader to Schopenhauer's thought as a whole and, particularly in the final chapter, to convey a sense of its lasting importance.

By the generous standards of nineteenth-century German philosophy, Schopenhauer's is short and to the point. He only wrote one work of systematic philosophy, *The World as Will and Representation*. To master this is to master the totality of his philosophy. (Admittedly this involves mastering, in English translation, 1221 pages.)

In its final version, *The World as Will* consists of two volumes. The first, the substance of which appeared in 1818, is divided into four books. The second, added in 1844, comprises four 'Supplements' to each of the four books of volume I. Usually, though not universally, the supplements are, as Schopenhauer claims, expansions rather than corrections of the ideas of the corresponding book in volume I. My book closely follows the fourfold structure of Schopenhauer's great work, a work Thomas Mann described as a symphony in four movements.

Book I, together with its supplement – the topic of my Chapter 2 – argues that the world of everyday experience is 'representation', merely; that it is only an 'appearance' or 'phenomenon' of reality, not reality itself. Book II – the topic of my chapters 3 and 4 – pursues the interesting topic of what that reality is which underlies the everyday world. Schopenhauer's master-word is 'will'. The metaphysical – meta-physical – essence of things is 'will'. Unfortunately, this turns out to be a depressing discovery, since, like Buddhism, a religion that greatly impressed him, Schopenhauer sees will as inextricably tied to suffering. The third book – the topic of my chapters 5 and 6 – discovers in art a partial escape from the world of suffering. And the final book – the topic of my chapters 7 and 8 – discovers in love, but finally in mystical asceticism, a permanent escape from the will and hence from suffering.

Schopenhauer wrote a number of satellite works which deal with localised regions of the synoptic vision presented in *The World as Will*. *On the Fourfold Root of the Principle of Sufficient Reason* (1813), his Ph.D. thesis, deals with the issues discussed in Book I, *On the Will in Nature* (1836) with those of Book II, while *On the Freedom of the Will* (1839) and *On the Basis of Morality* (1840) relate to the issues of Book IV. Schopenhauer's final book *Parerga and Paralipomena* (1851) is a collection of essays only some of which relate to his systematic concerns. ('On Din and Noise', for example, seeks to prove that all geniuses have been ultra-sensitive to noise pollution.) I have integrated my discussion of all of these works into the discussion of the main work at the appropriate places.

Wilfred Sellars, the teacher from whom I first gained an inkling of what philosophy really was, once said that to be able to criticise a philosophy you must first love it. This book attempts a judicious balance.

One

Life and Works

Theodor Adorno calls him 'peevish' and 'malicious',[1] Bertrand Russell 'shallow' and 'not very sincere'.[2] To Iris Murdoch, on the other hand, he is 'merry', 'sincere' and 'generous'.[3] Who, in fact, was Arthur Schopenhauer?

HAMBURG

He was born in the port city of Danzig (now Gdansk) in 1788, but was brought up in Hamburg. In his parents he could have scarcely have been less fortunate. His father, though wealthy, cultured and cosmopolitan, was a depressive who, in 1805, jumped to his death from the attic of his house, leaving behind a traumatised son. His mother, Joanna, a writer of sentimental popular novels, combined frivolity and selfishness in a way that led one acquaintance to describe her as possessing neither heart not soul.

Unsurprisingly, her marriage of convenience to a much older man was loveless. Though Arthur's arrival gave her the brief pleasure of, as she put it, 'playing with my new doll', she soon became bored, and resented the way his presence cramped her lifestyle. Adolescence did not improve relations between mother and son. More than usually alive to the pain and wickedness of life, Schopenhauer's no doubt inherited tendency to, as Johanna put it, 'brood on the misery of things' depressed her.

Schopenhauer was born, then, into a place without warmth or security. He records an occasion when, his parents having left the house, he experienced extreme anxiety that they would never return. Anxiety remained with him all his life: 'I always', he remarks with characteristic honesty, have an anxious concern that causes me to look for dangers when none exists' (MR 4: 507).

Schopenhauer was often gruff and did not suffer fools gladly. But unlike Friedrich Nietzsche, whose philosophy is dominated by his love–hate relationship with Schopenhauer, he was by no means unsociable. Conversation was one of his greatest pleasures. Yet since anxiety, watchfulness, precludes the trust necessary to close relationships, it is unsurprising that his life contained no really deep friendships. In a famous parable, he offers an account of human sociability which naturally tells us a great deal about its author. One cold winter's day, Schopenhauer writes, a number of porcupines huddled together quite closely

> in order through their mutual warmth to prevent themselves from being frozen. But they soon felt the effect of their quills on one another, which made them again move apart. Now when the need for warmth once more brought them together, the drawback of the quills was repeated so that they were tossed between two evils, until they discovered the proper distance from which they could best tolerate one another. Thus the need for society which springs from the emptiness and monotony of men's lives drives them together; but their many unpleasant and repulsive qualities and insufferable drawbacks once more drives them apart. The mean distance which they finally discover, and which enables them to endure being together, is politeness and good manners. Whoever does not keep to this is told in England to 'keep his distance'
>
> (PP II: 651–2).

Schopenhauer clearly had a powerful sex drive – as we will see, he views sex as 'the invisible centre point of all action and conduct (WR II: 513). But his sexual relations were consistently unsuccessful. The women he was disposed to love would not sleep with him, and the women who would sleep with him – whores and actresses – he did not love. The one exception is the actress-singer Caroline

Médon, with whom he had an on-off affair throughout the 1820s. Though he had a genuine and lasting affection for her – he remembered her in his will even though their contact had ceased many years before his death – his habit of distrust prevented him committing himself to the marriage he sometimes contemplated.

* * *

Parents, as Philip Larkin famously observed (in somewhat racier language), screw you up. And Schopenhauer's philosophy with, at its heart, we will see, the assertion that life is a painful 'error' from which we need to be 'saved', may well seem the product of a distressed childhood. In fact, I think, there is little doubt that it is. Had he been the offspring of different parents he would have written a different philosophy – or, more probably, no philosophy at all. The actual homelessness of his childhood is reflected in the metaphysical homelessness (and homesickness) of his philosophy.

This being said, it is important also to emphasise that the facts of Schopenhauer's life, of themselves, do nothing to bring into doubt the truth of his philosophy. For, as we shall see, he presents an array of insightful and substantial *arguments* for his pessimistic account of the human condition and it is upon these that his philosophy stands or falls. The facts of his life bear on the origin of his ideas but not on their validity.

GÖTTINGEN

Let us fast-forward; past Schopenhauer's early schooldays, past his two-year stay in France in 1797–9, past his grand tour of Europe in 1803–4 and past his unhappy commercial apprenticeships of 1804–7 undertaken out of respect for his father's wishes. Let us fast-forward to his final escape from the world of commerce and to his arrival at the University of Göttingen in 1809.

Schopenhauer spent his first year at Göttingen studying natural science. This, however, was by no means incompatible with his philosophical inclinations since, as we will see in chapter 3, he regards science as 'the corrected statement of the problem of metaphysics' (WR II: 178). In Schopenhauer's view, only a substantial grounding in science allows one even to *begin* as a philosopher.

Schopenhauer remained fascinated by natural science, and kept abreast of new developments all his life. Unlike most members of the Romantic movement with whom he otherwise has many affinities, he is not at all hostile to science – providing, as we shall see, it recognises that, at the most fundamental level, it can only complete itself by becoming philosophy. There is, as Nietzsche remarks, much science in Schopenhauer.

In his second and final year at Göttingen, Schopenhauer turned to philosophy proper. The philosophers he admired above all others were Plato and Kant. The quality of his relationship to the one, however, was very different from that of his relationship to the other.

* * *

Schopenhauer admired Kant as a supreme theoretician. (As a surveyor of the human heart, on the other hand, he regards him as fatally crippled by a lack of contact with the 'real' world, by a life spent in lecture theatres.) The *Critique of Pure Reason* (1781) is a source of so many fundamental and 'incontestable' theoretical truths as to make Kant's name indisputably 'immortal' (WR I: 437).

'Kant's greatest merit', Schopenhauer writes, 'is the distinction of the phenomenon from the thing in itself, based on the proof that between things and us there always stands the intellect' (WR I: 417). Kant's central achievement, in other words, was to show that rather than being a blank sheet on which reality simply stamps its character, the knowing mind is *active*, actively engaged in constructing intelligibility out of unintelligibility, consciousness out of sensations. From this it follows, Schopenhauer takes Kant to have shown, that the world of everyday experience, indeed the whole space-time world of 'nature', is 'appearance' or 'phenomenon', merely, utterly distinct from reality as such, from the 'thing in itself'.

What, then, Schopenhauer took from Kant is the conviction that the natural world is, in philosophers' jargon, 'ideal' rather than 'real'. ('Ideal' is confusing. Think of it in connection with 'idea' rather than 'perfection'.) To read and understand Kant's proofs of idealism, he says, produces a change so fundamental as to amount to an 'intellectual rebirth', an overcoming of that 'inborn realism which arises from the original disposition of the intellect' (WR I: xxiii). As we will see in the next chapter, Schopenhauer regards the human mind as an evolutionary product of the struggle for survival. From this point of view, 'realism' *has* to be built into the intellect. Creatures with a disposition to sit around doubting the reality of the tiger bearing down on them are likely to come to a tragic end before reproducing their kind.

If the space-time world is ideal, a mere construction of our minds, what is reality – *real* reality – like? Kant's frustrating answer (frustrating at least to his immediate successors) is that this question can never be answered. To know reality as it is 'in itself' we would have to possess what he calls 'intellectual intuition'. We would have to be capable of a direct encounter with the 'thing in itself', an encounter which bypassed the world-fabricating, 'story'-telling, activity of the mind. But as *human* beings, says Kant, intellectual intuition is something of which we are incapable. Only God has intellectual intuition – or would have if he existed. (Whether God exists is, for Kant, precisely one of those questions about ultimate reality we can never answer.)

Schopenhauer says that Kant's writings are illuminated by a 'brilliant dryness' (WR I: 428). But his own spirit was far from dry. It was flooded by a passionate yearning that there be 'something more'; something more than this mundane world which, already as a teenager, he perceived to be a place of pain, horror and boredom. This metaphysical homesickness, this yearning for, as Nietzsche would later call it, a 'true world' above and beyond this one, is what constitutes his spiritual affinity with Plato. Whereas he relates to

Kant as a theoretician, he relates to Plato as an existential philosopher.

* * *

Like Schopenhauer, Plato (about 428–347 BC) found the everyday world an unpleasant place in which to find oneself, and like Kant he found it to be less than fully real. In the *Republic* he propounds the famous simile of the cave. Our everyday conception of reality, he suggests, is like that of prisoners in a cave chained in such a way that they can only look at the play of shadows on the wall in front of them, the shadows being cast by objects behind their backs illuminated by a fire. Taking the 'virtual' objects on the screen in front of them to be reality itself (like the inhabitants of *The Matrix*) they do not even guess the existence of the objects and the fire behind their backs. And of the *truly* real world beyond the cave and of the sun which illuminates it, they have no inkling at all.

Truly real objects are, for Plato, what he calls the 'Forms' or 'Ideas'. These are the perfect originals of which the shadow-casting objects of the cave are, even at their best, imperfect copies. So the form of the mountain, for example, is a perfect, perfectly beautiful, mountain. The 'sun' which illuminates the world of the Forms corresponds to 'the good'. Plato is convinced that the world of the Forms is ordered and illuminated by a divine benevolence.

Unlike Kant, Plato held that access to the 'true world' was possible – not for the multitude of ordinary 'prisoners' of the shadow world, but for the enlightened few, the lovers of the Forms, the authentic 'philosophers'. In the *Phaedrus*, a work influenced, as Schopenhauer was to be a couple of millennia later, by Eastern thinking, he suggests that while ordinary people are condemned to perpetual reincarnation, the enlightened one can escape the cycle of rebirth and achieve permanent dwelling in a world beyond change and pain.

All this produced a powerful resonance in Schopenhauer. Already as a teenager (like Nietzsche) he loved mountain tops, especially at dawn. Climbing the Chapeau near Chamonix when he was sixteen, he records in his diary the 'indescribably wonderful imprint' of 'the enormity of nature', a nature that is 'no longer ordinary nature but has stepped out of its bounds [so that] one feels closer to it' (*Reisetagebücher aus den Jahren 1803 bis 1804*, p. 186). Already as a teenager, that is, Schopenhauer sought and sometimes achieved *ecstasy*: Latin: *ex-stasis*, standing out of, transcendence, transcendence of ordinary consciousness, absorption into a higher plane of reality. By 1813 Platonic transcendence has begun to dominate his philosophical notebook as the notion of a 'better consciousness':

> personality and causality exist in this temporal, sensory, comprehensible world. But the better consciousness within me lifts me up into a world where neither personality, nor subject not object, exist any more
>
> (MR 1: 44).

It is very important to see that the idea of Platonic ecstasy, of a 'better consciousness' that transports us to a 'true world', belonged to Schopenhauer's philosophical thinking from the very beginning. As we will see in chapter 8, his mature philosophy ends with an affirmation of the possibility of 'salvation', hinted at by art but achieved only through the will-'denial' of the mystical ascetic. Many interpreters follow Bertrand Russell in viewing Schopenhauer's 'salvation' as a last-minute failure of nerve; an 'insincere' twist stuck on to the end of a work whose true conclusion is bleak despair. In fact, however, the idea of ecstatic access to a Platonic domain belonged to the heart of Schopenhauer's thinking from the very beginning. This is why Iris Murdoch (one of Schopenhauer's greatest admirers and best readers) is right in saying that, though he totally rejects traditional Christian theology, Schopenhauer's fundamental concerns are, in a broad sense of the term, 'religious', and that 'his religious passion is sincere' (op. cit: 72, 62). Like all of us who are troubled by evil, pain and death, Schopenhauer was always intensely focused on the 'something more'.

BERLIN

In 1811 Schopenhauer moved from Göttingen to Berlin in order to attend the lectures of Johann Fichte, then at the height of his fame. Like all of Kant's immediate successors, the so-called 'German idealists', such as Jacobi, Schelling and Hegel, Fichte refused to accept the unknowability of the thing in itself. Not only did he claim to have the 'intellectual intuition' necessary to know it, he claimed to be able to capture it in concepts, to describe it in the sober medium of philosophical prose. (What Fichte's contemplation of 'the Absolute'[4] delivered were three fundamental principles: 'The ego posits itself', 'The ego posits the non-ego' and 'The ego posits a limited ego in opposition to a limited non-ego'. Quite evidently, understanding Fichte's philosophy is no easy matter.)

Schopenhauer was bitterly disappointed by Fichte's lectures. The frustrated complaint, recorded over and over again in the lecture notes he struggled to compile, is simple: Fichte's flights of conceptual fancy are unintelligible, 'lunatic babbling', 'raving nonsense', (MR 2: 134). Eventually, frustration gives way to satire. When Fichte reports that 'the Ego seats itself' Schopenhauer draws a picture of a chair. When Fichte reports that 'the Ego is not clarified by anything else', Schopenhauer comments: 'As today he only supplied the pure light but no taper [to light it with] these notes could not be continued' (MR 2: 211).

It is important to take note of the fact that Schopenhauer's objections to Fichte's pretentious obsurantism appear early in his life. After it became clear that he was not going to obtain a paid university position, Schopenhauer's writings start to overflow with frenetic abuse of the 'professors of philosophy' – Fichte, Hegel et al. The central objection is always to the mud-like unintelligibility of their prose. Expressing the sentiment – to which he always adheres in his own wonderfully lucid writing – that authentic philosophical writing should, like a Swiss lake, reveal its depth precisely through its clarity, Schopenhauer asserts as a fundamental principle that 'clarity is the good faith of philosophers' (FR: 4). It is this principle which he uses to convict Fichte and company, not just of ugly obscurantism, but of intellectual dishonesty. Since this is often put down to mere jealousy of those who managed to get paid to philosophise, it is important to see that the objection appeared long before personal disappointment could play any role.

Another reason it is important to take note of Schopenhauer's early dislike of Fichte is that his philosophy is sometimes dismissed as little more than reheated Fichtianism. Given the actual character of his encounter with Fichte, this is inherently implausible.

WEIMAR

In May of 1813 Schopenhauer left Berlin for Weimar, a town dominated by the figure of Johann Goethe. A universal man – lover of many women, scientist, politician, civil servant, poet and playwright of the highest genius, as well as being a person who inspired deep affection – Goethe had become, as a result of his novel The Sorrows of Young Werther, the first European superstar. When the novel appeared Europe was swept by a wave of suicides imitating the fate of its hero.

Joanna Schopenhauer had lived in Weimar since 1806, conducting a regular salon visited by the great and the good, including Goethe himself. Though the deterioration of his never-good relations with his mother made it prudent to withdraw to nearby Rudolstadt, Schopenhauer attended his mother's tea parties, where he met Goethe and for a short time collaborated with him on his anti-Newtonian theory of colours. This led, in 1815, to Schopenhauer's own On Seeing and Colours. Though the topic was relatively peripheral to the main line of his thinking, Schopenhauer was greatly flattered by the attention of the great man. Goethe is one of the few figures of his age for whom he never has a bad word. (The same is true of Nietzsche.)

A more philosophically significant encounter in his mother's salon was with the orientalist F. J. Majer, who, in 1813, introduced him to the Upanishads. Though Schopenhauer employs the phrase 'veil of Maya' taken from Hindu metaphysics in the first (1818) version of the main work, it was not however until after its appearance that his serious concern with Buddhism – which he came to regard as the greatest of all religions – began. That it took him some time to fully appropriate what he really wanted from Eastern thought helps explain, as we will see, certain changes that took place in the development of his philosophy.

While at Rudolstadt Schopenhauer completed his Ph. D. dissertation, *The Fourfold Root of the Principle of Sufficient Reason*, which was published in 1813. This is a technical, purely theoretical work devoted to simplifying the complicated machinery which Kant had postulated as the mind's method of transforming sensory input into intelligible output. According to Schopenhauer's (not, I think, very plausible) argument, all the mind ever does is to apply one of the, as he sees it, four forms of the principle that everything has a reason for being as it is. Though he always insisted that the work should be read as an introduction to *The World as Will*, it in fact contains hardly a hint of the vast imaginative construction that was soon to follow.

DRESDEN AND BERLIN AGAIN

After a final break with his mother, Schopenhauer spent the years 1814–18 in Dresden. This was the period of the most intense and sustained creativity of his entire life. What gave birth to it was that he thought he had cracked the problem of the 'thing in itself'. As he wrote in a note of 1815, it seemed to him he had made the revolutionary discovery that 'the will is Kant's thing in itself' (MR 1: 319). With the inspirational excitement of seeming to have solved the problem that preoccupied all his contemporaries – an excitement akin, perhaps, to Watson and Crick's excitement at beating everyone else to the discovery of the structure of DNA – the whole vast edifice of the first edition of *The World as Will* poured from his pen. Though he considered himself a good Kantian, and was, during the same period, criticising Schelling for claiming to know what Kant had shown to be unknowable, the nature of the thing in itself

(MR 2: 358–60), he does not seem to have been unduly troubled by the appearance that he was doing exactly the same thing himself. And neither does he at this stage seem to have been unduly troubled by the thought that the will, as the creative ground of a world of suffering, must itself be fundamentally evil – an account of ultimate reality hardly conducive to the admission of a realm of 'salvation' accessible to a 'better consciousness'.

Seeming to have solved the fundamental problem of philosophy, Schopenhauer decided, in 1820, to let the world know about it. The venue was the University of Berlin where he obtained the right to lecture. Deciding on a clash of Titans, he deliberately timetabled his lectures to coincide with Hegel's. The result was a fiasco. While over two hundred people listened to Hegel, almost no one turned up for Schopenhauer.

Given Schopenhauer's acumen in other fields – finance, character assessment and self-analysis, for example – his challenge to Hegel exhibited a strange naivety. For Hegel, then at the height of his power and influence, was the philosopher for the times. He was popular with the Prussian upper and middle classes because he digested for them the still uneasily remembered events of the French Revolution (1789) and the 'Terror' that followed. His telling of the history of the West as an inexorable, 'dialectical' process of self-education whereby the 'Absolute Spirit' embodied in human society proceeds from the primitive to the perfect, affirmed the shattering events of the Revolution yet, at the same time, endorsed the authoritarianism of the Prussian state as a still higher state of perfection. All, it seemed, was working towards the best in the best of all possible worlds. And though Hegel's notion of Absolute Spirit might not be exactly the transcendent God of traditional theology, its proximity to God's benevolent hand was close enough to keep both state and ecclesiastical authorities happy. (Since the Prussian king's legitimacy rested on the idea of 'divine right', his direct appointment by God, he was distinctly averse to the raising of doubts about God's existence.) In general, therefore, Hegel's philosophy was well calculated to appeal to an age of authoritarian complacency.

Schopenhauer, by contrast, with his assertion that, in Hegel's sense, 'history' doesn't exist, that life is – essentially, always and equally – suffering, his replacement of intelligent 'Spirit' with 'blind', irrational 'will', was thoroughly out of tune with the times. Had he scented the air even a little, he would not have dreamt of timetabling his lectures as he did.

WANDER-YEARS

The next decade of Schopenhauer's life was a period of frequent depression. Partly this was on account of the Berlin fiasco, partly on account of the deafening silence that had greeted the appearance of *The World as Will*, and partly on account of physical illness. It is permissible, however, suspect a cause deeper than any of these.

Like many great writers Schopenhauer felt that writing, rather than being something he *did*, was what he *was*. 'Who am I really?' he asks himself in a private note, and answers, 'He who wrote *The World as Will and Representation* and provided a solution to the great problem of existence' (MR 4: 488). But, as it seemed to him in the early 1820s, his work was not merely neglected, it was over, completed. So, therefore, was his life. One may suspect, in other words, that for most of the 1820s Schopenhauer inhabited every creative writer's greatest nightmare – the thought that he had nothing more to say. Thus 1825 find him attempting (unsuccessfully) to establish himself as a translator of other people's works – an indication that he had nothing of his own left to say but wished, nonetheless, to continue with the motions of writing.

The previous year Schopenhauer had recorded in his pocket book the following: '*to recognise* [give a name to] the *thing in itself* is a contradiction, because all cognition is [mind-processed] *representation*, whereas the thing in itself means the thing to the extent it is *not*' (MR 3: 195). Since everything that comes before the mind is processed by the mind, we can only ever know – Kant's point – how the world *appears*, never how it is in itself. When one compares this to the confident assertion of 1815 that 'the will is Kant's *thing in itself*' one sees an additional cause for Schopenhauer's depression: not only was his life's work over, it was a fundamental *error*. If the thing in itself cannot be known, it cannot be known, in particular, to be will. The great inspiration was a great delusion.

As he reflected on this, however, one can imagine Schopenhauer's mood slowly lightening. If the claim that the will is the thing in itself is, in fact, illegitimate, then there is, after all, work still to be done. Gradually, one can imagine, Schopenhauer recovered the will to work, the will to philosophise, once again.

FRANKFURT

In 1833 Schopenhauer's somewhat peripatetic existence came to an end when he settled in Frankfurt on the Main, where he remained for the final twenty-seven years of his life. This seems to have provided him with the secure and regular existence he needed. (Productivity as a writer generally requires a routine, even boring, life.) In 1836 he produced On the Will in Nature, 'A Discussion', as the subtitle put it, 'of the Confirmations which the Author's Philosophy has received from the Empirical Sciences since its Publication'. In 1839 he won first prize in a competition set by the Norwegian Royal Scientific Society with his essay On the Freedom of the Will, but the following year failed to win the prize set by the corresponding Danish society with his On the Basis of Morality – even though his was the only entry. This was largely because the judges, mostly ardent Hegelians, took exception to the essay's extreme rudeness about their master. Both essays are excellent presentations of particular regions of the grand philosophical scheme.

Most significantly, however, Schopenhauer produced, in 1844, a new version of The World as Will. This consisted of a revised version of the 1818 edition plus a second volume of the work that is in fact longer than (what now became) the work's first volume.

One of the received opinions about Schopenhauer is that he had worked out his entire philosophy by 1818 and thereafter never changed his mind. The chief source of this view is Schopenhauer himself, who insists in the 1844 preface to the expanded work that there is no change of substance, only of 'tone' and 'method of presentation', between the first and second editions (WR I: xxii).

On the whole, this claim is justified. In the main, the four component parts of the second volume genuinely are, as he calls them, 'supplements' to, rather than revisions of, the four books of volume I. There is, however, one significant exception to this, and it is absolutely fundamental. It concerns the status of the 'will'. One only has to set 1815's 'the *will* is Kant's *thing in itself*' against 1824's '*to recognise* the *thing in itself* is a contradiction' to see that a profound change is occurring at the very foundations of Schopenhauer's metaphysics. (The change that eventually results is, as we shall see, of some subtlety. Schopenhauer never abandons the *formula* 'the will is the thing in itself'. The change consists, rather, in the fact that by 1844 the *meaning* of the formula has become crucially different from what it had been in 1818.[5])

The crucial revision to the claim that the will is the thing in itself is carried out, as we shall see, in Chapter 18 of volume II, appropriately entitled 'On the Possibility of knowing the Thing in itself'. Quietly – and in formal contradiction of the claim that only changes in 'tone' distinguish the second from the first edition – the 1844 preface recognises this fact. There are occasions, he reluctantly concedes, when 'maturity' has provided 'correction' to the impetuous 'fire' of youth (WR I: xxii).

* * *

In 1851 Schopenhauer published *Parerga and Paralipomena*, which means 'complementary works and matters omitted', a collection of essays on topics as diverse as women, noise, suicide and fame. It also contained a set of 'Aphorisms on the Wisdom of Life', a collection of wise and witty observations on the art of conducting one's life as successfully as possible. *Parerga*, which pushes Schopenhauer's systematic philosophy, and particularly his pessimism, into the background, made him famous. After a lifetime of obscurity the last few years of his life saw him rapidly becoming the most famous German philosopher after Kant. His 'Aphorisms' became an ornament essential to every middle-class coffee table. Wagner and the youthful Nietzsche were drawn together by their mutual enthusiasm for Schopenhauer. (The former sent him a copy of his libretto for the *Ring* cycle to which, however, Schopenhauer responded by advising him to give up music and stick to poetry.) The University of Leipzig set up a course to interpret his philosophy, famous people came to visit him. To one of them, the poet Friedrich Hebbel, sensing the end of his life approaching, Schopenhauer described his feelings about his sudden fame. 'I feel', he told Hebbel,

> strange to my present fame. No doubt you will have seem how, before a performance, as the house-lights are extinguished and the curtain rises, a solitary lamplighter is still busy with the footlights and then hurriedly scampers off into the wings – just as the curtain goes up. This is how I feel: a latecomer, a leftover, just as the comedy of my fame is beginning
>
> (*Gespräche*: 380).

Schopenhauer was undoubtedly an often difficult person: rude, satirical, quarrelsome, sometimes depressed. On the other hand he is observant, funny, original, writes like an angel and is, as Iris Murdoch remarks, in his own way 'merry', '*fascinated* by the world and its bright diversity' (op. cit.: 62). He is, moreover, sharp-sighted and honest, honest with the reader, honest, in particular, about himself. Virtually all of the discreditable character traits and episodes in his life (his neurotic anxiety, his incapacity for friendship, his throwing of a noisy seamstress down a flight of stairs) we know from his own pen. Beneath the grim exterior of man and philosophy is someone for whom a surprising number of people (including this writer) experience considerable affection.

SUMMARY

Family background. Education at Göttingen and Berlin. Chief influences: Kant and Plato. Yearning for a 'better consciousness'. Takes himself to have 'solved' the problem of the 'thing in itself'. Settles in Frankfurt. Realises that after all he has not solved the problem of the 'thing in itself' and writes second volume to The World as Will and Representation. Becomes famous shortly before his death. Schopenhauer's personality described.

FURTHER READING

R. Safranski, Schopenhauer and the Wild Years of Philosophy.
D. Cartwright, Schopenhauer: A Biography.

Two

Metaphysics: The World as Representation

PARTIAL VERSUS RADICAL IDEALISM

In the first book of *The World as Will* (which, together with allied works, is the topic of this chapter) Schopenhauer says that the problem of philosophy is to say 'what' the world is. (WR I: 82). Sometimes he says that it is to solve the 'riddle' (*Rätsel*) of what the world is. Given the rootedness of this word in German folk tales where solving a 'riddle' is often a matter of life and death, this suggests that an answer to the question, rather than merely satisfying the curiosity of armchair investigators, will have existential implications, will have an effect on our lives.

Interestingly, in Book III, he says that the stance of art differs from the everyday stance to the world in that, in this stance, 'we no longer consider the where, the when, the why and the whither in things but simply and solely the what' (WR I: 178). This indicates that we are going to discover a strong affinity between art and philosophy, between *Dichten and Denken* (poetry and thought).

Why should the 'whatness' of the world be a *problem*? Why can't we just look and see? Because, in a word, of Kant.

For Schopenhauer, as we noted, Kant's 'greatest merit' is his 'proof' that since 'between things and us there always stands the intellect' (the 'veil of Maya' as the *Upanishads* calls it), that which is accessible to us in everyday experience is 'appearance' or 'phenomenon', merely, not the 'thing in itself'. In some way, then, the things of everyday experience are 'ideal', not, or at least not fully, real. This is why we cannot discover the whatness of things by just looking. The whatness of the world is in some sense 'beyond' what we can look at.

* * *

What exactly is it that Schopenhauer claims, and claims Kant to claim, to be 'mere appearance'?[1] As he recognises, idealism comes in two basic forms, forms which I shall refer to, respectively, as partial and radical idealism. Partial idealism concerns the way a material object appears to us, radical idealism concerns the object itself.

John Locke, for whom Schopenhauer has a great deal of admiration, is a partial idealist. He draws a fundamental distinction between, as he calls them, 'primary' and 'secondary qualities': secondary qualities are things like colours, tastes, sounds and smells, while primary qualities are the qualities physics talks about such as weight, mass, spatial and temporal extension. His claim is that, as we experience them, secondary qualities exist only in our experience, 'in the mind', and do not characterise objects in themselves.[2] Primary qualities, on the other hand, do characterise objects. So for Locke, though aspects of our experience of objects are ideal, material objects themselves are not. They are firmly and securely 'out there', albeit leading less colourful existences than we usually imagine.

Locke's British successor George Berkeley, however, was a radical idealist. Locke had argued for the in-the-mind-rather-than-the-world-ness of secondary qualities from the facts of perceptual relativity. Something that looks red in one light looks purple in another, so, he thinks, there is no *particular* colour a thing has and hence *no* colour it has. Berkeley accepts such arguments but points out that they apply equally well to so-called primary qualities: something that looks round from one perspective looks oval from another. So really, he concludes, *all* qualities are secondary qualities, and have no existence outside the mind. And since there is nothing to material objects save their qualities the same must be said of objects.

* * *

Schopenhauer takes Kant to be, like Berkeley, a radical idealist with respect to the status of material objects. Though many modern Kant scholars would reject this interpretation, it is far from silly. In evidence Schopenhauer quotes Kant's remark in the first edition of the *Critique of Pure Reason* that 'if I remove the thinking subject the whole corporeal world must at once vanish: it is nothing save an appearance in the sensibility of our subject and a mode of its representations' (*Critique of Pure Reason*, A 383). And this radical, or as Kant calls it 'transcendental'[3] idealism is, says Schopenhauer, his own position.

Berkeley's philosophy was ridiculed as contrary to obvious common sense. (Remember Schopenhauer's remark about 'realism' being an 'inborn disposition' of the intellect (p. 5 above).) Jonathan Swift refused to open his door to him on the grounds that he ought to be able to walk straight through, and Dr Johnson famously kicked a stone uttering the words: 'Berkeley – I refute him thus'. And Kant, too, was ridiculed, regarded as a 'German Berkeley'. So, Schopenhauer suggests, in the second edition of the *Critique* (the so-called 'B' edition), Kant attacks Berkeley – quite unjustifiably, since he really agrees with him. He obfuscates, tones down and tries to disguise the radical nature of his idealism,[4] producing, thereby a work that is 'disfigured and spoilt', a 'self-contradictory book whose sense could not be thoroughly clear and comprehensible to anyone' (WR I: 435). Hence, Schopenhauer claims, in stating his own idealism in the most uncompromising terms he is simply allowing the 'real Kant' to stand up.[5]

The world of nature, the world of space and time is, Schopenhauer says, just a 'phantom', a 'dream'. (Actually, as we will see, 'nightmare' would be a better word.) This does not mean that there is no distinction between reality and illusion within the world of nature. Though life and dreams are 'leaves from the same book'. there is an obvious distinction between the 'systematic reading' which is life, and the bits that don't fit into 'the continuity of life' (WR I: 11).

Schopenhauer's position, here, can be put in terms of theories of truth. Truth, we know, real truth, is correspondence to the facts. ('England won the World Cup in 1966' is true if and only if it is a fact that England won the World Cup in 1966.) In terms of real or 'correspondence' truth, therefore, all our everyday beliefs about shoes, ships and football matches are, for Schopenhauer, false since there are, in fact, no such things. Yet this does not mean that we can make no distinction between true and false beliefs *within* the world of everyday experience. We do so in terms of a *coherence* account of truth. True beliefs from this point of view are ones that cohere with the overall pattern of things, constitute the 'systematic reading' of experience, false beliefs the ones that do not. When you wake up from dreaming of wizards, flying automobiles and vanishing railway platforms you know you have been dreaming because in the rest of your experience there are no such things, and because, moreover, it would seriously upset a lot of assumptions vital to getting around in the world if you accepted that cars might fly or railway platforms suddenly vanish.

Officially, at least, Schopenhauer is, then, a radical, that is, as he understands Kant, a Kantian idealist. This being said, it has to be immediately added that he has, himself, a serious tendency to obscure the matter. This is largely due to the desire, which reveals itself in all areas of his philosophy, to make all his heroes say the same thing. In the case of idealism this manifests itself as a desire to make Locke and Kant say the same. Hence we find in Schopenhauer a sloppy use of metaphors to express his idealism. Sometimes he talks of 'phantoms' and 'dreams', which point to radical idealism, but at other times he uses 'veil' and 'illusion', which only point to partial idealism. (In illusions typically, the object – e.g. the stick half submerged in water which looks bent – though misperceived, exists. In dreams and hallucinations − 'Is this a dagger I see before me?' − there is nothing there at all.) As we will see, this sloppiness about the radical-partial distinction means that we will have to do some work to find out which sort of idealism is operative in which part of *The World as Will*.

READ KANT!

Why should we believe in radical idealism? Why should we believe the extraordinary thesis that, in the final analysis, material objects do not really exist? Mostly, Schopenhauer's answer is simply: 'Read Kant!' Read, in particular the 'Aesthetic', the first major section, of the *Critique of Pure Reason*. This, says Schopenhauer,

> is a work of such merit that it alone would be sufficient to immortalise the name of Kant. Its proofs have such a complete power of conviction that I number its propositions among the incontestable truths

(WR I: 437).

So what happens in the 'Aesthetic'?

Kant divides propositions into 'analytic' and 'synthetic'. Analytic propositions are true in virtue of the meanings, the definitions, of the words they contain: 'children are young', for example. For the same reason they are uninformative, in the end, uninteresting: though they may tell us something we did not know about the use of words, they do not tell us anything about the world. Synthetic truths, on the other hand, are not true in virtue of the definitions of words and so expand our knowledge: 'Greater Paris has nearly twelve million inhabitants', for example.

Most synthetic propositions are, as Kant puts it, 'a posteriori'. we can only know them after ('posterior' to) experience, experience of the way things are. But a few special, and very important propositions are, Kant claims, though synthetic, true 'a priori' rather than 'a posteriori': we can know them without ('prior' to) experience, without checking up on how the world actually is.[6]

This is because we have certain knowledge beforehand that they could never be disconfirmed by experience. Propositions that are in this way both synthetic and a priori are, according to Kant, the propositions of mathematics: for example, '7 + 5 = 12' and 'the angles of a triangle are equal to the sum of two right-angles'. Such propositions are, firstly, genuinely informative. The first of them, Kant holds, tells us something informative about counting the passage of time: if you count seven moments and then five more the result will be twelve. The second (this seems, perhaps, somewhat more plausible) tells us something genuinely informative about physical space: if you allow three straight lines (walls, perhaps) to intersect, the interior angles will form the sum of two right angles. But secondly, they are certain a priori. We do not go around measuring triangles to find out the sum of the angles because we know beforehand what that sum must be. Kant's question in the 'Aesthetic' is: How is mathematics possible? How is 'synthetic a priori truth' possible? The answer is radical idealism.

Kant's argument is the Analytic is essentially this. We have certain (a priori) knowledge about space in the form of Euclidean geometry. (I shall miss out time and arithmetic where Kant's discussion is much sketchier.) But this would be impossible if space and time possessed mind-independent reality, for in that case there would always be at least the possibility of future disconfirming experience. If space were real, that is, just as we *might* one day discover a bear that talked, so we *might*, one day, discover a triangle with angles summing to something other than a hundred and eighty degrees. So space and time are not real but are, rather, the 'pure forms of sensible intuition'.

By calling space and time forms of intuition Kant means that they are kinds of filters through which all sensory input to the mind is processed. That we can never meet up with a non-Euclidean triangle can only be explained by thinking of these filters as imposing Euclideanness on all the input to the mind rather in the way in which green sunglasses impose greenness on everything one sees through them. (Or, to change the analogy, the way in which a word-processing programme with the font set at 'New York' imposes 'New-York-ness' on all its output.) Spatiality and temporality, then, are *our* contributions to experience. We perceive things as spatial and temporal not because they *are* spatial and temporal but because of the way our minds work.

It is common to criticise Kant for misunderstanding the nature of mathematics. In truth, it is said, the propositions of Euclidean geometry are either 'analytic', true because of the way terms such as 'triangle' are defined and not, therefore, informative about physical space, or else key terms such as 'straight line' must be given a physical interpretation. But if we do that then it becomes a matter of empirical investigation as to whether space is Euclidean or not. And, in fact, it turns out that it is not. If we take the shortest distance between two points that we know of, the path of a light ray, and measure the interior angles of the intersection of three such paths, then the sum of the angles is actually considerably greater than a hundred and eighty degrees.

Kant was, then, wrong, it seems, in attributing synthetic a priori status to mathematical propositions. In fact, however, this is a rather superficial criticism, for all it shows is that Kant made a bad choice of examples from which to argue to the ideality of space and time. Schopenhauer for one, certainly believes that there are a great number of truths about space and time — fifty-four, to be exact — which are both certain and informative: that space and time are infinitely divisible, that time has one dimension and space three, that there is only one space so that all different spaces are parts of it, that there is only one time, that time cannot stop and space has no boundary, and so on (WR II: 48–52).

The real problem with Kant's argument is not, therefore, his mistake about the status of mathematical truth. It is rather the following.

Kant argues, we saw, that we perceive reality as spatial and temporal not because of the way it is (the way it is 'in itself', Kant would add) but because of the way our minds are constructed. Let us grant, for the sake of argument, that this is true. The problem is, however, that it *does not follow* from this that space and time are unreal. For it might be the case *both* that space and time are, as Kant claims, 'forms' of the mind which impose an a priori structure on all human experience *and* that space and time are real, that they characterise things as they are, out there, 'in themselves'. There might, that is to say, be either a complete or a partial *identity* between the way we experience things – the way they show up in what we might call 'phenomenal space' – and the way they are 'in themselves'.

The former possibility is entertained in a witty painting by the Surrealist René Magritte which has the sardonic title 'Free at Last'. The painting depicts the interior of a window on which is painted a landscape of meadow and hills. In the centre of the window is a jagged hole through which, we may suppose, someone has 'at last' broken through the 'veil of Maya' to the 'real' world beyond. The trouble, however, is that the colours and contours of the landscape one sees through the hole exactly match the colours and contours of the landscape painted on the inside of the window. As I, at least, read it, the painting pokes fun at Eastern or Schopenhauerian-type thinkers who take the point of everything to be 'releasement' (Heidegger) from the prison of the everyday into a mystical 'beyond'.

The trouble with the Aesthetic is, then, that while spatiality and temporality may well be 'forms' of experience, this does not establish the truth of radical idealism, since they may *also* characterise things as they are in themselves.

For Kant, himself, this problem is not too serious since he has a back-up argument to dispose of this possibility. This appears at towards the end of the *Critique*, in the first of what he calls the 'Antinomies of Pure Reason'. Here he argues that if space and time are real then they can be proved to be both finite and infinite. As

Schopenhauer summarises Kant's argument, he attempts to prove that space and time 'cannot even be *conceived*, when closely considered, as . . . an order of things in themselves, or as something absolutely objective and positively existing: for if we attempt to think it out to the end, it leads to contradictions' (WR II: 8).

The problem for Schopenhauer, however, is that he (actually quite rightly) *rejects* Kant's argument on this point, regards the attempt to prove that realism about space and time leads to insoluble contradictions as a transparent failure (WR II: 9). What this means is that to establish the truth of radical idealism Schopenhauer cannot rest on his Kantian laurels. He urgently needs something over and above what is to be found in Kant.

REALISM AS SELF-CONTRADICTORY

The first sentence of the main work is: 'The world is my representation'. This, as we may take it, statement of radical idealism is, says Schopenhauer, a truth so certain that it needs no proof (WR I: 3). This odd claim – odd, since radical idealism is so contrary to common sense – is illuminated in the second volume as follows:

> 'The world is my representation' is, like the axioms of Euclid, a proposition which everyone must recognise as true as soon as he understands it, although it is not a proposition that everyone understands as soon as he hears it
>
> (WR II: 3).

So, allegedly, all we need to do to see the truth of radical idealism is properly to understand the meaning of the assertion that 'space and time characterise things as they appear but not things in themselves'. Like Kant in the 'First Antinomy', Schopenhauer, too, in his own way, tries to argue that some kind of *contradiction* is involved in affirming the world of everyday experience to have mind-independent existence.

Schopenhauer says that it is 'remarkable' that Kant did not follow

Berkeley in tracing the 'merely relative' (i.e. mind-dependent) existence of everyday objects to 'the simple, undeniable truth . . . "*No object without a subject*" ' (WR I: 434). Why is it 'simple' to establish the truth of this realism-refuting principle? Because, as Berkeley showed, even though it at first seems quite easy to imagine an 'objective world' existing without there being any 'knowing beings' to experience it – earth before the first appearance of sentient life, bubbles in the primeval goo going 'plop' from time to time – concealed in the supposition is actually a 'contradiction'. For

> if we attempt to *imagine an objective world without a knowing subject*, then we become aware that what we are imagining at that moment is in truth the opposite of what we intended, namely nothing but just the process in the intellect of a knowing being who perceives an objective world, that is to say, precisely that which we sought to exclude
>
> (WR II: 5).

In short, you cannot imagine a world without someone perceiving that world because the very act of imagining it is imagining yourself as perceiving that world, 'the opposite of what we intended'. You cannot, for example, imagine a tree existing without anyone being conscious of it since imagining a tree you are imagining yourself as being conscious of it.

But this is outrageous. Here am I imagining a tree without anyone being conscious of it:

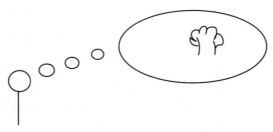

Figure 2.1

And here am I imagining myself being conscious of a tree:

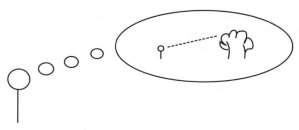

Figure 2.2

Obviously the situation represented by Figure 2.1 is different from that represented by Figure 2.2, and is a situation that can easily occur. The argument is, in short, little more than a sophism, a trick.

A 'postmodernist' would be inclined, at this point, to leap tiresomely to Schopenhauer's defence. 'The way you see the tree', he would likely point out, 'is profoundly determined by the constitution of your particular, culturally constructed, way of apprehending reality. The subject is, therefore, always present'. But this is like arguing that since we always see through our eyes we always see our eyes or that since we always talk in language we always talk *about* language. The medium, to be sure, must always affect the *character* of the message. But that does not mean it is always, or even usually, *part* of the message.

* * *

Why else might Schopenhauer think that 'no object without a subject' is a simple and obvious truth which places radical idealism beyond doubt? Maybe because, in a sense, 'no object without a subject' *is* an obvious and simple truth that 'needs no proof'. There can be, that is, no *object of consciousness* without a subject of consciousness. But whether *material objects* are nothing but objects of consciousness is, of course, the very point at issue. If, that is to say, 'no object without a subject' is a statement of radical idealism then it is not a trivial and obvious truth. If, on the other hand, it is a trivial and obvious truth then it is not a statement of radical idealism. The whole appeal to the principle is, in short, a disaster and cannot begin to do the job of replacing the rejected argument of Kant's 'Antinomy'. Schopenhauer, then, badly needs something else with which to support the truth of radical idealism.

EVOLUTIONARY IDEALISM

One further argument is to be found in his work, an argument which, while highly original, interesting, and (as we will see in the final chapter) influential with respect to the future development of thought, is at the same time deeply problematic.

Schopenhauer claims that by looking at what we know through natural science, through, in particular brain physiology and evolutionary biology, we can reach exactly the same conclusion – radical idealism – as Kant reaches through philosophical reflection (WN: 296, WR II: 285).

Science shows us, Schopenhauer boldly asserts, that the 'intellect' and the brain are one and the same thing: that our perceptual consciousness of the world is 'a physiological phenomenon, a function of the brain' (WR II: 285). Given this, Kant's view that the intellect constructs rather than simply registers experience of objects can now be supported by science. For the input to the brain, retinal images, a few twitches and tingles in the ears, nose, throat and fingers, is a 'poor, wretched thing' that 'cannot contain anything . . . resembling intuitive perception'. There is, that is, a massive gap between the input to the brain, sensations, and its output, perception of objects, a gap as massive as that between the colours on a painter's palette and the painting he produces out of them. It follows that the world of objects must be conceived, not as something that steps, 'already cut and dried', into our heads, but rather as something the mind 'creates' or 'constructs' out of the 'raw material' of sensation.[7] As mind-created it is, therefore, mind-dependent (FR: 76–9).

There are two problems with this argument. The first is that it seems to presuppose what we may call 'scientific realism'. It seems to presuppose, that is, that even though the entities of common sense, shoes, ships, cabbages and the like, might not have mind-independent existence, scientific entities like brains, nerves, retinas, etc. do. The *best* the argument can establish, therefore, is not the *radical* idealism it is supposed to be establishing but only *partial* idealism – something along the lines of Locke's position, the position which holds, remember, that while 'secondary qualities' have no mind-independent existence 'primary qualities' do. Schopenhauer is oddly insensitive to this point, regularly finding Kant to be unnecessarily reticent in referring always to 'the knowing faculty', never to the brain (e.g. WR II: 284–6). The truth of the matter, however, is that Kant was well aware of the futility of trying to prove *radical* idealism from a starting-point which *presupposes* the existence of material objects.

The second problem is the 'Magritte problem' once again. Surely, one might point out, the world as we experience it might *both* be a brain-construct *and also* correspond to the way reality in itself actually is. And in fact, one might continue, doesn't our evolutionary success suggest that this is no mere possibility but is actually *the truth of the matter*? Surely creatures whose representations of the world were habitually at variance with the way it actually is would have (to borrow W. V. Quine's memorable words) 'the pathetic but praiseworthy habit of dying out before reproducing their kind'?

* * *

Now concerning this second problem Schopenhauer has, in fact, an interesting and important reply. The brain, he says is simply the 'one great tool' (WR II: 280) whereby a physically weak animal with multiple needs survives in a highly competitive environment

(WN: 272–3, WR II: 204–6).[8] What follows is that 'the intellect . . . is designed for comprehending those ends on the attainment of which depend individual life and its propagation [but] . . . is by no means intended to present the true, absolutely real inner nature of . . . things in the consciousness of the knower'. Rather, it is 'thoroughly practical in tendency', a 'medium of motives' (WR II: 285–6). Contra the suggestion I have used Quine's words to express, it is the 'pedants', those who habitually seek the exact and precise truth about things, who get wiped out. In a word, truth-seeking is not an 'adaptive', survival-promoting trait. Why not?

I shall return to this question in greater detail in the discussion of art in chapter 5. Here, let me just cite a few of Schopenhauer's examples. To the traveller in a hurry, he says, the beautiful bridge over the Rhine appears as little more than a dash intersecting with a stroke (WR II: 381). To the engaged chess player the antique, beautifully carved, Chinese chessmen appear as nothing but 'the king', 'the queen', 'the knight' and so on. He is aware of nothing about the chess pieces other than the role they play in the game (PP II: 69). And it is the same with people: typically we are unaware of what kind of people they are, view them simply in terms of their social role – e. g. their 'job description' – particularly if we stand to them in power relations ('boss', 'secretary', 'tax inspector', 'policeman' etc.) (WR II: 372).

The point of these examples is to suggest that evolution favours economy of effort. Since in the jungle (where the basic structure of human consciousness was formed) time is of the essence, since speed of response is essential to survival, the brain processes only the minimum amount of information necessary to the job at hand. So things show up to us in a stripped-down, schematic way. They show up, in fact, simply as things which fulfil a given practical role, as equipment or (to borrow a term Heidegger was to invent a hundred years later to make the same point) 'ready-to-hand'. Nothing about the bridge is relevant to the traveller in a hurry other than that it will get him across the river, so he is aware of nothing about it other than that it is a 'thing for getting to the other side of the river'. In general, says Schopenhauer, in practical, instrumental consciousness the world appears 'just as a beautiful landscape appears on the plan of a battlefield' (WR II: 381).

It might be said that this only makes *simplification*, not *falsification*, an adaptive trait. But survival-promoting simplification often includes falsification. To the long-tongued frog, for example, both flies and dust motes show up as 'food'. Though only the former is in fact food, since the dust motes do no harm, the speed of reaction facilitated by the falsification promotes survival. To the fighter pilot in the heat of battle, all objects on the radar screen are liable to show up as 'danger' even though actually only some of them are. So he attacks them all – the 'collateral damage' and 'friendly fire' problems. Though this may be undesirable from most points of view, the speed of reaction it facilitates does promote the survival of the pilot. (On the survival value of falsification see further pp. 108–10 below).

* * *

Schopenhauer has, then, a rather compelling answer to the second of the above difficulties, the 'Magritte problem'. Concerning the first, however, he has nothing to say.

We might try to help him out by reconstructing his argument as a *reductio ad absurdum*. Let us suppose, we might interpret him as saying, that the scientific image of reality is true; that there really are things like human brains which are the product of evolutionary forces. Then, as we have seen, since falsification is an adaptive trait, human representations of the world are false. But the scientific image of reality is *itself* a human representation of reality. Therefore it is false. So the scientific image of reality auto-destructs – it entails its own falsity.

As I say, there is no hint of this argument in Schopenhauer himself. And, in fact, it is not one he himself could successfully deploy. The reason as we will see in chapter 5, is that he thinks that, though rare, it is possible for certain minds to rise above the 'practically' determined image of reality and attain a completely 'objective' apprehension of it. Schopenhauer says that the artistic or philosophical 'genius' can do this. But if they can, one must ask, why not the scientific 'genius'?

* * *

So far, I have argued that Schopenhauer fails to provide a convincing proof of radical idealism. On the other hand, I suggest, his appeal to evolutionary psychology does seem to provide a compelling case for partial idealism, does seem to suggest that the manifest or commonsense image of the world, the way things present them-selves in everyday experience, does not correspond to the way they are in themselves.[9] And this is sufficient to establish Schopenhauer's claim that we cannot establish the 'whatness' of things just by looking. The question remains, therefore: how *are* we to discover what the world is? If looking will not do what else will?

Given that perceiving and thinking are the only ways human beings have of gaining knowledge, the only possible answer that remains is: thinking. What, then, according to Schopenhauer, is thinking? What is the nature of the faculty of thinking, 'reason' (*Vernunft*) as Schopenhauer calls it? What can it do for us, and what are its limits? This is the topic that occupies the second half of Book I and to which I now turn.

REASON

'Reason', as Schopenhauer sees it, has a lot to answer for. In practical life the illusion that its possession gives us a special dignity and worth which marks a fundamental difference between us and non-human animals leads us to 'call them beasts or brutes [to give] . . . 'degrading names to all the vital functions they have in common with us and [to say] . . . they have no rights (FR: 146).

In philosophy, a similar overestimation of the importance of reason has lead to a similarly illusory self-importance. In the philosophical tradition, that is, reason has been treated as a kind of magic gift through the exercise of which 'rationalist' philosophers were able to penetrate into realms inaccessible to ordinary people and ordinary experience. Pure reason, it was thought – reason alone – could prove to us the existence of such things as God, freedom and immortality.

Following the example of the British empiricists, Locke, Berkeley and Hume, Kant devoted himself to beating back the pretensions of rationalism. 'Thoughts' without sensory 'content', 'concepts' without 'intuitions', he famously pronounced, are 'empty' (*Critique of Pure Reason*, A 51). The bounds of sense are the bounds of sense: the limits of sense-experience are the limits of what can be cognitively meaningful,[10] and hence of what can be known.

Surveying the contemporary scene, however, Schopenhauer observes that the insights of the empiricists and of Kant are being swept aside by the 'professors of philosophy' (Fichte, Hegel, Jacobi, Schelling etc.) who claim the 'oracular ability' (FR: 166–7) to bypass sense-experience and to have, through reason alone, direct encounters with 'the Absolute', with ultimate reality (see further pp. 49–51).

To some degree, he continues, Kant himself must bear some responsibility for this sorry state of affairs, since it was he who, via the 'categorical imperative'[11], turned reason into the supposed source of fundamental moral values. Kant having thus turned reason into a 'practical oracle', it required only a 'little audacity' on the part of the likes of F. H. Jacobi to associate with it a 'theoretical oracle', so that reason ends up as 'so to speak, a little window that admits us to the superlunal and even supernatural world' (FR: 180–1).

It is in opposition to this pompously inflated conception that Schopenhauer sees it as his task to return reason to the modesty of the empiricist insights that lay at the root of Kant's philosophy. Reason, he asserts – with his usual political incorrectness[12] – is essentially 'feminine', as can be seen from the fact that in both the Germanic and Romance languages the noun is a feminine one (*die Vernunft, la raison*). Reason, that is,

> can never furnish material from its own resources. It has nothing but forms; . . . it merely conceives, but does not generate
>
> (FR: 171).

Correctly understood, in short, reason, is in essence, nothing more than a computer programme. If you give it information it can calculate other information, but by itself it can generate no information at all.

Given this deflationary objective, Schopenhauer has two deflationary tasks. The first is to deflate the 'practical oracle', the illusion that pure reason is the source of *moral* knowledge. And the second is to deflate the 'theoretical' oracle, the illusion that pure reason is a source of *theoretical* knowledge.

PRACTICAL REASON

David Hume famously said that 'reason is and ought only to be the slave of the passions'. Reason, that is, can be 'practical' in the sense of telling you how to achieve the ends you desire, but as to what those ends are or should be it has nothing to say. In the sphere of value and action, that is to say, reason has a purely instrumental role.

For Kant, however, reason is practical in a much stronger sense: according to him, there are certain ends, specifically the ends of morality, which one has to have purely in virtue of being rational.

In his 'second' *Critique*, the *Critique of Practical Reason*, that is to say, Kant claims that (a) the 'categorical imperative' – 'act only on that maxim which you can at the same time will to be a universal law of nature' – is built into reason in the sense that a purely rational being would never infringe its requirement and that (b) the principle is adequate to generate precisely what we intuitively know to be our moral obligations. In a word, immoral action is always irrational action, wickedness is a failure in rationality.

Schopenhauer thinks that Hume's purely instrumental conception of reason is obvious good sense. Reason can influence action but by itself can never, he says, *motivate* (WR II: 148). And he thinks the Kantian view which reduces morality to rationality is just silly. Everyone, he says, 'except a few German savants' has always agreed that virtue is one thing, rationality another. Was Jesus Christ a paradigm of *rationality*? Is Machiavelli's prince – the ruthless, unscrupulous but consummately rational practitioner of statecraft – a paragon of *virtue* (WR I: 515–16)? (Naturally, these remarks are no more than opening skirmishes. Important philosophers such as Jurgen Habermas and John Rawls have devoted professional lifetimes to the – in my own view ultimately quixotic – task of defending Kant's elevated conception of practical reason.)

* * *

Digressing (as he often does) from the main line of argument, Schopenhauer asks: what ends *do* we have as human beings? Does it just depend on what kind of an individual one is? Not so. There is one end we all have – not in virtue of being rational, but simply in virtue of being *human* beings – and that is happiness. This Schopenhauer construes as 'peace of mind (*Geistesruhe*)' (WR I: 86).[13]

This makes the Greco-Roman philosophy of Stoicism (WR I: section 16 and WR II: chapter XVI) 'the highest point to which man can attain by the mere use of his faculty of reason' (WR I: 89). Since suffering consists in a disjunction between what we want and what we get, between desire and reality, and since only the former side of the equation is within our power, it follows, Stoicism holds, that we should minimise our desires – or at least our attachment to those desires. 'Practical philosophers' (those, who are, as we still say, 'philosophical' about things), those who manage to live without fear or hope, are indeed, says Schopenhauer, much less unhappy than the run of humanity.

In spite of this commendation, however, Schopenhauer's ultimate judgement on Stoic ethics is not favourable. One problem with it is that it cannot deal with intense bodily pain and so is forced to recommend suicide in these circumstances. This is symptomatic of the fact that the best it offers is a kind of hardening of the heart against the blows of fate rather than the true peace of mind, the 'blessed life', which, according to Schopenhauer, we all seek. (How this might be attained will be discussed later on.)

Another problem with the Stoics is that whereas their predecessors, the Cynics, lived lives of actual poverty (without money, the means of satisfying desire) the Stoics preached not the abandonment of but merely 'non-attachment' to one's desires; desiring but not being upset if one's desires are not satisfied. What, however, this attempt to make Cynicism compatible with bourgeois, 'well-fed' existence failed to notice, says Schopenhauer, is that habit begets dependence: everything to which we become accustomed turns into a necessity (WR II: 155–6).

PERCEPTION

Kant says not only that concepts without intuitions are 'empty' but also that intuitions without concepts are 'blind' (Critique of Pure Reason, A 51). The basis for this claim is his view that concepts are rules for organising sensations. The difference between having an experience of a red, round colour patch and seeing a tomato, is that the sensations in question have been 'brought under' the concept 'tomato'. The adult mind, that is, approaches the realm of its experience forearmed with a menu of concepts in terms of which it divides the sensory 'manifold' into objects. Without concepts there can be no experience of objects.

For Kant, therefore, there is a co-dependence between concepts and sense-experience. Concepts depend on sense for 'content', but sensations depend on concepts for intelligibility, for objectual signification. For reasons we will discuss in greater detail shortly, Schopenhauer enthusiastically endorses the first half of this dependence. But the second he rejects. Devoted, as he is, to the deflation of reason he is correspondingly devoted to elevating the status of unaided sense-perception.

* * *

Schopenhauer divides the 'intellect' (i.e., as he usually insists, the brain) into two faculties: the conceptual faculty of 'reason' (*Vernunft*) and the perceptual faculty of the 'understanding' (*Verstand*). Though Kant is right, he says, to insist on the 'intellectual' nature of our experience of the everyday world of objects – right to think, to repeat, that 'the objective world cannot just step into our heads from without, already cut and dried' but must rather be 'constructed' by the intellect – he is wrong to think that concepts play any role in its genesis. The reason is that the entire 'world of perception', 'empirical reality', is given to us by the completely non-conceptual faculty of the understanding. Though 'intellectual', everyday perceptual experience of reality is completely non-'conceptual' (WR I: 443–4).

* * *

So how does the concept-less 'understanding' construct our world of everyday objects? Schopenhauer's account of its genesis (formulated in FR section 21, WR I: chapter 4 and WR II: chapters 2 and 3) is that it does it by exercising its 'one function' of making causal inferences (WR I: 38).

Innate in the understanding, i.e. the part of the brain responsible for perception, are the 'pure intuitions' (WR II: 27) of space and time. Following Kant, Schopenhauer calls space and time 'pure intuitions' to counteract the disposition to think of them as nothings, as mere absences, absences of matter. Though we cannot see them directly, space and time are things with a definite nature which we discover when, for example, we do geometry. Together they constituted the ground plan on which the mind/brain 'constructs' its account of the external, natural world. The totality of our synthetic a priori knowledge of nature describes the character of this ground plan, reports the constraints on the brain's constructive activity. The brain cannot, for example, Schopenhauer would say, construct the perception of a house with four straight walls without the interior angles of the walls amounting to three hundred and sixty degrees.

It is helpful, in trying to grasp Schopenhauer's idea, to think of the ground plan on which the brain constructs our experience of objects as a kind of grid. At any point in time any given square on the grid is either empty or occupied. If a square is empty then we have empty space. If it is occupied then there is 'matter' at that point: a material object is located there.

So how does a square come to be occupied? By, according to Schopenhauer, the understanding's making a causal inference to the most likely explanation of the sensations the subject experiences in its own body – retinal images, pressure on the fingertips, sounds in the ears, and so on (WR I: 19).

Let us suppose, for example, that there is a red and round retinal image. The understanding refers it to a given square on the grid, in other words decides that it is in that part of space-time that the causal origin of the visual sensation lies. And let us suppose that the understanding also experiences a hard, smooth and cool tactile sensation which it refers to the same spot. This is what happens in the mind when we, for example, experience a billiard ball as being at a particular place.

Normally, we are completely unconscious of all this activity. It is, as it were, a software programme that operates automatically, below the level of consciousness. But sometimes we do become conscious of the nature of this sensation-processing activity as when 'in the dark, we touch a thing on all sides for a long time until, from the different effects on our hands, we are able to construct their cause as a definite shape' (WR II: 23).

The causal inferences discussed so far are inferences from states of the subject's body to the nature and position of objects in the world. As well as making these kinds of my-body → object inferences, however, the understanding also makes object → object inferences. It makes all those causal inferences on which everyday 'prudence' (WR I: 22) depends.

To mark the, as he sees it, non-conceptual character of the knowledge on which these inferences are based, Schopenhauer calls it 'intuitive' knowledge. Of this he has some nice examples. We know 'intuitively', for example, 'the mode of operation of the lever, a block and tackle, a cog wheel' (WR I: 53). An experienced billiards player has 'perfect knowledge of the laws of impact of elastic bodies on one another merely in the understanding, merely for immediate perception' though 'only the man versed in the science of mechanics has a real rational knowledge of those laws, that is to say a knowledge of them in the abstract' (WR I: 56).

Intuitive knowledge is what we share with the reasonless (but not intellect-less) animals, beings, clearly, which not only represent the world in terms of objects much as we do but also have a great deal of causal knowledge about it. For in spite of our abominable treatment of them, we often marvel at the 'great sagacity of the monkey or the fox', or at the elephant who refuses to cross a bridge it sees to be too flimsy to carry its weight (WR I: 21).

In sum, then, for both us and the non-human animals, the entire rich fabric or the world of objects is constructed for us by the understanding, entirely without the aid of concepts. The question arises, therefore, as to what, if anything, there is left for concepts to do.

CONCEPTS

What, first of all, *are* concepts? What — to repeat the question we asked some time ago — is 'reason'?

Just as the understanding has the 'one function' of causal inference, so reason has the one basic function of forming concepts

(WR I: 39). It does so – here Schopenhauer follows the British empiricists and in particular, John Locke almost to the letter – by means of a process of 'abstraction' (WR II: 66).

Perceptions, 'representations of perception', are, says Schopenhauer, 'complete'. They are, that is, fully determinate. A perceptual representation of a dog, for example, must be a representation of a particular dog – a terrier, sheepdog, dachshund or whatever.[14] Concepts, 'conceptual representations', on the other hand, are 'abstract'. To produce concepts reason surveys a number of perceptual representations and forms a new representation by leaving out what is peculiar to each and retaining what is common to all. To form the concept 'dog' for example, it leaves out what makes Frodo a poodle (Schopenhauer's favourite kind of dog) and Gandalf a sheepdog and retains only what they both share – being able to bark, being four-footed and furry, presumably. This makes universality the distinctive feature of concepts. Whereas a perceptual representation can only be of a particular dog the concept 'dog' applies to all dogs.

Concepts are, then, 'representations of representations'. They are 'copies or repetitions' of perceptual representations in an abstract or sketchy form (WR I: 40). They stand to perceptions, one might say, as a stick-drawing of a dog stands to a photograph.

Concepts are not yet thoughts, 'judgements', as Schopenhauer calls them. Reason, rather, turns them into thoughts by joining them together according to the formation rules of logic (FR: 156). Simple judgements, in other words, are formed by the logical function of predication represented by the verb 'to be' – 'Dogs are a man's best friend' – which then become more complex judgements through the operation of other logical functions such as negation – 'Dogs are not a man's best friend' – and implication – 'If dogs are a man's best friend then we should take better care of them.' And then the inferential rules of logic allow reason to move from sets of judgements to new judgements: 'If dogs are a man's best friend then we should take better care of them. Dogs are a man's best friend. Therefore, we should take better care of them.'

Schopenhauer says that it is 'impossible to think in opposition to [the rules of logic] . . . as it is to move our limbs in a direction contrary to their joints' (FR: 162). The science of logic which articulates these rules, that is to say, is 'the self-observation of the faculty of reason' (WR I: 45); as it were, its physiology. Though a standard nineteenth-century view, this account of logic is certainly mistaken since we often think illogically, make logical mistakes. As Frege and Husserl were to point out half a century later in their attacks on 'psychologism', the rules of logic are normative not descriptive: they describe how we *ought* to think, not how we invariably *do* think.

* * *

Concepts are, says Schopenhauer, the meanings of words. This is why animals, though they represent the world perceptually in much the same way as we do, do not have language. Though they have understanding they lack reason, the ability to abstract concepts from perceptions (WR II: chapter V). The essential feature of language is generality. Whereas I can only see *a* dog, in virtue of the abstract universality of concepts I can think about dogs in general.

* * *

Schopenhauer himself is conscious of a certain problem with the theory of concepts as thus far sketched. If concepts are manu-factured out of perceptual representations, perceptual images, that is to say, then they must themselves be images – albeit abstract or sketchy ones. But in fact, when we think, there are usually no such things in our consciousness: 'what a tumult there would be in our heads', Schopenhauer observes, if 'pictures of the imagination' were streaming through our heads every time we listened to a speech or read a book (WR I: 39).

Rather than questioning his account of what concepts are,

however, he deals with the difficulty by saying that we do not think in concepts but rather in 'representatives' of them, namely words (FR: 152, WR II: 66). The concepts themselves, we must suppose – Schopenhauer is rather indistinct on this point – exist as a kind of mental dictionary which the mind consults when it is in doubt as to the meaning of a word. Whether this constitutes an adequate treatment of the difficulty is a question to which I shall return.

INTUITIVE VERSUS CONCEPTUAL KNOWLEDGE

In line with his general ambition of deflating 'reason' ('an empty, poor thing' (FR: 147) 'suitably called "reflection" since that is all it is, a pallid reflection of perception' (WR I: 62)) Schopenhauer is in general concerned to emphasise not merely the difference between conceptual and intuitive knowledge but also the inferiority of the former to the latter. When it comes to practical, everyday coping, he suggests, intuitive knowledge is virtually always superior to conceptual knowledge. For two reasons.

The first, as he sees it, is a direct consequence of the origin of concepts in abstraction. Since they are thinned down, sketchy, impoverished 'representations of representations' they are related to perceptual representations 'as a mosaic to a painting' (WR I: 59). They are, as it were, a crudely digitalised version of an analogue reality. This means that it is generally foolish not to trust one's intuitions. The person who cannot do this is the *pedant* – someone who 'puts his understanding entirely under the guardianship of his reason, and makes use thereof on all occasions; in other words, he wants always to start from general concepts, rules, and maxims, and to stick to these in life, in art, and even in ethical good conduct' (WR I: 60).

Pedantic rule-following often hinders successful practice, 'for example, in the case of billiards-playing, fencing, tuning an instrument, or singing' (WR I: 56). Concepts are just too crude to deal with the subtle differences involved.

A particularly regrettable form of pedantry is 'moral pedantry'.

(Schopenhauer thinks that Kant's 'stilted maxims' embody and encourage a life of moral pedantry.) Since concepts are rough and ready and to some extent arbitrary abstractions from perception, they 'can never accurately apply to reality's fine shades of difference and innumerable modifications'. It follows that the moral pedant, however well intentioned, will often act in morally wrong ways since, acting from conceptual maxims, he will frequently be blind to 'the infinitely nice distinctions in the nature of the circumstances' (WR I: 60).[15]

The second general reason Schopenhauer offers for the superiority of intuitive to reflective knowledge has to do with the fact that reflection, thinking, takes time. It follows that it is a hindrance 'in all those cases which do not allow time for reflection' – for example, fencing and everyday chatter. (In the latter, Schopenhauer adds – one of his milder political incorrectnesses – women excel precisely because they do not think before they speak (WR II: 75).)

* * *

Though generally intent on deflating reason Schopenhauer does allow that it gives us one significant advantage over the reason-less animals. Since the essence of a concept is universality, reason enables us to make universal judgements. In the theoretical sphere this enables us to do things like science and philosophy (on Schopenhauer's somewhat ambivalent attitude to philosophy see pp. 165–8 below) and in the practical sphere it liberates us from the power of present perception. The animal, that is to say, has no option but to respond to the present stimulus – the sight, let us say, of ice cream. Humans, on the other hand can formulate general policies, abstract 'maxims', on which to act (WR II: 148): 'I will never eat fat-making food such as ice cream.' This enables them to 'navigate' a path through life as the animals cannot. Whereas the latter are tossed from one stimulus and the next, humans who act consistently from general policies (particularly Stoic or, better, Cynic policies) achieve a certain 'composure' (WR II: 85).

CRITICISM OF SCHOPENHAUER ON REASON AND PERCEPTION

As we have seen, the crux of Schopenhauer's humbling of reason is the division of the intellect into the conceptual and perceptual faculties, together with the claim that the whole world of objects is given to us entirely by the latter; that our basic knowledge of what objects are where, and of their everyday causal dispositions, is given to us without concepts playing any role at all. Is this claim true?

The first thing that needs to be said is that Schopenhauer's own account of what concepts are is actually quite hopeless. It is hopeless because whereas the abstractionist account of their origin demands they be regarded as mental images they are clearly – on Schopenhauer's own showing – nothing of the sort. Not only do we not find our heads full of pictures when we think, we do not find ourselves consulting mental pictures when we want to know the meaning of a word.

Quite trivially, therefore, our everyday knowledge of empirical reality is independent of concepts in *Schopenhauer's sense*, for the simple reason that *all* knowledge is so independent.

To answer the question properly, therefore, we need really to know what concepts are. One idea that might spring to mind is that concept-possession is essentially tied to language. To have the concept of an X is to be able properly to use the word 'X' (or some word in another language which means the same thing).

If this is what concepts are then Schopenhauer's discussion of the understanding and its 'intuitive' knowledge really does establish that we have a great deal of knowledge about the world that is non-'conceptual'. His examples of human intuitive knowledge – billiards-playing, fencing, responding to the uniqueness of a situation with moral sensitivity – hover between knowledge we *don't* articulate in words and knowledge we *can't*. It is the latter phenomenon, however, that is really crucial, which is what makes Schopenhauer's discussion of non-language-using animals the crux of the matter. As Schopenhauer says, their behaviour is quite evidently guided by perceptual representations of objects and knowledge of causal connexions between them that is similar, and sometimes superior, to our own. When the monkey uses a stick to reach the high-up banana it clearly sees, if not a banana, at least a food-object, and knows that hitting it with the stick is likely to dislodge it. If conceptual knowledge is knowledge which can be articulated in language then some non-human animals have non-conceptual knowledge.

There is, however, another understanding of what concepts are – Kant's understanding. According to Kant, concepts, at least at the most basic level, are rules for sorting, 'synthesising', the 'manifold' of sensations into objectual wholes (*Critique of Pure Reason* A 124–5). They are rules that enable us to tell where one object stops and another – or else object-less space – begins. To have the concept of an X on this approach is to be able to classify things into Xs and non-Xs, whether by linguistic or by other means.

Following this Kantian approach to concepts, we may note that, for human beings, the rules in question are generally produced by linguistic training. This is why they vary. To the visitor from Mars (or anywhere outside Melbourne) the scene reveals nothing but a lot of humanoid individuals running around like headless chickens. But to someone from the right sociolinguistic community, what is happening is an Australian Rules football match.

Yet that rules for constructing objects are *generally* produced in this way does not preclude that some of them are the biological products of evolution. And, to come to the point, it does not pre-clude that some such rules are 'hardwired' into non-linguistic ani-mals. If this is what concepts are then, clearly, animal knowledge, while 'intuitive' in the sense of being non-linguistic, is not intui-tive in the sense of being non-conceptual.

As far as Schopenhauer himself is concerned, it is concepts in this second sense that are relevant. For he is, remember (see pp. 36–7 above), attacking Kant, attacking his claim that 'intuitions' without concepts are 'blind', do not amount to experience of objects. His claim, as we have seen, is that his theory of the understanding's unconscious causal inferences does away with the involvement of Kantian concepts in the genesis of everyday experience.

The fact is, however, is that it cannot possibly do that. What Schopenhauer's theory possibly explains is, how, *given* that we are *already* disposed to organise sensations into things like, *inter alia*, billiard balls, we determine that there is a billiard ball at a particular place at a particular time. But as to how we come to populate our world with objects of this kind in the first place, he actually has no answer at all. The fact of the matter, in short, is that since his theory really *presupposes* the activity of Kantian concepts it cannot possibly challenge Kant's account of the genesis of perception.

MEANINGFULNESS

In spite of an unhappy three months in an English boarding school (in Wimbledon in 1803), Schopenhauer loved most things British. In particular, he loved the British philosophers of the eighteenth century, Locke, Berkeley and Hume. By contrast, as we have seen, the German philosophers of the nineteenth century – his contemporaries and near contemporaries, Fichte, Schelling, Jacobi, but above all, the 'mind-destroying' (WR II: 40) Hegel – he loathed. The British he loved for their clarity. Real philosophical writing, he says, to repeat his wonderful image, should resemble 'a Swiss lake which by its calm combines great depth with great clarity, the depth revealing itself precisely through the clarity' (FR: 4). And the Germans he hates for their turbid, muddy impenetrability.

The other thing he hated about the Germans – to indulge in a short digression – was that they were *professional* philosophers. Since he who pays the piper calls the tune, independence of financial means, Schopenhauer holds, is a precondition of independence of thought, of a genuine quest for truth. It is for this reason that '*professor* of philosophy' is always, for him, a term of contempt. The world, he holds, divides into those who live *from* philosophy and those who live *for* philosophy (FR I: 73). Though professional philosophers of every age, our own included, need to be carefully scrutinised for signs of economically based political correctness, Schopenhauer's observation had particular force in his own age. As was pointed out in the opening chapter, since the king's authority (in Prussia, for example) rested on his appointment by God, to challenge either God or his morality was to challenge the king. So in the interests of one's salary one was under a strong pressure to become, as Schopenhauer puts it, a 'petticoat philosopher' (FR: 74).

Schopenhauer saw – to return to his admiration for British philosophy – a connection between the style of British writing and its content. Locke, that is to say, emphasised that since concepts ('ideas' as he called them) are all derived by abstraction from sense-experience it must be possible to trace them back to their sensory origin, and that if this is not possible then the words for which those concepts supposedly provide the meaning are actually devoid of meaning, are empty verbiage. 'All those sublime thoughts', writes Locke, 'which tower above the clouds and reach as high as heaven itself take their rise and footing' nowhere but in 'in the senses' (*Essay on Human Understanding*, Book II, chapter 1, section 24). If words are used to which no 'idea' corresponds – as is common among 'the [rationalist] schoolmen and metaphysicians' – then the words they use are 'insignificant terms' (ibid. Book III chapter X, section 2).

Schopenhauer says exactly the same. For him, as for Locke, the theory of the origin of concepts provides a criterion of meaningfulness – and of fraudulence, a criterion that exposes Hegel, for one, as the 'repulsive and dull charlatan and unparalleled scribbler of nonsense' (WR II: 70) that he is. Since 'the whole structure of our world of thought rests on the world of perceptions,' says Schopenhauer, it must be possible

for us to go back from every concept, even if through intermediate stages, to the perceptions from which it has . . . been drawn . . . In

other words it must be possible to verify the concept with
perceptions which stand to abstractions in the relation of examples.

Where this is not possible 'we have in our heads not concepts, but
mere words. In this respect, says Schopenhauer (drawing, as he
frequently does, on his commercial background), 'our intellect is
like a bank of issue which, if it is to be sound, must have ready
money in the safe, in order to be able, on demand, to meet all the
notes it has issued' (WR II: 71). Perceptions are, in a word, the
'cash value' of words. Without being able to come up with perceptual examples of what he is talking about a philosopher is
'bankrupt', is engaged – Schopenhauer's complaint about Fichte's
lectures (see pp. 8–9 above) – in an 'algebra of mere [pseudo-]
concepts' (WR II: 88).

Genuine concepts and meaningful words are, then, distinguished
from fake concepts and fake words by their pedigree – by the
possibility of retracing that pedigree to their source in sense-
experience. This principle first enunciated by Locke is, says Schopenhauer, the beginning of a new 'epoch' in philosophy (WR II:
82), an epoch in which Fichte or Hegel's style of writing would
become 'history'. (Unfortunately, as we now know, this prediction
was seriously over-optimistic.)

OBSERVATIONS ON SCHOPENHAUER'S CRITERION
OF MEANINGFULNESS

I should like to conclude this chapter by making four observations
concerning Schopenhauer's criterion of meaningfulness.

The first consists in noting the duality in Locke's claim that all
genuine concepts take their 'rise and footing' in sense-experience,
a duality that carries over into Schopenhauer's criterion. Sense-
experience, he is claiming, provides both the *origin* and the *authentication* of genuine concepts. Authentication of the genuineness of a
concept, certification that a word is genuinely meaningful, like the
authentication of a Rembrandt, consists, for Locke, in checking up

on its provenance. But, in fact, the idea that a genuine concept must be 'footed' in sense-experience is independent of the idea that it 'rises' out of it. What this means is that although, as we have seen, the abstractionist theory of the genesis of concepts is thoroughly hopeless, the criterion of meaningfulness can survive its rejection. The general idea, roughly, that words are meaningful only if we can give them experiential 'cash value' is the foundational idea of 'empiricism' and can be retained even if, as we should, we reject the abstractionist theory of concept formation.

* * *

My second observation consists, however, in noting that Schopenhauer does not quite capture his intention in the formulation of the criterion he actually gives. Taken literally, the idea that it must be possible to authenticate concepts 'with perceptions which stand to abstractions in the relation of examples' would make the Harry Potter books meaningless (as well as bad), since no 'example' of such a boy can be given. But obviously Schopenhauer does not want to rule out the possibility of meaningful fiction. So what he really intends to say is that, for a meaningful word, it must be possible to give an example of what it stands for in actual *or possible* experience. Put less pedantically, Schopenhauer's criterion says that if a word is used meaningfully it must be possible to specify *what it would be like* to encounter such a thing, even if in fact we never will. J. K. Rowling's Harry Potter satisfies this criterion; Hegel's Absolute, Schopenhauer claims, does not.

* * *

My third observation concerns so-called 'intellectual' or 'rational' intuitions' (WR I: xxi, WR II: 192 *et passim*).

As mentioned in the first chapter, the notion begins with Kant's suggestion that, were God to exist, his knowledge would be completely independent of sensation and hence of the need for 'forming' mental activity to transform sensation into perception. Since there would thus be no intellect standing between consciousness and reality he would thus have unmediated access to reality just as it is in itself. He would have, in terms of the earlier analogy (see pp. 22–3 above), 'sunglasses'-free acquaintance with the thing in itself. (If he did not have such acquaintance he could never know his beliefs about the world outside his mind to be correct, which would be incompatible with both his omniscience and omnipotence.)

For Kant, since we can never know God to exist, intellectual intuition is, to repeat, a mere hypothesis. Certainly it is available to no human being and Kant never claimed it for himself. His successors, however, had no such modesty. At least as Schopenhauer reads them, they claimed their metaphysical systems to be reports of intellectual intuitions of the thing in itself, of 'the Absolute' – the absolutely 'unconditioned', the unmediated.

It is this move on the part of the 'professors' that repeatedly unleashes the full power of Schopenhauer's satirical scorn. He can never miss an opportunity to satirise their amazing 'oracular ability' to have an 'immediate rational intuition of the Absolute, or even *ad libitum* of the Infinite, and of the Infinite's evolution into the finite' (FR: 166–7), their supposed possession of 'little window[s]' through which to peer at the 'superlunal and even supernatural world' (FR: 165, 180–1). (Nietzsche, in a not unrelated context, satirised the idea of a telephonic hotline to the Divine.)

One can, I think, see Schopenhauer's point and share his scorn. As we have seen, the basic idea of empiricism is that if you can't encounter something in (actual or possible) sense-experience then you can't meaningfully talk about it. This idea has the ring of obvious good sense. But according to Kant's fundamentally inescapable discovery that 'between things and us there always stands the intellect' (WR I: 417), it follows that one cannot meaningfully talk about 'the Absolute', that metaphysics, at least as traditionally conceived, is impossible. So – metaphysics being the traditional heart of philosophy – the 'professors' who made a living 'from' philosophy faced, in the wake of Kant's work, the threat of joblessness.

Their solution, as Schopenhauer represents it: pretend that there is a little rent in the Kantian veil between us and the thing in itself through which the select few can peer, and set yourself up as one of them. Intellectual intuition – 'its correct names would be humbug and charlatanism' (WR I: xxi) – is what we would now call guruism.

There are two reasons why it is important to take note of Schopenhauer's contempt for intellectual intuition. The first is that he is right that there is no such thing – there is no stepping outside of the particular forming activities of our own minds; or at least, if there is, its deliverances cannot be communicated in language. The second concerns the traditional reading of Schopenhauer's philosophy which, seeing him as very much part of the 'German Idealist' movement, interprets him as basing his own metaphysics on direct encounters with the thing in itself; on, that is, in fact if not in name, intellectual intuition. To take proper note of Schopenhauer's contempt for the supposed faculty is to see that this interpretation should be resisted if at all possible.

* * *

My final observation on Schopenhauer's empiricist criterion of meaningfulness consists in noting that by subscribing to it he gives at least the appearance of setting himself up for failure. For his task, remember, just like that of the 'professors', is to get at the real 'whatness' of things, to say what it is which lies behind the veil of appearances. But given his empiricism, he finds himself in the same dilemma as the professors: since we never experience that which lies beyond appearances we can't talk about it. And given his scorn for intellectual intuition, the 'professors'' pseudo-exit from the dilemma is one he can never take. In chapter 4 I shall discuss how, in his mature years, Schopenhauer deals with this problematic area in his thinking.

SUMMARY

1   Schopenhauer's aim: to discover *what* the world is. What makes this a *problem* is Kant's *idealism*: in experiencing a world of natural objects we experience only 'appearances', never reality 'in itself'. *Arguments for idealism.* Kant's proof that space and time are located merely in the mind. Berkeley's argument that a mind-independent object is unimaginable. Schopenhauer's own argument that the mind is a product of evolution which falsifies consciousness in the interests of survival.

2   Schopenhauer's desire to reduce the importance attributed to *reason* by rationalist philosophers by

   (a) showing that in practical life it determines merely means, never ends

   (b) showing that reason's concepts play no role in the genesis of everyday perception of objects and

   (c) showing that reason does very little more than provide crude summaries of what is known through perception.

3   Schopenhauer uses the empiricist principle that concepts are dependent for meaning on sense-experience to dismiss the works of philosophers like Hegel and Fichte, which claim to describe the 'thing in itself', as *meaningless*. A problem, however, is that since he himself appears to be engaged in the same project of discovering the nature of ultimate reality he seems to be setting *himself* up for failure.

FURTHER READING

J. E. Atwell, *Schopenhauer on the Character of the World*, chapters 1 and 2.

P. Gardiner, *Schopenhauer* chapters 2 and 3.

C. Janaway, *Schopenhauer* chapters 2 and 3.

Three

Metaphysics: The World as Will

The task of Schopenhauer's philosophy, we saw at the beginning of chapter 2, is to get at the *whatness* of things, to get at that 'essence', 'kernel', or 'in-itselfness' that lies concealed behind their surface 'appearance'. So perhaps — the thought might present itself — we should turn for an answer to natural science. Perhaps it is here that we will find the 'inner' reality that lies beneath (or within) the 'outer' surface of things. Schopenhauer begins Book II of the main work, at which we have now arrived, by arguing that this is *not* the case. Physics, he argues, can never be placed on the throne of metaphysics (WR II: 175). The ultimate whatness of things can be discovered, if by anything, only by philosophy.

In a way, this is an odd beginning to Book II. For since it is supposed to have been already argued in Book I that the whole world of nature is radically ideal, a kind of 'dream', it would seem to follow immediately and obviously that *natural* science can at best be concerned with the world as it appears, and cannot have anything at all to say about the world as it is in itself.

Kant, after all, had made clear that the whole point of his idealism was to save religion from the challenge of science by confining the latter to the realm of 'appearance'. 'I have', he says in the introduction to the *Critique of Pure Reason*, 'found it necessary to deny *knowledge*, in order to make room for *faith*' (*Critique of Pure Reason* B, xxx) — to deny *scientific* knowledge to make room for, not indeed the *knowledge* that the world beyond space and time is the way Christianity says it is, but for, at least, the *possibility* that what Christians accept as a matter of faith might be true. So given, as we saw, that Schopenhauer accepts Kant's proof of radical idealism as incontestably true, the job of excluding science from access to the ultimate nature of reality has, he ought to accept, already been completed.

But Schopenhauer *does* argue the point in a new and quite different way. This suggests the hypothesis that radical idealism is not genuinely in play in Book II. That though a *partial* idealism is assumed, though the everyday or commonsense comprehension of the world is assumed to be ideal, idealism about the space-time world, about nature *as such*, is not in play. Only on this assumption is natural science even a *candidate* for the title 'that which reveals the ultimate whatness of things'.

This hypothesis, I shall suggest, represents the truth of the matter. For the project of Book II, radical idealism is fundamentally irrelevant. Though the book discovers *something* – Schopenhauer calls it, of course, 'will' – to lie beneath the everyday surface of things, this something is a *natural* entity, lies within the bounds of space and time.

This being said, however, it also needs to be emphasised that, as a young man, as the author of Volume I, Schopenhauer had a strong inclination to misinterpret his own project, to believe, as I put it in the opening chapter, that he had cracked the problem of Kant's thing in itself. Many times in Volume I, that is, he calls the 'will' the 'thing in itself', and never gives any clear indication that this term is being used in anything other than its established, Kantian sense. In the next chapter, however, I shall show how the more mature Schopenhauer, the author of Volume II, came to see that this is a mistake; how he came to admit that the 'will', though esoteric, though lying beneath the commonsense surface of things, remains a *natural* entity and as such distinct from Kant's *supra-natural* thing in itself.

COMPLETING THE SCIENTIFIC IMAGE

One reason, then, for beginning Book II with a discussion of natural science is that the scientific account of things *is* a candidate for being an account of their ultimate whatness – which would of course make philosophy in general, and Schopenhauer's own philosophy in particular, redundant.

Another, more interesting, reason is that for Schopenhauer, 'just what the sciences presuppose and lay down as the basis and limit of their explanation is precisely the real problem of philosophy' (WR I: 81–2), from which it follows that 'science is the corrected *statement of the problem* of metaphysics' (WR II: 178). For Schopenhauer, then, as mentioned in the first chapter, philosophers need to know a good deal of science (a sentiment all modern philosophers of science would endorse). 'No one', he admonishes, 'should venture [into metaphysics] . . . without having previously acquired a knowledge of all the branches of natural science which, though only general, is yet thorough, clear, and connected'. But this is not to find an *answer* to the question of metaphysics but simply because 'the problem must come before the solution' (WR II: 178–9).

Schopenhauer himself, as we saw, satisfied this condition by devoting his first year at Göttingen to the study of natural science. Though his yearning for a 'better consciousness' links him to Romanticism, it is an important fact, as we noted, that he does not share the hatred of science generally characteristic of Romanticism. Throughout his writings he preserves a strong interest in science, the *World as Will* being regularly punctuated by strongly expressed views on contemporary scientific issues: the impossibility, as he sees it, of reducing biology to physics, the superiority of Goethe's theory of colours to that of Newton, the wrong-headedness of atomism and so on. Schopenhauer did not like *scientism*, the claim that science is capable of answering every question that is of human interest. In particular, he disliked the 'fine airs' which misinterpreters of science sometimes adopt towards philosophy (WR II: 172). But science itself fascinated him.

All this suggests a non-hostile, collaborative relation between science and philosophy (traditionally known as 'the queen of the sciences'); that natural science, by itself is somehow incomplete, that '*physics* is unable to stand on its own feet, but needs a *metaphysics* on which to support itself' (WR II: 172). It suggests a conception of philosophy such that at least one of its fundamental tasks is, as we might put it, the completion of the scientific image of reality.

NATURAL FORCES

So how and why is natural science incomplete?

Science aims at explanation – at explaining particular phenomena by subsuming them under causal laws. So the essence of science is the discovery of causal laws. But what makes something a *law* as opposed to an accidental correlation? Why are we sure that smoking causes lung cancer but not so sure that eating red meat causes bowel cancer, even though in the latter as in the former case there is a strong statistical correlation between the two phenomena? Ultimately because in the first case but not the second we are able to give an account of *what* it is that connects the phenomena. We have, that is, some idea of what Schopenhauer calls the 'inner mechanism' (WR I: 100) connecting smoking with lung cancer. This, he holds, is always the case. In so far as we claim something to be a genuine law, we suppose there to be some 'inner conditioning' (FW: 34) in which that law is grounded, something which authenticates its status as a law. Even if we do not know what this 'conditioning' is, our conviction that there is a law is the conviction that such a 'conditioning' exists. When we get down to the fundamental level of matter these items which make laws laws are what Schopenhauer calls 'natural forces'. Putative examples he gives are gravity, impenetrability and electricity (WR I: 97, 141).

Forces are neither causes nor effects. They do not belong to, but rather preserve and 'express' their natures in, lawful patterns of cause and effect. They preserve 'the unalterable constancy' of those laws through time (WR I: 97). That small objects are attracted towards the centres of large objects, for example, is both an expression of, and is constituted as a law by, the force which we call 'gravity'.

Science, then, committed as it is to laws of nature, is committed to the existence of natural forces. But what are these forces? What is gravity? To this question it gives no answer. So far as science is concerned gravity is a '*qualitas occulta*' an 'unknown X', (WR I: 125, WR II: 318, WN: 317–20). Hence, though fascinating and useful, the image of the world produced by science is essentially facile, two-dimensional. It is like 'a section of a piece of marble showing many different veins side by side, but not letting us know the course of the veins from the interior of the marble to the surface' (WR I: 98). Though a distinction is generally made between explanatory sciences such as physics and chemistry and descriptive and classificatory sciences such as botany, really, all science is merely descriptive. It shows the 'orderly arrangement' of natural phenomena but explains none of them (WR I: 96–7).

Schopenhauer acknowledges, of course, that in science one theory often gets absorbed into a more fundamental one. Forces such as solubility and rigidity inherent in gross bodies (sugar lumps) may be explained in terms of those bodies being structures of more refined objects (molecules) together with the laws governing the behaviour of the latter. Theory reduction can go, however, only so far. Sooner or later science must reach a bedrock level of entities and a bedrock level of most fundamental laws governing the behaviour of those entities. It is the forces presupposed by these laws, the ultimate, 'original' forces of nature, which Schopenhauer claims to constitute the fundamental mystery, the 'insoluble residuum' (WR I: 123–4) of natural science.

It might be objected that since theory reduction, explanation, must stop somewhere, it is of course the case that, ultimately, one will arrive at laws grounded in forces which are incapable of further explanation. But this is to misunderstand Schopenhauer's account of the incompleteness of natural science. His objection is not that science cannot *explain* fundamental forces, but rather that it can't attach any *meaning* to its fundamental terms.

The background to this is Schopenhauer's empiricist criterion of meaningfulness discussed in the last chapter. According to that principle, 'it must be possible to verify the [meaningfulness of a] concept with perceptions which stand to abstractions in the relation of examples'; it must be possible to specify in experiential terms, what it would be like to come across whatever it is that is being talked about. As we saw, Schopenhauer uses this empiricist principle to debunk pseudo-philosophical 'scribbling' about 'the Absolute' and 'the Infinite's evolution into the Finite'. But, he now observes, left to its own devices, science is in the same boat. Just like Hegel's 'Absolute', gravity is, to science, a mere 'X'. It uses empty words so that, quite literally, it doesn't know what it is talking about.

In Michael Frayn's play *Copenhagen*, which concerns a meeting in 1941 between Niels Bohr and Werner Heisenberg, the founders (along with Einstein and Max Plank) of quantum physics, Bohr raises an objection against Heisenberg's 'Indeterminacy Principle' (if you know the position of a subatomic particle you can't know its momentum and vice versa) and against his approach to fundamental science in general. His complaint is that he, Heisenberg, doesn't care what his theory *means*, only that the sums come out right. This I think is Schopenhauer's complaint about natural science as such. At its fundamental level, he suggests, it doesn't know what it *means*.

So, left to its own devices, it is 'inadequate' (WR II: 176). It needs help, 'is unable to stand on its own feet but needs a *metaphysics* on which to support itself' (WR II: 172).

THE NATURE OF MATTER

So physics needs metaphysics, science needs philosophy. But equally, as we saw, metaphysics needs science, since it is the latter that is the 'corrected statement of the problem of metaphysics'. Why does philosophy need science? Why does philosophy, in particular, need to get its fundamental science right in order to even start its thinking from the right place?

Schopenhauer has decided views about the nature of matter. Matter, he says, is 'pure causality' (WR II: 305). Its 'whole essence consists in acting (ibid.). It is 'not extended [in space] and is consequently incorporeal' (WR II: 308). It cannot itself be perceived but merely 'exhibits itself as body' (WR II: 305, 309). These interesting remarks are intended to oppose 'atomism' – the view that the world's ultimate constituents are tiny chunks of matter in terms of whose behaviour everything else is to be explained. This view, which Schopenhauer calls a 'revolting absurdity', though propounded by Locke (and two thousand years before him by Democritus), finds particular favour in France due to 'the backward state of [French] . . . metaphysics' (WR II: 302), the inability of French philosophers to think seriously about the foundations of natural science (an inability, one might be tempted to add, which continues to this very day.)

Putting these remarks together, we can understand Schopenhauer's view to be that what the best science does is to dematerialise or desubstantialise matter. Opposing the 'chunky' view[1], Schopenhauer understands good science to hold that the ultimate constituents of matter are extensionless centres of 'pure causality', in other words of force. The natural world is nothing but space filled with (as modern science calls them) force fields. These fields of force, as Schopenhauer puts it, 'objectify' themselves – are experienced by us – as perceptible bodies, yet outside the human mind such bodies have no existence. When we say that a body is 'hard, heavy, fluid, green, alkaline, organic and so on', we are merely reporting the 'action or effect' of force fields on the human mind (WR I: 458).

This account of the status and nature of material bodies casts the theory of perception discussed in the last chapter (pp. 36–9) in a new light. According to that theory, it will be remembered, the 'understanding' constructs its account of the external world by inferring from sensations to objects as their external causes. In this way it produces what we might call the 'manifest' or 'common sense' image of the world. In fact, however, according to what Schopenhauer takes to be good science, all these inferences (inferences that are absolutely necessary to human survival) are mistaken. Nothing object-like exists outside the mind. According to the best science, bodies are nothing but 'spaces filled with force' (WN: 207).[2]

* * *

There is, then, a relation of mutual dependence between science and philosophy. On the one hand physics needs some further discipline to attach meaning to its fundamental terms (and if not 'meta-physics' what else?) for otherwise it is, at root, a meaningless, though technologically useful, enterprise. But on the other hand, philosophy needs science to tell it, with precision, just what the problem of understanding the whatness of the world amounts to. The problem, we now know, is to describe the character of the fundamental forces of nature and thereby to do what science itself cannot do, complete the scientific image. How might it set about doing this? By, Schopenhauer suggests, turning from science's necessary 'objectivity' to something which he calls 'subjectivity'.

THE SUBJECTIVE VERSUS THE OBJECTIVE STANDPOINT

Schopenhauer observes, correctly, that there are different standpoints from which we may think about reality. We may, he says, adopt either the 'subjective' or 'objective' view of things.

At the beginning of his *Meditations* about what he really knows, René Descartes (1596–1650) observes that he certainly has experiences which seem to be of houses, trees, sky and so on. But since he has had such experiences during dreams, and since he can't absolutely prove he's not dreaming now, he concludes that he can't be certain that there is anything outside his mind (his 'representations', as Schopenhauer would put it) that corresponds to his experiences. This is a paradigm of the 'subjective' approach to things: consciousness – experiences, representations – is certain, objects problematic.

The 'objective' view looks at things the other way round. It 'takes as its object, not our own consciousness, but the beings that are given in external experience' (WR I: 97). From this point of view it is the existence of objects that is certain, the existence of consciousness problematic. It is, in fact, entirely discounted. Though the objective inquirer himself has of course conscious states, he pretends to be 'a winged angel's head (Engelskopf) without a body' (WR I: 99) and views what is, in fact, his body 'as if . . . [it] were something foreign' (WN: 294). In other words, he pretends that, as a subject of consciousness, he is not in the field of enquiry. In the field, he pretends, there is no consciousness. Just bodies and their behaviour. Hence another name for the objective view is 'materialism', that position which 'abstracts from the subjectivity of the subject' (FR: 52, WR I: 33–4).

The objective view represents, says Schopenhauer, the methodology of science. (He anticipates, here, the orthodoxy of contemporary science. The requirement that a scientist's experimental results should be repeatable by other scientists is taken to mean that they should be confined to data available from the objective point of view.) We can therefore describe the incompleteness of science – the fact that it offers a mere 'X' at precisely the crucial point where we want to know what the world really is – in a new way: it is the incompleteness of the objective viewpoint, its failure to discover the ultimate nature of things.

And what this shows, since this is the only remaining option, is that if – if – we are going to be able to fathom the ultimate nature of reality we have only one place to turn: to the subjective point of view. How might this help?

THE BLACK BOX PROBLEM

Let us, says Schopenhauer, perform a thought-experiment with respect to the knowledge we have of ourselves. Let us pretend that we have no knowledge about our own body and its behaviour other than that which is provided by the objective viewpoint. On this assumption, our own body becomes

> a representation like any other, an object among objects. Its movements and actions are so far known to him [the objective investigator] in just the same way as the changes of all other objects of perception; and they would be equally strange and incomprehensible to him, if their meaning (*Bedeutung*) were not unravelled for him in an entirely different way. Otherwise, he would see his conduct follow on presented motives with the constancy of a law of nature just as the changes of other objects follow upon causes, stimuli, and motives. But he would be no nearer to understanding the influence of the motives than he is to understanding the connexion with its cause of any other effect that appears before him. He would then also call the inner, to him incomprehensible, nature of those manifestations and actions of his body a force, a quality or a character, just as he pleased, but he would have no further insight into it
>
> (WR I: 99–100).

A word of explanation. Schopenhauer, as we know, views causality as a three-term phenomenon: there is cause, effect and the natural force in virtue of which the cause is the cause of that effect. As he puts it here, the force is that which accounts for the 'influence' of the cause. Of causes, however, he has a threefold classification. There are causes in the 'narrow' sense, the kinds of causes one finds in the field of mechanical, inorganic nature (a billiard ball moving because struck by another). Then there are 'stimuli', the kind of causes one finds operating in vegetable nature. Stimuli differ from mechanical causes in that the effect is not proportional to the cause. Increases in the velocity with which one billiard ball hits another are precisely correlated with increases in the distance travelled by the second ball. But increases in the heat to which a plant is subjected are not so proportional: a small increase in heat may result in the death of the plant. Finally 'motives' are the kind of causes one finds in the animal and human domain. They presuppose an intellect, that is, a brain. I have already briefly mentioned 'motives' and will have more to say about them later on, but for the present discussion let us just say that they are inputs of information to the brain of an organism which cause it to act. The deer or the human being has its eyeballs irradiated with an image of a unfriendly-looking tiger which causes it to run (FR: 70–1).

So, Schopenhauer suggests, by imagining that we only have objective knowledge of our own bodily behaviour, we reproduce the situation science finds itself in with respect to the fundamental laws of nature. In principle, he thinks, if we observed our bodies long and hard enough we would come up with laws governing all of their behaviour – 'whenever he sees a tiger on the loose he runs', for example. But as to why those laws obtain, why that 'motive' has that particular 'influence', we would be none the wiser. We would take it that there was something there, a 'force or character', but just like fundamental forces to science, it would be a '*qualitas occulta*', an 'unknown X'.

'All this, however', says Schopenhauer – releasing us now from the conditions of the thought-experiment – 'is not the case'. Since, in reality, we have subjective as well as objective access to our own bodies, the answer to the question of what it is which explains why we run when we see tigers – a question which is, from the object-ive point of view, an insoluble 'riddle' – is transparently obvious:

> this answer is given in the word *will* (**Wille**). This and this alone gives him [the human inquirer] the key to his own phenomenon, reveals to him the meaning (*Bedeutung*) and shows him the inner mechanism of his being, his actions, his movements. To the subject of knowing, who appears as an individual only through his identity with the body, this body is given in two entirely different ways. It is given in intelligent perception as representation, as an object among objects, liable to the laws of these objects. But it is also

given in quite a different way, namely as what is known immediately
to everyone and is denoted by the word *will*

(WR I: 100).

This is a crucial passage.[3] First, its *strategic* importance.

From the objective point of view, we have seen, the forces which
sustain – and are expressed in – the laws governing the behaviour
of bodies are a complete mystery. This is as true of 'my' body as of
any other. In reality, however, there is something unique about my
access to that body: I have subjective access to it, too. And this
subjective access *discloses* the nature of the force in question: it is a
perfectly trivial piece of everyday knowledge that I run from tigers
because I don't want to be eaten – I 'will' not to be eaten (Schopenhauer says that the most fundamental aspect of the will is the
'will to live'). So, in at least one case, the 'riddle' as to the character
of forces is solved. The force in question is disclosed by the subjective perspective to be will. In one case, then,

a way *from within*, stands open to us to that real inner nature of
things which we cannot penetrate *from without*. It is, so to speak, a
subterranean passage, a secret alliance, which, as if by treachery,
places us all at once in the fortress that could not be taken from
without

(WR II: 195).

And perhaps, here, we find the essential 'clue' (WR II: 274) to the
'deciphering' (WR II: 182) of the riddle of the fundamental whatness of things in general. Perhaps, that is, if 'inner experience is
connected to outer' (ibid.) in the right way we will find 'will' to be
the answer not just to the question of the nature of the force that
sustains the laws governing the behaviour of my body, but to the
question of the nature of forces in general. Perhaps, that is, the
world which appears in human representation as objects is, from a
deeper point of view, *in its totality*, 'will' and nothing else.

And this, of course, is Schopenhauer's audacious thesis. Notice, how, on the face of things, 'will' looks to be very well adapted to the task of completing the scientific image. Good science, we know, rejects the 'chunky', substantival view of reality shared by both atomism and common sense. Though it cannot tell us their nature, science, in Schopenhauer's view, really does show that natural reality is not made up of objects of any kind but rather of immaterial forces. So, if we are to give an account of those forces we need something that does not have the nature of an object. At least on the surface, therefore, 'will' — 'striving' Schopenhauer often says — might well look to be a good candidate.

* * *

But what, really, is the 'will'? The problem that interests Schopenhauer is what we might call a 'black box' problem. On the objective view of things – and, here, it doesn't make any difference whether the things in question are rocks, daffodils, dogs, other human bodies or my own body – we observe the body in question affected by a cause which produces as an effect a given piece of behaviour. Something about the body in question ensures that that cause produces precisely that effect (the same cause would produce different effects in other bodies) but we have no idea what it is; it is a *'qualitas occulta'*. So we have an input and an output mediated by, as it were, a black box which we cannot open. Its 'inner mechanism' is as unintelligible as (to a computer-ignoramus such as myself) is the inner mechanism of the elegant little iBook laptop on which I am writing this book.

This would be the end of the story were it not for the single, dramatic exception of my own body. Here, on account of the 'double knowledge' I have of its 'action and movement following on motives' (WR I: 103), on account of the subjective as well as objective access I have to it, I *can* see inside the black box. I can get 'behind the scenes' with regard to causality: *'motivation* [understanding why given "motives" lead to given actions] *is causality seen from within'*, says Schopenhauer, an insight which, he adds, 'is the cornerstone of my whole metaphysics' (FR: 213–4). And what I discover when I look inside the black box is 'will'. Yet what, to repeat the question, is 'will'?

WILL AS CHARACTER

What really interests Schopenhauer about action in general and human action in particular, is *difference*. Why does a rock behave one way when you hit it with a hammer and a sponge in another? Why do two humans – twins, perhaps, brought up in identical circumstances – respond differently to identical motivational (informational) imputes? Why does one invest in low-risk but low-return bank deposits, the other in the high-return but high-risk futures? Why does one pass indifferently by the beggar in the street, the other give him the entire two hundred dollars she has just withdrawn from the ATM machine? Because they have different 'wills', that is to say *characters*. 'The particularly and individually constituted nature of . . . [a person's] will . . . makes up what one calls his character' (FW: 51). It is, then, will as 'character' that mediates between 'motive' and action: 'Only on the presupposition of my . . . character is the motive a sufficient ground of explanation of my conduct' (WR I: 106).

What, then, is character?

* * *

A person's character is, says Schopenhauer, both innate (in the genes, as it were) and unalterable (FW p. 54).[4] At different times in his life, to be sure, a person may pursue different goals. The petty criminality of youth, for example, may, in adulthood, give way to the bloody conquest of nations (see WR I: 138–9, 158–9). But this is always attributable to a change in circumstances, never to a change in the fundamental goal of acquiring, for example, as much wealth as possible.

Since character never changes it follows that every life has a fundamental unity to it (WR II: 35). Schopenhauer represents this underlying unity in terms of 'a maxim [principle] characterising my willing as a whole, a maxim that expresses what I will 'in general' (WR I: 106). (Jean-Paul Sartre – who learnt more from Schopenhauer than he ever acknowledges – calls this a person's 'fundamental project'.) The whole of a life, Schopenhauer says, can be thought of as flowing from a single act of choice (FW: 96). So the idea is that one's choices form a kind of pyramid. At the top is one's most fundamental choice which, together with knowledge of the circumstances one finds oneself in, lead to less fundamental choices, and so on down to those choices which form the base of the pyramid.

At the beginning of Shakespeare's *Richard III*, Richard declares that he is 'determined to prove a villain', to dedicate his life to destroying the happiness of the 'house of York' which he hates. Though few people (other than Schopenhauer himself) possess such ruthless honesty about themselves, this, I think, is an example of the kind of fundamental maxim Schopenhauer has in mind. An absolutely contrasting maxim would be to 'harm no one, on the contrary to help everyone as much as possible' which is, as we shall see, the maxim on which the saint acts. It might be objected that most lives are far too muddled for there to be any such fundamental maxim, that possessing a 'fundamental maxim', whether directed towards good or towards evil, is a significant *achievement*. This is an issue to which I shall return on pp. 160–4 below.

'Motives' are, says Schopenhauer, the 'occasion[s] on which my will manifests itself' (WR I: 106). So, for example, if my fundamental maxim is the saintly one and I see a beggar in the gutter, I will give him the money I have just withdrawn from the ATM machine. If, on the other hand, it is to be a villain or a sadist, I will give that beggar a kick in the guts. If my fundamental maxim is simply one of self-interest, I will merely pass by. As we will see (pp. 175–6 below), Schopenhauer thinks that, on an at least preliminary classification, the three fundamental ingredients of the human will are self-interest, altruism and malice. Leaving aside the limiting cases of the pure villain and the pure saint, every human character is some mixture of the three. (WR I: 303).

Since a person's actions are entirely determined by motives together with character, and since character is innate and unalterable, it follows that freedom, in the sense of my being able to act otherwise than I actually do, is a myth.[5]

EXTENDING THE WILL

Let us recapitulate the strategic situation. Material bodies, for Schopenhauer, are, in essence, black boxes. They are devices which, in response to given inputs (causes) produce given outputs (effects) in a way in which, if we know them well enough, we know to be entirely lawful. Since laws are the expression of underlying 'natural forces', bodies are therefore, in essence, forces. More precisely – since a number of laws govern the behaviour of any material body – they are constellations of such forces – rigidity, impenetrability, gravitational attraction and so on. To bodies in general, we have only 'objective' access. And this means that the nature of the fundamental forces which, in reality, they are, is unknown to us.

This had two bad consequences. For science it means that, ultimately, it does not know what it is talking about. Since it is unable to specify, in experiential terms, the meaning of its fundamental terms, those terms have, in fact, no meaning. And for Schopenhauer himself it means that the project of discovering the basic whatness of things looks to be facing shipwreck.

Help, however, is at hand. For there is one unique case where, on account of our subjective access to it, we are able to decipher the nature of the force-constellation that a body is. This is the case of our own body. And what we know here is that what is, from the 'outside', designated as 'force', is, from the 'inside', will; that is to say, 'character'. Here, then, Schopenhauer hypothesises, we perhaps find the Archimedean point, the decisive 'clue' to 'deciphering' the nature of forces in general, to rescuing both science and the whatness-discovering project of philosophy. Perhaps what that which 'objectifies' itself to us as a world of bodies really is, is, through and through, nothing but will. Perhaps, as Schopenhauer often puts it, the nature of the 'macrocosm' is given in the 'microcosm'; perhaps what I know to be the case in respect of my body is really the case with respect to all bodies. Schopenhauer's task is now to convince us that this is indeed the case.

* * *

He calls this process of discovering the inner nature of absolutely everything to be 'homogeneous' (WR I: 105) with my own, the 'extension' (WR I: 111) of the concept of 'will' beyond its normal sphere of application. The extension is, he says, 'paradoxical' (WN: 216), incongruous with familiar modes of thought. But actually only part of it is. The non-paradoxical part is the acceptance that the actions of other human beings are, like my own, manifestations of a will. The paradoxical, audacious, part is the extension of 'will' to explain the behaviour of non-human beings. I begin with the former.

BYPASSING SOLIPSISM

I have, we know 'double knowledge' (WR I: 103), objective and subjective, of my own body. This doubleness is unique: there is no other human body to which I have subjective access. This, says Schopenhauer, faces me with a choice: either I must assume that my *access* is unique – that other bodies are, like mine, manifestations of will but that I cannot 'see' their wills in the same direct way as I can see my own – or I must assume that my *body* is unique – that the reason I cannot 'see' any wills other than my own is that *there are no wills other than my own*. The latter position, which he calls 'theoretical egoism' (solipsism), can, he says,

> never be refuted by proofs, yet in philosophy it has never been
> positively used otherwise than as a sceptical sophism i.e. for the
> sake of appearance. As a serious conviction, on the other hand, it

> could be found only in a madhouse: as such it would then need not
> so much refutation as a cure
>
> (WR I: 104).

So of course we must extend 'will' to other human beings. Not to
do so would be 'mad'.

Schopenhauer is sometimes accused of being 'soft on solipsism'.
His claim that solipsism cannot be 'refuted by proofs', it is suggested, is superficial and unacceptable. But this seems to me to
ignore the interesting remark that 'theoretical egoism . . . regards as
phantoms all phenomena outside his own will, just as practical
egoism does in a practical respect' (WR I: 104). 'There are no other
wills, no other beings capable of experiencing desire and frustration, pain and pleasure', as an explicitly articulated belief is found
only in madhouses. Yet it is this very same doctrine, Schopenhauer
suggests, which is expressed in selfish action. And such 'practical
egoism', as we will see in chapter 7, he *does* 'refute'. He argues that
it is based on metaphysical illusion. So there *is*, after all, a refutation
of solipsism in Schopenhauer. It is just that it is to be found in his
ethical philosophy, in Book IV of the *World as Will*, rather than in
Book II.

ORGANIC NATURE

Given that we have rejected theoretical egoism, 'will' is accepted as
extending throughout the human domain. And so far as the higher
animals are concerned – dogs, elephants, and apes, for example – it
is obvious that no significant distinction can be made between the
grounds or their behaviour and the grounds of human behaviour. It
is obvious, that is, that they respond to 'motives' (although not
'abstract' motives (see p. 43 above)) in accordance with their will,
just as humans do.

It is when one moves beyond the higher animals to the rest of
nature, to insects and plants and the non-voluntary processes of the
human body (breathing, the beating of the heart and so on), that

one might well find the extension of the will to be, as Schopenhauer says, 'paradoxical'. One might well think, that is to say, that will is essentially tied to 'motives'; that it does not make sense to speak of desiring, willing, or striving for some goal except where there is an intellect (brain) which can (a) represent the desired goal and (b) the means of achieving it. One might well think, in short, that will is essentially tied to what Schopenhauer calls 'knowledge (*Erkentniss*)'.

But Schopenhauer denies this. He thinks that the affront to ordinary modes of thought has to be accepted for the sake of truth. The reason is that 'we see at once from the instinct and mechanical skill of animals that the will is also active where it is not guided by knowledge' (WR I: 114). And again:

> The truth that will can exist without knowledge is apparent, we might say palpably recognizable, in plant life. For in it we see a decided striving, determined by needs, modified in many different ways, and adapting itself to the variety of circumstances – yet clearly without knowledge
>
> (WR II: 295).

Why is Schopenhauer so confident about this, as one might think, mind-boggling idea that even though plants don't have brains or consciousness they have something like the desires that we have? The answer has to do with Schopenhauer's understanding of teleology, of purpose-directedness.

ORGANIC NATURE AND TELEOLOGY

Organic nature is, Schopenhauer observes, universally purposive. It is permeated by 'in order to's, by what, using Aristotle's terminology, Schopenhauer calls 'final causes'. Every feature of an organism, of either its behaviour or its 'form and shape' (WR II: 327), has a purpose or final cause that contributes, ultimately, to its survival and capacity to reproduce (WR II: 329). So, for example, the heart beats in order to circulate the blood, the giraffe has a long neck in order to reach the leaves of tall trees, the spider spins a web in order to catch flies, and the sunflower turns towards the sun in order to photosynthesise. But how is it that final causes are effective? Isn't there something terribly paradoxical about the idea of some future state causing something to happen in the present? Isn't it the one thing we know for certain that causes always happen before their effects, that causation can never happen backwards?

Indeed so, says Schopenhauer. It follows from this we must reduce final causation to 'efficient' (ordinary) causation, show that talk of final causes is just a shorthand for something that can be stated entirely in terms of ordinary causes. But how are we to do that?

In fact, we use final causation as a shorthand for ordinary causation all the time. 'Harry went to the post office (in order) to get some stamps', we know, is just an abbreviation of 'Harry went to the post office because he wanted ("willed") to get some stamps.' This pattern, says Schopenhauer, represents the only way we know of reducing final to efficient causation: 'we cannot clearly conceive a final cause except as an intended aim or end i.e. as a motive' (WR II: 332)[6], in other words, as the content of a willing. What follows from this is that the 'universal suitability [purpose-directedness] relating to the continued existence of every being cannot easily be associated with any philosophical system except that which makes will the basis of every natural being's existence' (WR II: 327).

What follows is that when dealing with the instinctive behaviour or physiological features of organisms

> we must not shrink from a contradiction and boldly state that the final cause is a motive which acts on a being by whom it is not known. For nests of termites are certainly the motive that has called into existence the toothless jaw of the ant-eater, together with its long, thread-like, and glutinous tongue. The [desire to break out of the] hard egg-shell, holding the chicken a prisoner, is certainly the

motive for the horny point with which its beak is provided, in order
with it to break through that shell; after this the chicken casts it off
as of no further use

(WR II: 332).

Really, however, Schopenhauer continues, there is no 'contradiction' in such cases since we are dealing with 'the transition from
the physical to the metaphysical' (ibid.). What is going on here?

There are two questions we have to ask. First, why does it *seem* a
'contradiction' to say that, for example, the chicken embryo has a
horny point because of a will, 'intention' or 'motive' of breaking
out of the egg? And second, why does the transition to 'the metaphysical', whatever that might be, remove the appearance of
contradiction?

* * *

Schopenhauer says, in explanation of his use of the word 'will', that
'not only willing and deciding in the narrowest sense' – acts of will
such as 'I shall *now* raise my arm' – 'but also all striving, wishing,
shunning, hoping, fearing, loving, hating, in short all that directly
constitutes our own weal and woe, desire and disinclination, is
obviously only affection of the will, is a stirring, a modification, of
willing and not-willing' (WR II: 202). A few pages later he compares the will to a sultan sitting on a couch, before whom the
'intellect' places various projects for action and who then simply
expresses his 'monotonous approval or disapproval' (WR II: 207).
It seems, then, that willing is simply saying 'yes' or 'no' to possible
courses of action. But what that means is that one has to have some
content to say yes or no *to*, has to be capable of cognitive states, has
to possess, in other words, an 'intellect'. Yet clearly the chicken
embryo, having no brain, has no intellect. The apparent 'contradiction' is then, that we seem to be attributing and intending or
willing to a being that cannot possibly will or intend.

Why does the 'transition to the metaphysical' remove that

apparent contradiction? Because, says Schopenhauer, 'this [the metaphysical] we have recognised in the will' (WR II: 332).

In other words, we don't have to say that the intellect-less chicken embryo wills the goal of breaking out of the egg. Rather, it is the 'metaphysical' will that acts in the chicken, or acts 'on' it, as Schopenhauer says, making a significant choice of word.

The next question that needs to be answered, obviously, is: what is this metaphysical will? Before trying to answer it, however, I should like to attend, briefly, to the final step in the 'extension' of will throughout nature, its extension to the inorganic realm.

INANIMATE NATURE

Schopenhauer believes, as we have seen, that we cannot make sense of teleology without appeal to a will. The extension of the will throughout organic nature is, therefore, non-optional. When it comes to the final phase in the portrayal of the whole of nature as will, however, the extension of the concept to inorganic nature, he concedes that a degree of optionality creeps in. The reason is that 'in inorganic nature . . . the final cause remains problematic' (WR II: 334), 'ambiguous', in that we may wonder whether the appearance that teleology is at work here is 'merely a view' (WR II: 335).

Certainly we can view inorganic nature as permeated by purpose and will. Let us merely observe

> the powerful, irresistible impulse with which masses of water rush downwards, the persistence and determination with which the magnet always turns back to the North Pole, the keen desire with which iron flies to the magnet, the vehemence with which the poles of the electric current strive for reunion and which, like the vehemence of human desires, is increased by obstacles . . . [l]et us observe the choice with which bodies repel and attract one another . . .
>
> (WR I: 118),

the 'perpetual struggle between the magnet and gravitation' (WR I: 146), the 'contest', 'strife' and 'subjugation' of each other which occurs between, for instance, centrifugal and centripetal forces (WR I: 118), and 'it will cost us no great effort of the imagination to recognise again our own inner nature even at so great a distance' (WR I: 118). So we *could* make the final extension of the will, but why *should* we? Why should we regard the above picture of things as anything more than the fanciful projection of an overheated, romantic imagination?

Schopenhauer has, I think, two reasons to offer. The first has to do what he calls 'the law of homogeneity' sanctioned by no lesser person than 'the divine Plato'. This tells us to seek out the highest genus under which all the species of natural things can be subsumed (FR: 1), to search out 'knowledge of the identical in different phenomena' (WR I: 111). Applied to a metaphysical theory of nature, this fundamental constraint on philosophical method requires that it should unify, should 'spread a uniform light over all the phenomena of the world, and bring even the most heterogeneous into agreement, so that the contradiction may be removed even between those that contrast most' (WR II: 184). Schopenhauer repeatedly makes the same point by quoting the ancient axiom that 'nature makes no leaps'. If, then, we refuse to extend will to (so-called) inorganic nature the result is a sharp division between the organic and the inorganic. So if we *can* make the final extension of the will we *should*.

The second reason Schopenhauer seems to give for taking this final step is to remind us, once again, that physics requires completion by metaphysics, that it is the task of philosophy to complete the scientific image of the world. To refuse to extend will to the inorganic realm is to condemn the physical sciences to ultimate meaninglessness, to leave the forces in which fundamental physics deals shrouded in incomprehensibility. For since we know that the nature of those forces cannot be deciphered objectively, the only possibility of doing so lies in the subjective. And all that we find there, the only material available to us for rescuing science, is will. As Schopenhauer asks rhetorically: to what other kind of 'existence or reality' could we turn? 'From what [other] source could we take the elements out of which to construct [the inner nature of the] . . . world? Besides will and representation absolutely nothing is known or conceivable for us' (WR I: 105).

In the end, therefore, we have no choice. The will must be extended all the way into the inorganic realm. Schopenhauer sums up the consequence of this final extension of the will in a witty way:

> Spinoza . . . says that if a stone projected through the air had consciousness, it would imagine it was flying of its own will. I add merely that the stone would be right
>
> (WR I: 126).

THE WORLD-WILL

Back, now, to the question of just what it is that acts 'on' all those intellect-less organisms which can't will things for themselves.

So far, our discussion of 'will' has been pluralistic. We have seen Schopenhauer constructing a metaphysical account of the world which amounts, in the first instance, to the view that 'bodies are spaces filled with force' (WN: 207), and in the second (when philosophy renders the concept of force intelligible) to the view that bodies – those things that 'objectify' themselves in our experience as bodies – are in reality locations or centres of 'will'.

This talk, as I say, is pluralistic. There are *many* bodies and hence *many* centres of force i.e. will. Often, however, Schopenhauer talks of, not wills, but rather of a single, unitary entity which he calls 'the will'. Over and above the will in this and that body there is what I shall call, to avoid confusion, the 'world-will'. Schopenhauer has a number of motives for this metaphysical monism, but so far as Book II is concerned, what is important are his views on teleology.

Organisms, as we have seen, are defined by the fact that every part fulfils a purpose which contributes to the survival of the whole. And Schopenhauer, believes, as we have seen, that this, as he sometimes calls it, 'inner suitability' (WR I: section 28 *passim*) can only be made intelligible by appeal to a will. Additionally, however, organisms exhibit an 'external suitability' (ibid.). All parts of nature are in 'harmony' with each other, as they must be to render its continued existence possible. There is a mutual adaptation between each organism and the environment, both organic and inorganic, in which it finds itself: 'every plant is well adapted to its soil and climate, every animal to its element and to the prey that is to become its food, that prey also being protected to a certain extent against its natural hunter' (WR I: 159). But what this means is that *nature as a whole* exhibits 'inner suitability', that every part contributes to the existence of the whole. Schopenhauer believes, in short, that nature as a whole is an organism. He subscribes in other words to what has come to be known as 'the Gaia hypothesis'. Hence, just as the individual organism must be conceived as the product of a will, so must nature as a whole. It objectifies what I call the 'world-will'.

THE PLATONIC IDEAS

To represent the overall 'suitability' of nature Schopenhauer employs the notion of the 'Platonic Idea'. The Platonic Ideas correspond for Schopenhauer, as they do for Plato, to the species of things, both organic and inorganic, that there are in nature. They are the natural kinds (WR I: 156).[7] Over and above the Ideas of the particular species, however, is a further Idea which 'is related to the other ideas as harmony is to individual voices' (WR I: 158). Schopenhauer says that the particular Ideas may be regarded as 'individual, in themselves simple acts of will in which [the world-will's] . . . inner being expresses itself' (WR I: 155). According to this, the Platonic ideas are individual acts of will of the form: 'Let there be lions', 'Let there be antelopes' and so on.

Really, however, he says, all these individual willings are parts of

a single, complex act of will which constitutes the character of the
world-will in the same way in which, as we saw (pp. 66–7 above), the
'maxim' characterising what I will 'in general' constitutes my character (WR I: 158–9). This foundational act of will is one in which
the world-will's selection of particular Ideas is governed by the
consideration that they must be jointly realizable. Its content is the
overarching Idea in which all the individual Ideas are harmonised.

Notice how closely this conception of the world-will – or of
'nature' conceived as the 'mother' of all things – mirrors the
Christian version of Platonism, according to which the scheme of
Ideas represents the content of God's creative intention. There are,
however, two major differences.

THE INFLUENCE OF SPINOZA

The first of these differences is due to the influence of Spinoza, one
of the few Western philosophers, other than Kant, Plato and the
British, for whom Schopenhauer almost always has a good word.

In Christianity, as in Plato's theology, the world-creating being is
as separate from its creation as is the watchmaker from the watch.
(Plato actually calls his world-creator a 'craftsman'.) Following
Spinoza, however, Schopenhauer rejects this. The world-will is not
separate from but rather is the world.

In talking about one's own bodily action, Schopenhauer
emphasises, as we have noted (note 3 above), that it is not *caused* by
an act of will. Rather, the act of will ('I shall *now* pull the trigger') is
the bodily action, but the action seen from the 'subjective' rather
than 'objective' point of view, seen from within. This is true not
only of what the body does but also of what happens to it:

> Every true, genuine, immediate act of the will is also at once and
> directly a manifest act of the body; and correspondingly, on the
> other hand, every impression on the body is also at once and directly
> an impression on the will
>
> (WR I: 101).

In general, for Schopenhauer as for Spinoza, the 'inner' and the 'outer' are not separate entities, but rather two aspects of one and the same entity, are one and the same thing seen from different points of view.

What is true of the relation between my will and my body – 'the microcosm' – is also true of the relation between the world-will and its 'body' – 'the macrocosm'. The world-will is the world. When we describe it as a network of causally, spatially and temporally interconnected bodies we are describing it from the outer point of view, when we describe it as will, we describe it from the inner perspective.

For Schopenhauer, then, the world-will both creates and is the world. It is a self-creating entity (a *causa sui*, in the terminology of traditional metaphysics.)

NATURE-PESSIMISM

The second major way in which Schopenhauer's world-creator differs from that of Christianity is that its character is 'not divine but rather demonic', 'devilish' (WR II: 349–50). (With this remark he rejects not just the Christian God but also Spinoza's 'pantheism' – the world is God. He suggests, however, that Spinoza only designated his world-creator 'God' in an (unsuccessful) attempt to avoid persecution (WR II: 350).) In the affirmation of a demonic world-creator we arrive at the pessimism which is the hallmark of Schopenhauer's philosophy.

As we saw in the first chapter, pessimism goes back to his earliest years of reflection. 'When I was seventeen', Schopenhauer writes in an unpublished note,

> I was affected by the *misery and wretchedness of life* . . . The truth which the world clearly and loudly proclaimed . . . was that this world could not be the work of an all-powerful and infinitely good being, but rather a devil . . . as far as it could see[8] such a view was right

> (MR IV: 119).

Why does the world 'clearly proclaim' this truth? I shall look, here, at Schopenhauer's pessimism in so far as it concerns the condition of nature as a whole, his 'nature-pessimism', as I call it. In chapter 8 I shall look at a different set of arguments which are directed to a pessimistic account of, specifically, the human condition.

* * *

A little thoughtful observation shows, says Schopenhauer, that 'nature' (in other words, the world-will) cares not for individuals but only for the species. All it cares about is the continuance of its system of Ideas with which it seems 'thoroughly satisfied' (WR II: 351–2).

Schopenhauer's nature-pessimism focuses on the means by which nature chooses to preserve her system of Ideas. What she does is to overpopulate the world with members of one species – say, antelopes – so that there are sufficient individuals to maintain that species but also a surplus left over to feed another – say, lions. What follows from this is two things. First, that fear horror, pain and death are not accidental malfunctions of a generally benign order of things. Bellum omnium contra omnes, war, all against all, the struggle for survival and the survival only of the fittest, are, rather, the essence of the system, the means the world-will has chosen in order to realise its scheme of things.

The second thing that follows is that the source of this world of suffering is something which, properly understood, cannot be viewed with anything but moral horror. For what it does in treating individuals as mere canon fodder for the realisation of its grand design is to infringe the fundamental moral principle of, as Kant puts it, treating individuals always as 'ends', never merely as 'means'.[9]

Were it the case, Schopenhauer continues, that nature was evolving towards some higher state to which the suffering of individuals could be seen to contribute, such moral horror might be to some degree ameliorated. But this is not the case. There is no moral progress in the history of the world, the reason being that the world-will has no goal whatsoever beyond realising, in perpetuity, its system of Ideas (WR I: 163–4).[10]

* * *

The traditional 'argument from design' for God's existence observes, first, the amazing 'harmony' of nature, the amazingly complete mutual adaptation between organisms and their environment. (Cacti are just the way they need to be to survive in deserts, deserts are just what you need to sustain cacti.) All the parts of nature seem to be mutually adapted just like the parts of an intricate watch. And just as it is inconceivable that there should be a watch without a watchmaker so it is inconceivable that the 'design' that the world manifests should exist without an all-powerful, world-creating designer. Moreover, since the order of things in the world is such a benign order we must conclude that the world-creator is not only all-powerful but also wholly benevolent.

In effect, Schopenhauer agrees with all of this argument save for one crucial point. If we actually look at nature with honest, 'candid'[11] eyes, if we look at it without the theological need to prove it the creation of an all-powerful, wholly good God, and hence without the need to prove that it is, in Leibniz's words 'the best of all possible worlds', then we will see that it is actually the *worst* of all possible worlds. Far from being a sign of benevolence, the adaptation of the different parts of the world to one another that Christianity makes so much of is actually nothing more than the *minimum conditions of its existing at all*. If things were even a little worse if, for example there was even a small increase in the average temperature of the globe, then all sentient life would be wiped out. The minimal degree of design that exists in the world is actually something that a completely sadistic god, bent on creating beings for the sole purpose of entertaining itself through the sight of their pain, would be forced to maintain (WR II: 583–5).

* * *

Schopenhauer's horror at nature, his horror, in particular at the fate of animals, comes over particularly strongly in the following passage[12] in which he renders, in his own way, a report from Java by a European explorer, F.W. Junghuhn. Junghuhn saw, Schopenhauer writes,

> an immense field entirely covered with skeletons, and took it to be a battlefield. However they were nothing but skeletons of large turtles, five feet long, three feet broad, and of equal height. These turtles come this way from the sea, in order to lay their eggs, and are then seized by wild dogs (*canis rutilans*); with their united strength, these dogs lay them on their backs, tear open their lower armour, the small scales of the belly, and devour them alive. But then a tiger often pounces on the dogs. Now all this misery is repeated thousands and thousands of times, year in, year out. For this then, are these turtles born. For what offence must they suffer this agony? What is the point of the whole scene of horror? The only answer is that the will-to-live [the world-will] thus objectifies itself
> (WR II: 354).

One final twist of the knife. The world-will is the perpetrator of all this horror. So it is evil. But since it is the world it is also the victim of its own evil. It bears all the suffering it itself creates. Since every part of the world is part of the world-organism, every time an animal sinks its teeth in the flesh of another, the world-will sinks its teeth in its own flesh. The world-will, that is to say, is like the Australian bulldog ant whose sharp-toothed head and stinging tail engage in a fight to the death (WR I: 147). For 'at bottom, the will must live on itself, since nothing exists besides it, and it is a hungry will' (WR I: 154). The world-will is thus not only bad. It is also, in a clear sense, mad.

CAN THE WILL BE 'BLIND'?

This completes my exposition of the second Book of The World as Will. I should now like to take a closer and more critical look as certain aspects of the metaphysical vision it presents. The first issue I want to examine is Schopenhauer's persistent association of 'will' with 'blindness'.

Schopenhauer says that while many philosophers have postulated a 'world-soul (*Weltseele*)' as the 'inner being' of the world (Hegel, for example, postulates a world 'Spirit' on a learning curve as the inner essence of world-history) his world-will should not be confused with any such entity. This is because while a 'soul' is an '*ens rationis*' (being with reason), a being in which 'knowing and willing [are] . . . in inseparable connexion', his world-will is without 'knowledge', without, that is to say, an intellect (WR II: 349).

Though most commentators have accepted this 'blindness' of the will without demur, it seems to me important to take note of the fact that it is, fairly clearly, a mistake. For at least two reasons. First, Schopenhauer treats it as a suitable object of moral evaluation and condemnation which a blind, 'knowledge-less' being could not possibly be. And second, in at least in the central passages we have been examining, the world-will is very clearly a *designer* of things, a being equipped with the full range of the human faculties, with reason as well as will. Thus, as we saw (pp. 72–4 above), in the case of the chicken embryo the metaphysical will (a) *knows* that the chicken will be imprisoned in the egg, (b) wills that it should escape (c) *knows* that horny points are good tools for breaking egg-shell and so (d) provides it with such a tool.

So Schopenhauer misdescribes the world-will. The question is: why? The answer, I think, goes back to the very first introduction of 'will', the thought-experiment we examined on pp. 61–6 above.

When it was first introduced, 'will' appeared as the 'inner mechanism' that spanned the gap between cause and effect, 'motive' and action. The crucial question that needs to be asked is; what exactly is meant, here, by 'motive'?

Almost always Schopenhauer uses 'motive' to refer to the conscious registering of information about the environment. 'Motives' are, that is to say, 'representations' (FR: 70–1, 111–2, 212–3; WR I:

114 *et passim*). On that understanding, 'will' is indeed that which explains the 'influence' of the cause, why a particular cause led to a particular effect. You and I both see an apple on a table but you reach out for it and I don't. Why the difference? Because you are hungry — will to get food — and I am not.

The trouble is, however, that in the crucial thought-experiment (pp. 61–2 above) 'motive' cannot legitimately be used in this way. Thus, given Schopenhauer's 'disembodied-angel's-head' hypothesis that one only has 'objective' access to one's own body, one would, to repeat,

> see his conduct follow on presented motives with the constancy of a law of nature, just as the changes in other objects follow upon causes, stimuli, and motives. But he would be no nearer to understanding the influence of the motives than he is to understanding the connexion with its cause of any other effect that appears before him.

Here 'motives' are things observable from the *objective* point of view, things that exist in what is, so far as the objective observer is concerned, a mind-less universe. So they cannot be *registerings of information by a conscious mind*, but only causal impingements on the body — irradiation of the eyeballs, and such like.

So actually, what Schopenhauer should have said here is that the 'inner mechanism' connecting 'motive' with action is *not will alone but rather will plus 'knowledge'*. That is, the 'inside story' available to me but not to the objective observer, the inside story that explains why the irradiation of my eyeballs by light reflected from an apple is followed by my grabbing and munching the apple, is not just that I have a will to eat. It is, rather, this will *plus the knowledge* that there is an apple at a certain place which can be reached by extending the arm in a certain direction, and that apples are good things for reducing hunger. Of course, knowledge such as this is typically too obvious for us to mention in everyday explanations of action. Normally one would simply say 'I grabbed the apple because I was hungry.'

Nonetheless it is actually an essential part of the 'inner mechanism' of action.

But, tricked by the ambiguity in his use of 'motive', Schopenhauer is led to think of the inner mechanism of action as *will and will alone*, will *without knowledge*; 'blind' will, as he often puts it (WR I: 115).[13] This is why he thinks himself able to say that 'the force which attracts a stone to the earth is . . . will' without being committed to the 'absurd meaning that the stone moves itself according to a known motive' (WR I: 105), thinks himself able to reject Bacon's assertion that the movements of bodies must have been preceded by 'perceptions' (ibid. note), and thinks himself able to describe the world-will as will without knowledge. The reason he thinks the proposition 'absurd', of course, is that since, for him, the intellect is identical with the brain, its affirmation would require the attribution of brains to stones.

But Bacon was right. Will alone can never be the 'inner mechanism' of action. It can only explain action in conjunction with 'knowledge'. Hence, in spite of his protests, the world-will has to be, as, in crucial passages, Schopenhauer implicitly treats it, a world soul, a personal entity.

SCHOPENHAUER AND DARWIN

The crux of Book II's metaphysics of will is, as we saw, teleology: will is the underlying reality of nature only to the extent that the latter exhibits 'in order to's; goal-directed behaviour or physiological features of organisms that fulfil specific purposes. Schopenhauer says, remember, that only to the extent that we are prepared to see 'final causation' at work in inorganic as well as organic nature do we have any reason to extend the will to that domain (WR II: 335). It is only, for example, to the extent that we are prepared to see the movement of the iron filings as directed towards the goal of contact with the magnet that we have any reason to attribute to them the 'keen desire' for such proximity (see p. 74 above).

The reason teleology demands will, as we saw (p. 72 above), is that 'we cannot clearly conceive a final cause except as an intended aim or end'. Backwards causation is impossible, so when we say the giraffe has a long neck in order to reach the leaves of tall trees, 'reaching the leaves' has to be somehow located in something that happened *before* the giraffe's neck came into existence, and the only way we can do that is by locating reaching the leaves in the content of the world-will's creative desire.

Notice, however, a certain unease in 'we cannot *clearly* conceive . . .' and also in 'the universal suitability of organic nature cannot *easily* be associated with any philosophical system except that which make a will the basis of every natural being's existence' (WR II: 327; my emphasis). The same unease is expressed in Schopenhauer's endorsement of Kant's statement in the *Critique of Teleological Judgement* that purposiveness in non-human nature *might* be a mere human projection (WR I: 533). There might, that is, be a purely mechanical explanation of the giraffe's long neck and hence no need to postulate a designing will.

Such unease is, of course, well founded, indeed prescient. For a mere fifteen years after the completion of Volume II, Darwin's *Origin of Species* appeared.

* * *

Schopenhauer is sometimes hailed as a forerunner of Darwin. And in so far as he emphasised the struggle for survival he is. (Others had, however, preceded him in this: Hobbes with his view of life in nature as universal war, and, probably, a couple of millennia before him, Heraclitus, in his remark that 'War is the father of all things'.) As I have already remarked, however (note 10 above), Schopenhauer did not anticipate the continual *evolution* of the species. And neither, in the crucial case of teleology, did he anticipate Darwin's revolution.

For what Darwin showed was precisely how to eliminate the puzzle of final causation *without* appeal to a 'world-will' of either benevolent or malevolent intent. What he showed was that statements of the form 'Xs do or have Y in order to Z' are reducible to 'Xs without Y, and which can't therefore Z, tend to get wiped out in the struggle for survival before reproducing themselves'. So, for example, the giraffe has a long neck simply because giraffes deprived of long necks in the random distribution of characteristics (genes) starved in tall-tree country.

For us, for whom the Darwinian mode of explanation has become part of common sense, it is quite hard to appreciate either the nature or the world-shaking force of Darwin's revolution. The primary impact of *The Origin of Species*, it seems to me, was not scientific, was not the thesis that human beings are descended from the apes. Rather it was conceptual – the demonstration that the apparent 'design' of the world could be produced by purely natural causes. Before Darwin, almost everyone – even the sceptical Voltaire – had been forced to accept the inescapability of the 'argument from design' to God's existence. After Darwin there remained no compelling theoretical reason for believing in God at all.

In a sense, therefore – since Schopenhauer's argument to the world-will is, as already remarked, a deviant version of the argument from design – Book II has a certain quaintness about it. Reading it is studying the 'archaeology' of thought, studying how the world looked to a pre-Darwinian mind – albeit one vividly aware of the fatuousness of calling this 'the best of all possible worlds'.

SUMMARY
Schopenhauer's argument in Book II

Science presupposes, but cannot understand, 'natural forces'. So it needs philosophy to complete its account of the world. Its incompleteness, however, more precisely defines the philosophical problem of grasping the 'whatness' of the world: the problem is to grasp the nature of natural forces. This requires a turn to inner experience, a turn to will. I know that the 'inner mechanism', the underlying reality, of my bodily action is will. And since the character of the 'microcosm' can reasonably be supposed to reveal that of the 'macrocosm', it can be inferred that the underlying reality of everything is will. But as the designer of this world of suffering the will has to be 'not divine but demonic'.

Criticism of Schopenhauer's argument

1   The will cannot be, as Schopenhauer often describes it, 'blind'. As the explanatory 'inner mechanism' of behaviour it must be accompanied by 'knowledge'.
2   The crux of the metaphysics of will is teleology; the idea that purpose-directedness in nature 'cannot be clearly conceived except as an intended aim'. Darwin, however, showed that it can be.

FURTHER READING

J. Atwell, *Schopenhauer on the Character of the World*, chapters 3–6.
C. Janaway, *Schopenhauer*, chapters 3 and 4.
P. Gardiner, *Schopenhauer*, chapter 4.
S. Gardner, 'Schopenhauer, Will and the Unconscious' in *The Cambridge Companion to Schopenhauer*, pp. 375–421.

Four

Metaphysics: Ultimate Reality

In chapter 2 we saw Schopenhauer arguing that the everyday world is ideal. This raised the 'whatness' question, the question of what it is which lies beneath the everyday surface of things. In the last chapter we saw how Book II of *The World as Will* provides an answer to this question: that which lies beneath the surface of things is will. What, however, is the *status* of this answer? In particular, is 'will' really intended as an account of the nature of Kant's 'thing in itself'? Is 'will' Schopenhauer's answer to the question of the nature of *ultimate* reality?

THE EARLY VIEW

In the *Critique of Pure Reason* Kant argues, in a nutshell, the following. (1) The world of human experience is ideal, 'appearance' merely. (2) 'Concepts without intuitions are empty': one cannot talk with cognitive intelligibility about (and so cannot know) what lies beyond experience. So (3), reality 'in itself' is unknowable: 'metaphysics' (understood as the study of ultimate reality) is impossible.

As we saw in the first chapter, for all his contempt for his German contemporaries, Schopenhauer, at least as a young man, shared with them one characteristic: he wanted to crack the problem of Kant's thing in itself. Yet he wanted to do so while remaining true to the heart of Kant's teaching. In no way, that is to say, did he want to deny (2) in the above argument. On the contrary, as we have seen (pp. 32–4 above), he enthusiastically endorses it. Terms such as Hegel's 'Absolute', since we are provided with no account of what it would be like to encounter such a thing, are empty verbiage. Moreover, as we have seen (pp. 49–51 above), Schopenhauer has nothing but contempt for 'intellectual intuition', for the claim that while most human experience is ideal, highly paid 'professors of philosophy' have a special, exotic ability to penetrate the Kantian veil and come face to face with the thing in itself. Intellectual intuition he (rightly) regards as a betrayal of Kant.

As a young man, Schopenhauer thought he had done it: cracked the problem of the thing in itself while yet remaining true to the essence of Kant's teaching. (Nietzsche notes, with a kindly but critical eye, this young man's exhilarating sense of having made a major breakthrough, of having discovered, in the word 'will', the 'philosopher's Stone'[1].) Book II claims more than thirty times that 'the will' is the thing in itself with virtually no indication that 'thing in itself' is being used in anything other than its established, Kantian meaning.[2]

Why was Schopenhauer so confident of this? Here is my hypothesis.

In Book I of Volume I, as we saw, though not always too clear about the difference between it and partial idealism, Schopenhauer takes himself to have established radical idealism: that the empirical world – the world of both common sense and natural science – is ideal. In his own language, it exists merely as (the content of) representation, the representation of a representing subject. But, as we have seen, he takes Book II to have established, early on, that we have 'double knowledge' of our own bodies – we know them 'as representation' and 'as will'. But knowing them as will is knowing them as non-representation, as something 'toto genere [utterly] different' from representation (WR I: 110). Yet within the dualism of appearance and reality everything must be either representation or thing in itself. Hence, knowing one's own body 'as will' is knowing it as thing in itself:

What Kant opposed as *thing in itself* to mere *appearance* – called more decidedly by me *representation* – this *thing in itself*, this substratum of all phenomena, and therefore of the whole of nature, is nothing but what we know directly and intimately and find within ourselves as *the will*

(WN: 216).[3]

QED.

As a young man, therefore, Schopenhauer denies the first premise of Kant's argument to the impossibility of metaphysics. What Kant missed in claiming *all* human experience to be merely ideal was the fact that we have *inner* as well as outer experience of ourselves and that here we encounter something that is non-representation.

Notice that the experience Schopenhauer is talking about here, the experience of our own motivational states, is utterly common-or-garden. There is nothing exotic or difficult about it, nothing that could be regarded as the special province of the 'professors of philosophy', nothing dubious or faked. So the younger Schopenhauer thinks he can remain true to the empiricist heart of Kant's philosophy, premise number two, in the argument at the beginning of this section, *and* avoid the 'charlatanry' of 'rational intuition', and yet still crack the problem of the thing in itself.

* * *

So he thinks. In fact, however, the above line of reasoning is thoroughly mistaken, trading, as it does, on a crucial ambiguity in the use of the word 'representation (*Vorstellung*)'. I shall mark the ambiguity by speaking of 'representations A' and 'representations B'.

Representations A are any mental content. To experience an orange circular patch or a high-pitched whine is to experience a representation A. Crucially, those mental items which Schopenhauer identifies as states of the will – itches, pains, feelings of pleasure, emotions and desires (WR II: 202) – are representations A.

Representations B are a subset of representations A; those that have been processed – as Schopenhauer puts it 'worked up' by the understanding – into experiences of *objects* that belong together with other objects in public space (see pp. 36–9 above). This is the use of 'representation' that occurs, for example, in the title of *The World as Will and Representation*.

Schopenhauer's youthful mistake is to confuse what I shall call 'pure' representations A (things that are representations A but not representations B) with the thing in itself. Correctly seeing that we have subjective as well as objective self-knowledge, he confuses the having of pure representations A with encounters with Kant's thing in itself. Implicitly he reasons: encounters with states of the will are not representations (and here he, as it were, forgets to add to 'B'); everything that is not a representation is thing in itself; so, in encountering the will we encounter the thing in itself.[4] This, however, is a ground-level mistake since while all representations A are subject to the form of time Kant's thing in itself is *atemporal*. The whole of our inner experience, that is to say, is temporally organised: this pain has to happen before, after or during that burst of lust. But according to Kant's transcendental, i.e.[5] radical, idealism, as we know, space *and time* are properties merely of appearances, not of the thing in itself.

Schopenhauer's mistake is, in fact, so bad as to constitute a sufficient ground for failing 'Kant 101'. For as everyone learns right at the beginning, it is not just the thing in itself that is, for Kant, beyond space, time and knowledge but also the *subject* in itself. The real self is every bit as inscrutable as the real object.

QUALIFICATIONS

By the time he came to write the second edition of *The World as Will* (published in 1844) Schopenhauer had seen his mistake and decided to address it. He does this in several places[6], but above all in chapter 18 of Volume II, appropriately entitled 'On the Possibility of Knowing the Thing in itself'. The chapter is, however, oddly written. Rather than presenting a clear and coherent statement of his considered view on the question posed in its title, it offers a kind of dialogue, almost an argument, between his younger and older self.

The crucial passage (WR II: 195–8) starts off with a forceful expression of the youthful view:

> On the path of *objective knowledge* . . . we shall . . . remain on the outside of things; we shall never be able to penetrate into their inner nature, and investigate what they are in themselves. . . . So far I agree with Kant. But now, as a counterpoise to this truth I have stressed that . . . *we ourselves are the thing in itself.* Consequently, a way *from within* stands open to us to that real inner nature of things to which we cannot penetrate *from without.* It is, so to speak, a subterranean passage, a secret alliance, which, as if by treachery, places us all at once in the fortress that could not be taken by attack from without. Precisely as such, the *thing in itself* can come into consciousness only quite directly *by itself being conscious of itself*
> (WR II: 195).

So Kant made a mistake when he claimed that 'since perception (*Anschauung*) can deliver only *appearances*, not things in themselves we have absolutely no knowledge of things in themselves'. 'I admit this of everything', says Schopenhauer, 'but not of the knowledge each of us has of his own willing' (WR II: 196).

Now, however, the voice of 'maturity' chimes in, reminding the 'fire of youth' (WR I: xxii) that casting itself like a veil even over inner experience 'there still remains the form of time' (WR II: 197). So, after all, we do not encounter the thing in itself in inner experience.

Eventually, the argument is resolved by a kind of synthesis of the two positions. Though, being subject to the form of time, the thing in itself 'does not appear quite naked' in inner experience, nonetheless, having at least escaped the form of space, it has 'to a great extent cast off its veils'. It is, therefore, our 'nearest and clearest' encounter with the thing in itself for which reason 'I call the will the thing in itself' (WR II: 197).

This seems to say that though Kant is ultimately right that the thing in itself is unknowable, nonetheless 'will' constitutes our best guess as to its character. For at least two reasons, this is not really a very satisfactory position. The first is that the 'dance of the veils' argument is not a good one. Since, for example, a yellow filter superimposed over a blue one produces a more accurate representation of the colour of objects than a blue one alone, it cannot in general be argued that the fewer the filters ('veils') through which one views something the closer one comes to experiencing it as it is in itself. And the second is the general observation that the very idea of an atemporal will seems self-contradictory. Something that is 'will' surely, has to perform acts of will (which indeed, as we have seen, the will that appears in Book II does.) But acts of will are events and events happen in time.

METAPHYSICS AS 'DECIPHERING'

In chapter 17 of Volume II, entitled 'On Man's Need for Metaphysics', Schopenhauer offers what is in fact a quite different approach to the question of the status of the metaphysical will to the unsatisfactory approach of Chapter 18 that we have just discussed. This is the approach of what we might (with some reservations) call the 'hermeneutic' Schopenhauer.

'The whole of experience', Schopenhauer writes,

> is like a cryptograph [or 'riddle'], and philosophy is like the deciphering of it, and the correctness of this is confirmed by the continuity and connexion that appears everywhere. If only this whole is grasped in sufficient depth, and inner experience is connected to outer, it must be capable of being *interpreted, explained* from itself
> (WR II: 182).

This 'deciphering of the world', Schopenhauer continues,

> must be completely confirmed from itself. It must spread a uniform
> light over all the phenomena of the world, and bring even the most
> heterogeneous into agreement, so that the contradiction may be
> removed even between those that contrast most. This confirmation
> from itself is the characteristic stamp of its genuineness; for every
> false deciphering even though it suits some phenomena, will all the
> more glaringly contradict the remainder. Thus, for example, the
> optimism of Leibniz conflicts with the obvious misery of existence;
> Spinoza's doctrine that the world is the only possible and absolutely
> necessary substance is incompatible with out wonder and
> astonishment at its existence and essential nature . . .
>
> (WR II: 184).

This justification of Schopenhauer's metaphysics of will in terms of
its power to 'make sense' of the totality of experience accurately
describes the actual procedure of Book II. It fits particularly well his
discussion of the need to complete the scientific image, of what we
must do to make sense of teleology, and of the justification of the
extension of the concept of will to inorganic nature. In all these
cases, as we have seen, Schopenhauer asserts not so much that we
are compelled to acknowledge will to be at work but rather that will is
the only way we can make sense of things in a comprehensive and
unified way.

The question that concerns us here, however, is that of the *status*
of the will viewed as the key to 'deciphering' the riddle of experience. Schopenhauer says of his metaphysics of will that it 'remains
immanent, and does not become transcendent; for it never tears
itself entirely from experience, but remains the mere interpretation
and explanation thereof'. His metaphysical deciphering of the
world is, he continues,

> like an arithmetical sum that comes out, although by no means in
> the sense that it leaves no problems still to be solved, no possible

question unanswered. To assert anything of the kind would be a
presumptuous denial of the limits of human knowledge in general.
Whatever torch we kindle, and whatever space it may illuminate, our
horizon will always remain encircled by the depth of night. For the
ultimate solution of the riddle of the world would necessarily have
to speak merely of things in themselves, no longer of phenomena
(WR II: 185).

Schopenhauer is asserting three things in these passages. First, that
metaphysics as deciphering is a kind of 'reading' of experience as a
whole. Yet although this anticipates the postmodernists' treatment
of everything as a kind of 'text', Schopenhauer clearly has no time
for their assertion that any text has indefinitely many readings each
as good as the other. Schopenhauer is firmly convinced – this is his
second assertion – that his metaphysics of will is the uniquely 'correct' ('true' (WR II: 183), 'right' (WR II: 184)) deciphering, that all
of its rivals deal, at best, with only part of experience, that his is the
only reading that allows the 'sum' to 'come out'. Schopenhauer's
third claim is that in spite of its unique 'correctness', his metaphysics is a 'mere interpretation and explanation' of experience and so,
in the final analysis, *makes no claim about how reality actually is in itself.*

How can we make sense of the idea of a 'true' deciphering of the
riddle of experience which, remember, results in the claim that the
'thing in itself' is will, but which does not make any claim about
ultimate reality? *The World as Will* provides no answer to this
question.

* * *

Towards the end of his life, however, Schopenhauer finds himself in
dispute with his somewhat long-suffering friend, disciple and
future literary executor, Julius Frauenstädt. In a letter, Frauenstädt
(clearly no fool) suggests that, like Kant, Schopenhauer should have
left undetermined what the thing in itself is. Schopenhauer replies
(in 1852):

Then I could immediately throw my whole philosophy out the window. It is precisely my great discovery that Kant's thing in itself is that which we find in self-consciousness as the will, and that this [will] is completely different from and independent of the intellect, therefore without this is present in all things. But *this will is thing in itself merely in relation to appearance*: it is what this is, independently of our perception and representation [representation B!] which means precisely in itself . . . The thing in itself you are always to seek only in appearance, as present merely in relation to it not therefore in . . . cloud-cuckoo-land (emphasis added).

In a letter written the following year Schopenhauer adds:

My philosophy never speaks of the cloud-cuckoo-land, but of *this world*; that is, it is immanent, not transcendent. It spells out the world lying before us, like a hieroglyphics-tablet (whose key I have found in the will), and shows its interconnection throughout. It teaches what appearance is, and what the thing in itself is. This [latter] however, is the thing in itself merely relatively, i.e., in its relation to appearance; and this is appearance merely in its relation to the thing in itself. Beyond this *it* is a brain-phenomenon. *What, however, the thing in itself is outside that relation I have never said, because I don't know it*; but in that relation it is will to life (emphasis added).[7]

The crucial point that emerges from these letters is, clearly, the distinction between two senses of 'thing in itself': the thing in itself 'in its relation to appearance', or simply 'in appearance', and the thing in itself 'outside its relation to appearance'. Though he muddies the waters by quite wrongly suggesting that the former is Kant's sense of the term, what Schopenhauer is in fact doing here is introducing a new, non-Kantian sense of 'thing in itself'. If we take the Kantian distinction between appearance and reality, what Schopenhauer is doing is admitting (grudgingly) that the 'thing in itself' which he claims to be will, though providing a *more* fundamental description of nature than its description in terms of objects, is still not a description of reality as it is quite apart from any human modes of representation. It belongs, in the final analysis, to the realm of appearances. What Schopenhauer is in fact doing, in other words, is offering is a three-tiered picture of things. There is, in ascending order of fundamentality: first, the world as represented from the 'objective', third-person point of view, the world as representation B, i.e. the 'objectively' apprehended world of objects; second the world as pure representation A, i.e. the 'subjectively' apprehended world of will; and finally the world as it is 'in itself' in the *Kantian* sense which, Schopenhauer now *agrees* with Frauenstädt and Kant, is unknowable by us. 'Will', therefore, to put the point metaphorically, characterises *penultimate*, not ultimate reality. In the *final* analysis, if it is *Kant's* appearance/reality distinction we are talking about, it belongs on the side of appearance.

Notice that what the mature Schopenhauer has achieved is a subtle[8] reconciliation between intellectual honesty, on the one hand, and, on the other, a stubborn personality unwilling to admit that the central claim of his philosophy – that the will is the thing in itself – rests on a fundamental error. The reconciliation consists in retaining, to the end, the *formula*, the *words*, 'the will is the thing in itself' but in attaching to them, a meaning fundamentally different from the meaning they had possessed in the first edition of *The World as Will*.

THE POSSIBILITY OF 'SALVATION'

At the end of the Volume II discussion of 'the possibility of knowing the thing in itself', more up-front about things than in the cross and somewhat obfuscatory letters to Frauenstädt, Schopenhauer aligns himself clearly and unequivocally with Kant. He says that the question of

> what that . . . which manifests itself in the world and as the world is
> ultimately and absolutely in itself, in other words, what it is, quite

apart from the fact that it manifests itself as will, or in general
appears, that is to say, is known in general . . . can *never* be
answered, because . . . being-known of itself contradicts being in
itself, and everything that is known is as such only appearance
(*Erscheinung*)[9]

(WR II: 198).

To the youthful Schopenhauer this would count as an admission of
defeat, of the failure of the task of philosophy, that of uncovering
the ultimate 'whatness' of reality, of cracking the problem of the
Kantian thing in itself. But, as we are about to see, the mature
Schopenhauer realises that not only *can* he allow his philosophy to
end on a 'negative' (WR II: 612) note, to end with a confession of
ignorance, but that it actually it *demands* that it should; demands, at
least, that 'will', should *not* be the final word on the character of the
(Kantian) thing in itself, that there should be a domain 'beyond'
the will.

* * *

In 'On Man's Need for Metaphysics' (chapter 17 of Volume II),
Schopenhauer discusses the relation between religion and philosophy. Religions, he says, 'are necessary for the people, and are an
inestimable benefit to them' (WR II: 168) because they offer
answers to the 'unfathomable and ever disquietening riddle' (WR
II: 170–1) of existence; a riddle that is created by the fact that a force
powerful enough to bring the world into existence ought, surely,
to be able to eliminate, or at the very least reduce, the overwhelming quantity of suffering it contains (WR II: 172). The great religions satisfy 'man's need for metaphysics' because, in a popular i.e.
allegorical form, their promises of immortality, heavenly bliss etc.
provide an account of things that reconciles the believer to (at least
the big picture of) existence.

But religions are no longer believed; they are collapsing under
the weight of their own contradictions (such as that human beings

are both free and created by God), together with a rise in the general level of education which means that it has become much harder to pull the wool over people's eyes. Assessing the spiritual climate of his times, Schopenhauer writes in *The Fourfold Root* that

> A long predicted epoch has set in; the Church is tottering, indeed so badly, that it is doubtful whether it will recover its centre of gravity; for faith has been lost. It is with the light of revelation as with other lights; some darkness is the condition. The number of those rendered unfit for belief by a certain degree and extent of knowledge has become considerable. This is testified by the general dissemination of that shallow rationalism which is showing ever more openly its bulldog face
>
> (FR: 179).

In other words – the words Nietzsche was to use some forty years later – 'God is dead'. The conclusion Schopenhauer draws from this is that it is up to 'metaphysics' proper – the literal rather than allegorical expression of ultimate truth (WR II: 166), in other words philosophy – to fill the gap, to attempt itself to satisfy 'man's need'. The task of philosophy is to reconcile humanity to its existence despite the overwhelming presence of suffering and evil. Like Boethius, Schopenhauer conceives the task of philosophy as, ultimately, that of providing a 'consolation' for life as a human being, of providing, in the words of his youth, a 'better consciousness' (see further p. 140 below).

Given this conception of the philosophical task, Schopenhauer has to have a doctrine of, as he indeed calls it, 'salvation'. This, as we shall see in chapter 8, consists in the mystical realisation that the entire knowable world, the knowable world including the metaphysical will, is nothing but a (very bad) dream. Salvation consists in a kind of awakening from the nightmare of temporal existence.

But an awakening to what? To nothing, 'nothing' in the sense of 'nothing comprehensible to the rational mind', nothing comprehensible to philosophy. Salvation is accessible only to mystical practice and insight. Yet, Schopenhauer observes, 'if the will were positively and absolutely the [Kantian] thing in itself, then this nothing would be *absolute*, instead of which it expressly appears to us . . . only as a *relative* nothing' (WR II: 198).

What the mature Schopenhauer realises is that if ultimate reality really were the evil will, if Book II was the absolute end of the story, then there would be not just *nothing knowable by us* but *absolutely nothing* beyond the will. He realises that the claim that his metaphysical will represents *ultimate* reality commits him to an absolute nihilism – existence is both evil and eternally inescapable – in which case there would be no point in his bothering to write his philosophy. What Schopenhauer realises, in other words, is that his youthful claim that in Book II he had cracked the problem of the Kantian thing in itself is inconsistent with the doctrine of salvation propounded in Book IV and, for this reason, too, has therefore to be abandoned.

SUMMARY

Is the 'will' of Book II *really* intended as an account of the ultimate 'whatness' of things, of ultimate reality? Is it *really* intended as an answer to the question of the nature of Kant's 'thing in itself'?

As a young man Schopenhauer intends it as such an account. He thinks, moreover, that he can offer will as an account of the thing in itself *and* remain a good Kantian. He thinks this because he believes that in encountering ourselves 'as will' we encounter something that is non-'representation' and must therefore be the thing in itself. This is a bad mistake since inner experience, though non-spatial, is subject to the form of time and hence, for Kant, cannot be the atemporal thing in itself. The mature Schopenhauer realises this and modifies his position so that the will, while still being offered as a deeper account of reality than that provided by objectual consciousness, is acknowledged to be, in the final analysis, an account of the world as appearance rather than an account of Kant's thing in itself.

Given that he holds that the principle task of philosophy is to provide 'consolation' in the face of pain and mortality, one motive Schopenhauer has for this modification is to make room for his doctrine of 'salvation'. Were the evil will really to be *ultimate* reality, he realises, there would be no possibility of salvation.

FURTHER READING

J. Atwell, *Schopenhauer on the Character of the World*, chapter 5.

M. Nicholls, 'Schopenhauer, Young, and the Will' *Schopenhauer Jahrbuch* 72 (1991), pp. 143–157.

M. Nicholls, 'The Influence of Eastern Thought on Schopenhauer's Doctrine of the Thing-in-itself' in *The Cambridge Companion to Schopenhauer*, pp. 171–212.

J. Young, *Willing and Unwilling*, chapter 3.

Five

Art

SCHOPENHAUER VERSUS HEGEL

The closing pages of Book II of *The World as Will* mark the low point of the work. The world as will is a world of pain governed by a force that is 'not divine but rather demonic'. This force, moreover, is one that seeks no final satisfaction has no 'final goal' but is, rather, 'an endless striving' (WR I: 164). The significance of this latter statement becomes clear when it is conjoined with Schopenhauer's hatred of Hegel, of, in particular, the 'shallow optimism' of 'Hegelian pseudo-philosophy' (WR II: 442).

A theologian at heart, Hegel rewrote the Christian story of the last judgement for a secular age. The metaphysical essence of things, 'Absolute Spirit', is, he holds, historical. Realised in human society as the spirit of successive ages, it is on a long learning curve, is undergoing an inexorably progressive development from the primitive to the perfect. When this process completes itself 'history' will have come to an end. That end will be the realisation of a kind of city of God on earth, a state of society which everyone realises to be, as the phrase has it, 'as good as it gets'.[1] As we noted in the first chapter, many people, including Schopenhauer (WR II: 442), have understood Hegel as saying that it is the Prussian state (which paid Hegel's salary) that constitutes this triumphant 'end of history'.

This is what Schopenhauer abhors as a failure of both head and heart. It is a failing of the head, of philosophy (and is therefore mere 'pseudo-philosophy'), because, as we know from Kant, ultimate reality is atemporal. So the idea (originally Heraclitus') of a *process* as constituting the essence of reality represents a 'crude and shallow realism' which, Schopenhauer believes, has been disposed of, for ever, by Kant.[2] And it is a failure of the heart because any kind of 'optimism' is a callous mockery of the 'obvious misery of existence' (WR II: 184).

Schopenhauer's point is, then, that eschatology as a lie. The world-will isn't going anywhere. It is the 'will to life', the will, that is, to the eternal maintenance of its unchanging system of Ideas. And since horror, fear, pain and death are written into that system, it is the will to their eternal maintenance. Pain is not a valley of tears through which we will pass to (that politician's promise) a 'new dawn'. It will be with us always, undiminished and undiluted, the world's eternal fate.

Things are, then, extremely bleak at the end of Book II. If Camus is right that the fundamental question of philosophy is whether or not to commit suicide, then philosophy – if the vision of Book II is correct – is something we had better avoid.

* * *

Unexpectedly, however, the transition from Book II to Book III, to which I now turn, brings an immediate lightening of the atmosphere. Schopenhauer himself notes this. 'Now', he says with relief at the end of the Supplement to Book II, for 'our third book with its bright and fair content' (WR II: 360). And, in fact, the improvement in tone basically continues throughout the remainder of the work, terminating in the vision of 'salvation' at the end of Book IV. The work as a whole is shaped, therefore, like a valley. Books I and II descend to its depths, Books III and IV rise up out of them.

What I have just been saying is that, *inter alia*, Schopenhauer is a great artist. (Thomas Mann treats him as a great composer describing *The World as Will* as a 'symphony in four movements'.[3]) This helps explain the deep insight of many of Book III's observations on its central topic, art. Concerning what he calls 'the riddle of art', Martin Heidegger says that 'the task is to *see* the riddle' not to 'solve' it. His point, which is surely right, is that if one attempts to write about art without the experience of being genuinely moved by it, one will not, ultimately, know what one is talking about. (The one exception here is Kant who, as Schopenhauer notes, wrote profoundly about art in spite of the fact that, 'having little susceptibility to the beautiful', art was something essentially 'foreign' to him (WR I: 529). Kant's personal taste in music, for example, seems to have run to brass bands and no further.)

THE QUESTION: WHAT IS ART?

Book III of the *World as Will* falls into two halves. The first, sections 30–42 in Volume I, sets out Schopenhauer's general theory of art, while the second, sections 43–52, applies the general theory to the particular arts. The order of their presentation is determined by the idea that the Platonic Ideas of the species of natural things (see pp. 77–8 above) form a hierarchy which corresponds to the 'grades of the objectification of the will' (WR I: 130). The top of the hierarchy is that in which will is most obviously manifested, the human being, the bottom that in which its presence is least obvious – the natural forces inherent in non-living things like rocks.[4] Particular ideas form the objects of particular arts. Architecture, for example, is concerned with the Ideas of rigidity and gravity. So the individual arts form a hierarchy according to the grade of the objectification of the will with which they are concerned.

The rigidity of this system generates a great deal of nonsense. The scheme entails, for example, that landscape painting is somehow 'lower' than animal painting since the will is more 'obviously' present in animals than trees, and that architecture is inferior to landscape gardening – in fact the 'lowest' of the arts – since the Ideas with which it deals are at the very bottom of the hierarchy of Ideas. And Schopenhauer's discussion of the individual arts is uneven. He has for example almost nothing interesting to say about landscape gardening or animal painting but feels obliged to discuss them on account of the system. In what follows, I shall refer to his discussions of the individual arts only in so far as they illuminate the general theory. (The exception here is music, which he regards as not representing any Idea at all. Not being covered by the general theory, he takes it to require a special theory of its own. I shall discuss Schopenhauer's philosophy of music at the end of chapter 6.)

* * *

The first and central question of Book III is: What is art? Unlike modern aestheticians, however, Schopenhauer has no interest in thinking about the art/non-art distinction. (Is Duchamp's 'Fountain' – a urinal set up in a gallery – art or not?) He takes the difference to be obvious – as it usually is. What interests him, rather, (along with the other giants of the philosophy of art such as Kant, Hegel, Heidegger and Nietzsche) is the nature of *great* art. This comes to be treated as equivalent to the question of the nature of *art* because Schopenhauer operates with a dichotomy between 'genuine' (WR II: 406) art on the one hand and the work of 'imitators, mannerists, the slavish mob' (WR I: 235) on the other.

Like Kant, Schopenhauer has a healthy contempt for 'the art world' – the chattering classes who turn up to gallery openings and those who pander to, or seek to shock, their tired tastes (Damien Hurst etc.). In contrast to these, he sets up the authentic canon of the few great – i.e. 'genuine' – artists. (The canon is bound to be small because, as we are about to see, authentic art represents an extraordinary transcendence of the nature and the normal limitations of the human mind.)

Although Schopenhauer is quite right in saying that the art world is full of people who – to borrow his categorisation of philosophers – live *from* rather than *for* art, the exclusiveness of the great/ fraudulent dichotomy gets him into trouble. At least it does so together with the fact that he has just one paradigm of what great art is like. As I shall suggest in the next chapter, he needs to recognise types of art which do not fit his paradigm yet are both valuable and entirely genuine.

* * *

Schopenhauer defines art (i.e. great art) as the product of a certain state of consciousness; 'the aesthetic method of consideration' (WR I: 195), the, as I shall say, 'aesthetic state'. The artwork is that which is produced out of this state and tends to recreate it in the spectator (see particularly, WR I: 185, WR II: 407–8).

Though most people are occasionally and lightly touched by the aesthetic state – otherwise we would have no appreciation of art at all – only a few have the capacity for the intense and sustained habitation of the state that is necessary to the production of genuine artworks (WR I: 185–7, WR II: 389). Hence, agreeing with Kant (The Critique of Judgement section 48), Schopenhauer holds that art is the product of 'genius'. (Many of the main planks of Schopenhauer's philosophy of art are phrases recycled from The Critique of Judgement to which, however, he attaches his own distinctive meaning.)

Obviously, since the great artist is not just an inspired dauber but rather someone who can communicate his vision of the world, Schopenhauer would agree that, in addition to the capacity to enter the aesthetic state, the production of a 'genuine and successful work' (WR II: 406) also requires technique. But he devotes very little attention to this topic, holding, no doubt, that questions of technique are the province of art teaching and criticism, not of philosophy.

So, for Schopenhauer, the philosophically interesting part of the 'What is art?' question boils down to the question of the nature of the aesthetic state. Since he regards this as something extraordinary, it becomes natural for him to elucidate its character by means of a contrast between it and ordinary consciousness. Accordingly, he begins the discussion of art with a kind of clarifying summation of what has been learnt about ordinary consciousness in Books I and II.

EVERYDAY CONSCIOUSNESS

As we have seen (pp. 28–32 above), Schopenhauer's account of ordinary consciousness is told from the perspective of evolutionary physiology. The brain, and hence the consciousness it produces, is the 'one great tool' (WR II: 280) that enables a physically weak creature to survive in a competitive environment. It follows that our consciousness is entirely in the 'service of the will', the 'will to live', from which it sprang 'so to speak, as the head from the trunk' (WR I: 177). And though we no longer live in the original jungle, this legacy of our evolutionary past survives: ordinary consciousness is, through and through, 'interested' consciousness. It presents to us only those things that are 'interesting' (WR I: 177) to the will and only in ways that are interesting to the will. ('Interesting', here, means 'bears on our well-being', on what Schopenhauer calls our 'weal' or 'woe' (WR II: 202).)

So what is 'interested' consciousness? What does the individual human being need to know in order to know how the world bears on its welfare? Schopenhauer says that it needs to know the 'relations' in which things stand, specifically their spatial, temporal and their causal relations (WR I: 177).

Obviously, to know how things bear on one's welfare one needs to know where they are in space-time. But not just any spatio-temporal locating of things will do. To know that there is a tiger at latitude X and longitude Y is no use to me unless I know where X and Y are in relation to where I am. Hence ordinary consciousness is self-consciousness in the sense that I belong within my representation of the world. I belong there as 'an object among objects' to which, 'by a shorter or longer path' all spatio-temporal relations 'always lead back' (WR I: 176).

Schopenhauer's point here[5] is that I am the focal point, the 'centre' (WR I: 332) of my world. In ordinary, will-serving con-

sciousness, all spatio-temporal locating of things is relative, ultimately, to a *here* and a *now* that is determined by my own location in
space-time as an embodied being. All lines of direction, as it were,
radiate out from myself as the world's 'centre'. I shall call this first
mark of ordinary consciousness its 'egocentricity'.

In addition to knowing where things are, will-serving, consciousness also needs to know how they stand causally to its needs
and desires: what they can do to and for the individual and what he
can do to and with them. This means that in everyday perceptual
experience something gets added to the intrinsic properties of
objects. Schopenhauer calls these additions 'relative essences' (WR
II: 372).

'Relative essences' encapsulate how things stand to us causally.
Schopenhauer's idea, I think, is that they present things in one of
three ways: either as actual or potential *threats* to the will, or as actual
or potential *allurements* (see p. 114 below) to the will, or, thirdly, as
means of warding off threats or obtaining allurements. So, for
example, when an object shows up in ordinary consciousness as a
tiger, it shows up not, à la William Blake or Douanier Rousseau, as a
wonderfully blazing orange contrast to the black-green foliage of
the jungle, not as a burning-bright-in-the-forest-of-the-night kind
of tiger, but rather as *danger*. When something shows up as an *apple* it
shows up, not, à la Cézanne, as a delicately variegated display of
nature's wondrous infinity of greens, but as *food*. And when a piece
of greenstone shows up as a *knife* it shows up not as a beautiful,
ready-made sculpture, but as *equipment*, as something for killing
tigers or cutting apples.

Relative essences represent additions to the intrinsic nature of
objects in the sense that it is only on account of us, only on account
of our needs, desires and technological practices, that they are true
of things. While they constitute what we might call the 'being for
us' of things, they do not belong to their 'being in itself'.[6]

As well as adding 'relative essences' to things, ordinary consciousness (as we saw in discussing 'evolutionary idealism' in

chapter 2) also subtracts: it subtracts their 'absolute essence' (WR II: 372), in other words, their intrinsic nature or 'being in itself'. Since only the relative essence of a thing is 'interesting' to the will, ordinary consciousness does not attend to 'absolute essences': 'The ordinary man does not linger long over the mere perception' but 'quickly [and typically unconsciously] looks for the ['relative'] concept under which it is to be brought just as the lazy man looks for a chair' (WR I: 187–8).[7] So the Amsterdam stockbroker is oblivious to the background roar of the exchange though he hears every word of the neighbour with whom he is doing a deal (WR II: 381–2), the absorbed chess-player, as we saw, is oblivious to the beauty of the Chinese chessmen, the traveller in a hurry sees the beautiful bridge over the Rhine as a dash intersecting with a stroke, in general, the world shows up to practical consciousness as a beautiful landscape shows up on the general's plan of a battlefield (WR II: 381). In general, then, objects get 'thinned down' in ordinary consciousness, drained of their 'being in itself'. Their intrinsic properties (as Heidegger puts it) disappear into usefulness.

Schopenhauer calls this combination of addition and subtraction, the reduction of things to their 'relative essences', the 'subjectivity' of ordinary consciousness (WR II: 373). This is the second of its defining features.

The third and final mark of ordinary consciousness is what Schopenhauer calls its 'unhappiness'. Since ordinary consciousness views everything 'in relation to the will' (WR I: 177), the world shows up as full of dangers that threaten to engulf us and allurements, objects or desire, which, as desired, are not in our present possession. We are constantly being pushed and pulled here and there by danger and desire. Hence 'care (*Sorge*) for the constantly demanding will . . . continually fills and moves consciousness' (WR I: 196). Even at its best, there is a permanent undertone of 'discomfort or disquiet' (WR II: 368); 'anxiety' is the 'keynote of our disposition' (WR I: 373).[8] It follows that so long as we inhabit ordinary, 'interested' consciousness, 'lasting happiness or peace is impossible' (WR I: 196). (This is merely a preliminary account of Schopenhauer's argument for the unhappiness of ordinary human existence. The argument will be expounded in detail in chapter 8.)

THE AESTHETIC STATE

Aesthetic consciousness, which happens only very rarely, consists in the disappearance of each of the three features – egocentricity, subjectivity and unhappiness – definitive of everyday consciousness. Quite 'suddenly', and in a way that can never be *made* to happen, we are captivated by the breathtaking beauty of, perhaps, the sun rising through the mist over Lake Constance or setting over New Zealand's Bay of Islands, or by a Cézanne forest glade. When this happens, says Schopenhauer, 'we *lose* ourselves entirely in th[e] object, to use a pregnant expression';

> in other words, we forget our individuality, our will, and continue to exist only as pure subject, as clear (*klaren*) mirror of the object, so that it is as though the object alone existed without anyone to perceive it, and thus we are no longer able to separate the perceiver from the perception, but the two have become one, since the entire consciousness is filled and occupied by a single image of perception
>
> (WR I: 179).

In ordinary consciousness, as we saw, I am in the world of my experience as an 'object among objects', indeed the object to which all others are related as the world's 'centre'. In the moment of aesthetic entrancement, however, the usual 'egocentricity' of consciousness disappears. The 'I' vanishes from the scene (which therefore becomes 'decentred', of which more in a moment). I am no longer, as we might put it, 'in the picture'.

When we cease to perceive as an embodied individual in the world we cease to perceive things 'in relation to the will'. If I am no longer in the world then nothing that happens there can either threaten or attract me. And if that is so then nothing in the world can be 'interesting' to me as a means of warding off threats or gaining allurements. What follows is that the additions and subtractions of 'subjectivity' disappear and we become instead an innocent eye, a 'clear mirror' of the object.[9] We become, that is to say, completely 'objective' (WR II: 368). We 'no longer consider the where, the when, the why and the wither of things, but simply and solely the *what* (WR I: 178).[10]

A final consequence of the loss of our normal identity is that the unhappiness of ordinary consciousness disappears. Since, not being in the scene, we can no longer relate things to our will, it follows that nothing that happens there can be an object of fear or desire, nothing can any longer move or distress us. So we enter a state of absolute equanimity. We achieve that 'bliss and peace of mind (*Säligkeit und Geistesruhe*[11])' (WR I: 212) which is 'always sought but always escaping us on [the] . . . path of willing'. We enter that

> painless state, prised by Epicurus as the highest good and as the state of the gods; for [a] . . . moment we are delivered from the miserable pressure of the will. We celebrate the Sabbath of the penal servitude of willing; the wheel of Ixion stands still
>
> (WR I: 196).

The *subject* of aesthetic experience undergoes, therefore, a radical transformation. It becomes the '*pure* will-less, painless, timeless [and spaceless] *subject of* ['objective'] *knowledge*. 'Simultaneously and inseparably' (WR I: 197) connected with the transformation of the subject, however, is a transformation of the object. Since the ego-centricity of ordinary consciousness has disappeared it follows that the object is not seen *from* a position in space-time. But that means that it is not seen *at* any position in space-time. Yet space and time are, says Schopenhauer, the '*principium individuationis*', the 'principle of individuation' (WR I: 112–3, 128; BM: 205–7). For something to be an individual is for it to belong to a world of individuals, distinguished from other individuals by occupying its own unique place in space and time, by charting its own unique course through that world. Hence the object of aesthetic contemplation has ceased to be an individual. It has become instead the 'Platonic Idea' of the kind of thing it is. So the aesthetic state in fact involves a *double* transformation: 'at one stroke the individual thing becomes the *Idea* of its species and the perceiving individual the pure subject of knowing' (WR I: 179). It was this double transformation Spinoza had in mind, suggests Schopenhauer, when he wrote that '*mens aeterna est, quatenus res sub aeternitatis specie concipit* (the mind is eternal insofar as it conceives things from the standpoint of eternity)' (ibid.).[12] In aesthetic perception one becomes, as it were, God.

Thus, in outline, Schopenhauer's general theory of art. Plainly, there is a great deal that requires detailed discussion. For the remainder of this chapter I shall look more closely at what he has to say about the aesthetic *subject*, and in chapter 6 I shall turn to what he has to say about the aesthetic *object*.

AESTHETIC PLEASURE

The transformation of the subject from ordinary consciousness to the will-lessness of aesthetic perception provides Schopenhauer with his account of 'aesthetic delight (*Wohlgefallen*)' (WR I: 199), the delight we take in the aesthetic contemplation of nature or art. The absolute equanimity which comes to us when we escape the anxiety of ordinary consciousness is what we give expression to when we call something 'beautiful'. (More exactly, it is what we express when we call something beautiful in the 'subjective' sense. As we will see when we come to discuss the aesthetic object, there is also an 'objective' sense of 'beautiful' which, unlike the subjective sense, refers to the nature of the object (WR I: 200–1, 209–10, 212–3).)

Schopenhauer gives some interestingly non-standard examples of occasions when we take this kind of delight in things. Nostalgia is one: the return, for example, of a scene from childhood recalled in a charmed light as a 'lost paradise' (WR I: 198). Another is the 'picturesque' – *malerisch*, literally the 'painterly' – the 'magic gleam' of a foreign city (Paris, Prague, Salzburg), the charm it has for the visitor but not its inhabitants. Schopenhauer explains both kinds of delight in terms of 'the blessedness of will-less perception'. In the case of nostalgia this is the product of a kind of 'illusion' or 'self-deception' since in reality (as Freud later emphasised) childhood is as wracked by the anxieties of the will as adulthood (WR I: 198–9). In the case of the foreign town, no such deception is involved since, unlike the town of one's daily existence, the foreign town really does stand out of all relation to one's will and is hence perceived 'purely objectively' (WR II: 370–1; see too PP II: 424).

Since the point of art is to be beautiful – to facilitate the 'feeling of the beautiful'[13] (WR I: 202) – it follows that it must seek to promote 'disinterested' perception, perception which occurs 'under the complete silence of the will' (WR I: 187). What follows from this is that art must never be calculated so as to rouse the appetites.

This provides Schopenhauer with a criterion for distinguishing between art and, roughly speaking, pornography – 'the alluring (*das Reizende*)'. Semi-draped nudes in suggestive poses as well as photo-realistic portrayals of 'prepared and served up dishes of oysters, herrings, crabs, bread and butter, beer, wine and so on' (WR I: 208) – the *mouthwatering*, both figuratively and literally – are inadmissible in art. Inadmissible, too, is the 'negatively alluring' (ibid.), the deliberately disgusting (rotting sheep's heads and other such delights from Damien Hurst.)

This seems a compelling way of making the distinction but raises the following general problem: if genuine art demands the 'silence of the will', and if, as Schopenhauer seems to claim, all emotions are 'modification[s] of the will' (WR II: 202), is not his theory committed to the complete exclusion of emotion from art – from both the proper effect of art and from the state from which it properly arises?[14] Yet is it not, in fact, quite certain both that art, good and great art, often arises out of intense emotion and that it causes us to feel intense emotion?

Moreover, is not the capacity to cause emotion the most natural explanation of the *expressiveness* of art? What, one might well ask, is 'sad' or 'joyful music' other than music which makes us feel sad or joyful (though possibly not quite in the usual way)? What is a 'happy ending' to a novel other than an ending that makes us feel happy, or a 'scary movie' other than a movie that makes us feel scared? In sum, is it not the case that Schopenhauer's theory results in the emasculation of art, the excision of one of its most characteristic and valuable features?

Another way of stating the problem is this. Emotions entail desires. To be angry at or in love with X is to have desires concerning X. (Though I *say* I am in love with Julia Roberts I don't have any desire to do anything about it, which shows that I am not *really* in love with her but rather indulging in a flight of whimsy.) Yet the blissful equanimity of will-less perception consists precisely in the absence of desire: it is something 'always sought but always escaping us on the path of willing'. How, then, one might ask, can Schopenhauer possibly allow emotions such as sadness, hope, fear and joy to have any proper place in art?

Schopenhauer effectively confronts this problem in two places: in his discussion of 'the sublime' (WR I, section 39) where the emphasis is on the question of an emotional *response* to the aesthetic object, and in his discussion of lyric poetry (WR I: 248–50), where the emphasis is on the place of emotion in the *creation* of art. Since the two discussions say essentially the same thing, they allow us to infer, I think, to a *general* Schopenhauerian account of the place of emotion in art, an account, it seems to me, full of aesthetic sensitivity and philosophical insight.

THE SUBLIME

Schopenhauer's discussion of the sublime is, he says, built upon Kant's 'excellent' but incomplete discussion in the *Critique of Judgement*.

An object is sublime when it is apt to produce the 'feeling of the sublime' (WR I: 201–2). This occurs when three conditions are satisfied. The first is that the object of contemplation (a hurricane or avalanche, perhaps, either in nature or as represented by art) stands in a 'hostile (*feindlich*)' relation to the will, that it be something 'threatening and terrible' (WR I: 204) to the will. Not to the subject's individual will – for then he would break off contemplation and be disposed to flight – but rather to 'the human will in general' as expressed through 'its objectivity, the human body' (WR I: 202). The object must be something that human beings in general find threatening and terrible. The second condition is that the subject must be *aware* of this hostile relation – the feeling lasts only as long as the awareness lasts (WR I: 202). And yet – this is the third condition – the subject 'quietly contemplates, as pure, willless subject of knowing, those very objects so terrible to the will' (WR I: 201), experiencing a special feeling of 'exaltation beyond the known hostile relation of the contemplated object' (WR I: 202). The feeling of the sublime is, in short, the seemingly paradoxical phenomenon of delight in the terrible. When we have understand just what is 'terrible' about the sublime and why, nonetheless, its contemplation produces an ecstatic state, we will have understood the nature of the sublime.

* * *

Kant calls the sublime a 'bitter-sweet' feeling. Along with the 'exaltation' there is a feeling of having been humbled, made to feel 'small'. Following Kant, Schopenhauer distinguishes two ways in which the object humiliates one, is 'hostile' to the will, two species of the sublime: the 'dynamical' and the 'mathematical'.

The dynamically sublime – 'nature in turbulent and tempestuous motion; semi-darkness through threatening black thunder clouds; overhanging cliffs shutting out the view by their interlacing; rushing, foaming, masses of water; complete desert; the wail of the winds rushing through the ravines' (WR I: 204)[15] – is that which makes us aware of our *causal* insignificance, 'reduces us to nought'

(WR I: 205), in the face of the gigantic causal powers (Book II's 'natural forces') inherent in nature. The mathematically sublime, on the other hand – the Pyramids, the night sky, the dome of St. Paul's Cathedral seen from the inside – is experienced when vast spaces remind us of our speck-of-dust minuteness, of the 'vanishing nothingness' (WR I: 206), of our tenure within the infinity of time and space. The mathematically sublime is that which, as it were, reminds us that our entire lives are but a blink of the divine eye.

* * *

Actually, however, I think there is a third species of the sublime implicit in Schopenhauer's discussion that is not captured by either of the Kantian categories. Schopenhauer observes that most human beings do not like to be alone in nature. They need company or a book. This is because, unable to escape the 'interested' stance to the world, their entire consciousness is permeated by, 'like a ground-bass',

> the constant inconsolable lament, 'It is of no use to me'. Thus in solitude even the most beautiful surroundings have for them a desolate, dark, strange, and hostile appearance
>
> (WR I: 198).

Suppose however you are aware of this kind of 'hostility' of the object yet contemplate it with the absolute equanimity of the pure subject. Then according to Schopenhauer's account of the circumstances under which it comes about, you experience the sublime. Yet though the feeling of humiliation, of being 'reduced to nought', which Schopenhauer says is common to both the dynamically and mathematically sublime (WR I: 205), may be present here, what is salient for you, as I imagine the case, is neither your causal puniness in the face of the great forces of nature nor exactly your spatio-temporal 'nothingness'. You feel 'small' neither in a causal nor in a spatio-temporal sense. Rather, what makes you feel small is the total *indifference* of nature to oneself. It doesn't *care* (as Schopenhauer has indeed emphasised throughout Book II) whether one lives or dies – whichever it is, its processes carry on just the same. It is, I think, this humbling of one's pretence that one's existence *matters*, this indifference – bitter, yet at the same time obscurely wholesome – which attracts us to the ocean, to great rivers and to trees. And also to the moon which, as Schopenhauer indeed says, is sublime 'because, without any reference to us, it moves along eternally foreign to earthly life and activity' (WR II: 374).

* * *

Notice that the underlying theme common to all species of the sublime is one's own death. It is this bringing forth of death (a topic which, normally, we studiously avoid) that constitutes the 'hostility' of the sublime object, the 'bitter' part of the feeling of the sublime. The dynamical reminds one of one's fragility, of death's inevitability, the mathematical reminds one that it is almost here, while the indifferent reminds one of nature's lack of concern for one, of how, as Rilke puts it, it 'ventures' one forth without any 'special cover'.[16] This makes it even more paradoxical that we should *value* the experience of the sublime, regard it as a species of aesthetic *delight*. So why do we? This question can be approached by looking at Schopenhauer's account of the difference between the feeling of the sublime and that of the beautiful. (The distinction is, he says, not an absolute one. The two feelings can merge into one another; they form a continuum (WR I: 202.)

* * *

Schopenhauer's word for the sublime is *das Erhabene* – literally, 'the being raised up above', raised up above one's everyday, embodied self. Of course, the feeling of the beautiful (in the 'subjective' sense of 'beautiful'), too, consists in one's rising above the everyday self to become the 'pure' subject. The difference though, according to Schopenhauer, is that whereas, with the beautiful, the subject is so completely absorbed into the object of perception that 'not even a recollection of the will remains', the sublime requires a 'constant recollection of the will'. This is necessary since 'the feeling of the sublime is distinguished from that of the beautiful only by an addition, namely, the exaltation beyond the *known* hostile relation of the contemplated object to the will in general' (WR I: 202; emphasis added).

But how, to repeat our question, is it possible we should experience the sublime object as obscurely *threatening* and yet *welcome* the experience? Why is there some kind of deep satisfaction in the experience, a deep kind of 'sweetness' that completely outweighs its 'bitterness'? Because – here is the crux of Schopenhauer's answer – of the split, 'twofold' (WR I: 204) nature of consciousness of the sublime. On the one hand the subject 'feels himself as individual, as the feeble phenomenon of will . . . a vanishing nothingness' threatened with 'annihilation'. 'Simultaneously', however, 'he also feels himself as the eternal, serene subject of knowing who, as the condition of every object, is the supporter of this whole world . . . [it] being only his representation' (WR I: 204–5).

There are two things to notice in this crucial passage. First, that in confronting the sublime object we *experience fear*. Not fear that we as individuals will be annihilated by it here and now, but fear in the face of the annihilation that is the inescapable fate of all human beings. The second crucial point is that while we experience fear, it is, in an important sense, *not our fear*. Since our primary identification is with the pure subject rather than with the threatened individual, we feel its fear rather in the way we might empathise with the fear of another person or a character, in a play. (As we will see in the next chapter, Schopenhauer regards tragedy as the highest form of the feeling of the sublime.) Ourselves we experience as 'raised up above' the sublime object and so immune to the threat it discloses. This 'contrast' (WR I: 204) between feeling the precarious predicament of the individual and at the same time one's own absolute security is the ground of our feeling of 'exaltation'.

Here, finally we arrive at what is special about the feeling of the sublime. It is an intimation of immortality. We experience the illusory nature of identification with the fragile individual that lies within the world of experience and come to the intuitive realisation that 'we are one with the [eternal and indestructible] world'. In experiencing the sublime we intuitively realise that, as the *Upanishads* puts it, 'I am all this creation collectively, and besides me there exists no other being' (WR I: 205–6). What we realise, in short, is that what we are, in truth, is Kant's 'thing in itself'.[17] Kant makes a similar point in his own more sober manner and style. In experiencing the sublime, he says, we become alive to the 'supersensible' side of our being (*Critique of Judgement*, section 27).

* * *

So, to summarise, we began by wondering how Schopenhauer could allow for an emotional response to art (or nature) given that he insists on the 'will-lessness' of the art-creating and art-receiving state. In the case of the sublime the answer, in brief, is: we are will-less in the face of the sublime because, *though we feel emotion, in particular humiliation and fear*, it is *disassociated* emotion, emotion we, as it were, feel for another rather than for ourselves. And because it is thus experienced it does not prompt any act of will such as breaking off contemplation or running away. It is not a 'modification of the will'.

THE LYRICAL

The second occasion on which Schopenhauer explicitly discusses the place of emotion in art is in his reflection upon the nature of lyric poetry.

'Lyric' is distinguished from 'epic' poetry in virtue of the fact that whereas the latter is mainly a narrative of outer action, the former is concerned with the evocation of inner, usually sad, feeling – feeling that is often projected onto nature. The problem

Schopenhauer implicitly confronts in his discussion is the follow-ing. Since the lyric poet, literally or metaphorically, 'sings' of, for example, his own lost love, what he does is to feel an intense emotion to which he then gives voice in verse. But since all genuine art is a product of the 'pure, will-less subject of knowing', the appearance arises that Schopenhauer's will-lessness requirement commits him to consigning about half of all the world's great poetry to the category of 'fake art'.

Schopenhauer's effective answer to this problem begins by *seem-ing* to accept the consequence. In lyric poetry, he says, it seems that 'the depicted is also . . . the depicter' so that 'a certain subjectivity is essential to poetry of this kind' (WR I: 248). For example, the poet, as he writes, wills the presence of the beloved and so feels the pain of her having run off with another man. ('Yesterday, all my troubles were so far away . . .'.)

So, he continues, the lyric form is the easiest type of poetry to produce: while true art is the work of the rare 'objectivity' of genius, 'even the man who is not very eminent can produce a beautiful song' since he needs only a 'vivid perception' of his own agitated emotional state (WR I: 249).

So the lyric poem is autobiographical, self-obsessed, usually self-pitying. Actually, however, Schopenhauer is referring, here, only to the *undistinguished* lyric poem. For he continues by saying that 'the lyrics of genuine poets reflect the inner nature of the whole of mankind'. This makes the 'genuine' lyric poet 'universal man', since his subject is 'all that human nature produces from itself . . . all that dwells in any human breast' (WR I: 249). In *great* lyric poetry, that is, it is not *personal* but rather *universal* emotion that is expressed. The great lyric poet speaks about and for *all* of us. How is this possible?

In the lyric, says Schopenhauer, the 'singer's' own willing – his 'joy', but much more often his 'sorrow' – fills his consciousness. 'Besides this, however, . . . the singer, through the sight of sur-rounding nature, becomes conscious of himself as the subject of pure, will-less knowing whose unshakeable, blissful peace now appears in contrast to the stress (Drang) of always impeded, always needy willing' (WR I: 250).

The great lyric poem is, says Schopenhauer, an 'alternate play' between these two points of view. We feel the singer's pain but then 'pure knowing comes to us, so to speak, in order to deliver us from willing and its stress'. In turn, however, we are recaptured by 'personal aims', torn away from 'peaceful contemplation', but yet 'again and again the next beautiful environment, in which pure will-less knowledge presents itself to us, entices us away from willing'. In the lyric

willing . . . and pure perception of the environment . . . are wonderfully blended with each other, Relations between the two are sought and imagined; the subjective disposition, the affection of the will, imparts its hue to the perceived environment, and this environment again imparts in the reflex its colour to that disposition

(WR I: 250).

As expressions of 'this mingled and divided state of mind' (ibid.) Schopenhauer cites all of Goethe's 'immortal songs'. By name he mentions, inter alia, 'On the Lake', which reads, in (my) prose translation, as follows:

And fresh nourishment, new blood
I suck from the open world;
How sweet and kindly is nature,
Who holds me to her breast.
The waves rock our boat
Up and down in time with the oars,
And mountains, rising to the clouded sky,
Stand before our course.

Oh, my eyes, why do you droop?
Are you returning, golden dreams?

Away you dream, golden though you are;
Here too, there is life and love.

On the waves there glitter
A thousand drifting stars,
Soft mist drinks up
Surrounds the towering skyline;
A morning wind wings around
The shadowed bay,
And in the lake are mirrored
The ripe fruit.

Schopenhauer concludes the discussion by citing a poem of J. H. Voss which he regards as an amusing yet insightful parody of the lyric state. The song describes, he says,

> the feelings of a drunken plumber, falling from a tower, who, in passing, observes that the clock on the tower is at half past eleven, a remark quite foreign to his condition and hence belonging to will-free knowledge

(WR I: 250).

The thing to notice in this discussion of the lyric poem[18] is that emotion is allowed to enter into the aesthetic state and into art in essentially the same way as in the discussion of the sublime: it enters via a 'twofold', that is, a 'mingled and divided' state of mind. In both cases one experiences an emotion but, qua artist or art-receiver, becomes disassociated from it. This repetition of the same pattern of analysis strongly suggests that we should accept it as offering Schopenhauer's *general* account of the proper place of emotion in art: emotion is properly present in both the creative and receptive states provided it is, in the sense explained, *disassociated* emotion.

This principle – to return to the point at which this discussion started – will give us, for example, an account of the difference between erotic art and the masturbatory images of pornography.

And it will also distinguish between horror films and tragedy. Whereas the former rouse one to acts of will – cringing, closing the eyes, leaving the cinema – the latter does not. Another, more controversial consequence, is that it will lead to a sharp distinction between art and propaganda: however necessary and morally justified the latter may be, if its representation of oppression and cruelty is calculated to send us to the barricades (Diego Riviera's intention, for example), it is not, from a Schopenhauerian point of view, great art.[19]

Notice, finally, that disassociated emotion, since it is not, according to my primary sense of identity, *mine*, is rather *everyman's*. The person who has lost his love or is terrified by the vastness of the night sky is not me but all of us. This, I think, is the point Schopenhauer is making when he says that the sublime object is 'hostile' to 'the human will in general' (WR I: 204) and that the great lyric poet is 'the universal man' whose real topic is not his own state but rather 'human nature' (WR I: 249). This idea that the great artist expresses *our* joys, fears and sorrows, the lesser one *his* joys, fears and sorrows, captures, perhaps, something of the difference between Goethe and Paul McCartney.

And it captures, too, the intuition that there is something *morally* elevating about the expressiveness of great art. For on the Schopenhauerian account, authentic art trains us to feel from the point of view of humanity as a whole, to transcend the limits of narrow egoism.[20]

CRITICISM OF SCHOPENHAUER ON THE SUBLIME AND THE LYRICAL

Although Schopenhauer's treatment of the sublime and the lyrical is subtle and compelling, his deployment of Kantian metaphysics seems to me to lead him astray in one major respect.

In the sublime state, as we saw, the subject has abandoned his primary identification with the threatened individual. Instead, according to Schopenhauer, he 'feels himself as the eternal serene subject of knowing, who as the condition of every object is the supporter of this whole world . . . [it being] only his representation' (WR I: 205). In other words, the smallness, fragility, insignificance, in general the 'dependence' (WR I: 204) we previously felt in the face of the vastness, power and indifference of nature 'is now annulled by its dependence on us' (WR I: 205).

Schopenhauer claims, as we saw, that this captures the sense that 'we are one with the world' which occurs in the sublime or lyric state; that it is an intuitive grasping of the wisdom of the Upanishads, which holds that 'I am all this creation collectively, and besides me there exists no other being' (WR I: 205).

Whether or not this is a correct account of the Upanishads, it seems to me that Kantian idealism is not the right framework in which to interpret the sublime or the lyrical. For the feeling of the sublime, the redemptive feeling engendered by lyric poetry, is what Freud aptly called the 'oceanic' feeling.[21] It is, that is, an *expansion* of the self, a flowing *out* of the individual ego so that one becomes the totality of all things, becomes nature as a whole.[22] But representing the sublime or lyrical state as a matter of realising that everything is 'my' representation turns it into precisely the opposite: a *contraction* of the vastness of being into the content of my consciousness. To do proper justice to the sublime and the lyrical, it seems to me, one needs a different metaphysics, one that does not reduce the world to 'my representation'.[23] One needs some kind of realism – but that is another story.

THE POSSIBILITY OF GENIUS

Authentic 'genius' the capacity for sustained 'objectivity', sustained habitation of the perspective of the 'pure subject of knowing', is, we have seen, extraordinarily rare. 'Vulgarity', the 'strict subordination of their knowing to their willing'[24] is the condition of nearly everyone nearly all of the time, 'the stamp of commonness . . . impressed on the great majority of faces' (WR II: 380).

There is, Schopenhauer emphasises, a difference, not of degree but of kind between genius and talent. While genius belongs only to someone who has freed himself from subjectivity, talent remains within the province of ordinary, will-governed consciousness. The person of talent is simply someone who 'thinks more rapidly and accurately than do the rest', and is therefore more effective in practical affairs; 'the genius perceives a world different from them all – though only by looking more deeply into the world that lies before them also – since it presents itself in his mind more objectively' (WR I: 376). 'Talent is like the marksman who hits a target which others cannot reach; genius is like the marksman who hits a target . . . others cannot even see' (WR II: 391). ('Women', Schopenhauer predictably adds, 'can have remarkable talent, but not genius, for they always remain subjective' (WR II: 392). A feminist might reply that since, historically, women have been excluded from the arts and sciences and have been compelled to care for 'subjective' things like children and household management, the subjectivity of women lies not in their genes but in their oppressed historical situation.)

Schopenhauer observes that even the most sublime genius inhabits ordinary consciousness uninterruptedly for long periods of time. Consequently, 'the action of genius has always been regarded as an inspiration, as the name itself indicates, as the action of a superhuman (*übermenschlich*) being different from the individual himself, which takes possession of him only periodically' (WR I: 188).[25]

The question, however, is how, on Schopenhauer's account of the human mind as an evolutionary tool designed for survival rather than 'comprehending the inner nature of things', genius is possible at all.

Schopenhauer's answer is simply that though the genius is indeed a freak, a '*monstrum*', someone whose intellect operates against its 'destiny', a *monstrum* is not the same as an impossibility. Biology, though a destiny, is not always a fate. He also adds that the genius is a '*monstrum per excessum*' rather than a '*monstrum per defectum*', a freak by way of excess rather than deficiency. The genius is that rare individual with a 'superfluity and abundance' (WR II: 410) of intellectual energy, enough to satisfy the demands of the will but also with a 'surplus' available for objective perception (WR II: 376–8). This preserves Schopenhauer's account of genius against the objection that from the perspective of his evolutionary psychology, geniuses (though they indeed have, he says, very little interest in practical affairs (WR I: 187) would likely get wiped out before completing any artworks.

SUMMARY
Schopenhauer's general theory of art

Art, aesthetic consciousness, is an extraordinary transcendence of ordinary consciousness. The latter is defined in terms of three characteristics:

(a) it is 'egocentric' – things show up always in relation to me, a being in the world as its spatio-temporal 'centre',
(b) things show up always in their utility, 'in relation to the will', and
(c) it is full of unhappiness, anxiety.

Aesthetic consciousness is marked by the disappearance of these three features. The 'I' disappears from the scene so that things show up no longer in their utility but as they are in themselves and cease, therefore, to be objects of anxiety. Since they are not seem from a place in the space-time world they are not seen at a place in it. So they cease to be seen as individuals but become, rather, the 'Platonic Idea' of their species.

Difficulties and details in the theory

(1) Does not Schopenhauer's exclusion of 'will' from the aesthetic state mean that *emotions*, which he appears to regard as 'modifications of the will', are excluded from art? His account of the sublime and the lyric suggest a general answer to this question: emotion can

play a powerful role in the genesis and reception of great art provided it is *disassociated* emotion.

(2) *Genius*, the capacity for intense and sustained habitation of the
aesthetic state, which looks to be an impossibility on Schopenhauer's evolutionary account of human consciousness, is accounted for
in terms of energy. The genius is someone with enough energy to
attend to the needs of practical consciousness, but with a surplus
left over for aesthetic contemplation.

FURTHER READING

See the suggestions at the end of chapter 6.

Six

Art (continued)

THE PLATONIC IDEAS

The last chapter was concerned with Schopenhauer's account of the subject of the aesthetic state. I want to turn now to his exploration of its object. As we have seen, he describes the object of art as being the Platonic Idea, that is to say, 'the immediate objectivity of th[e] will at a definite grade' (WR I: 170). At first sight, this seems to imply the odd notion that when Cézanne looks at an apple what he sees is something other than the apple bought the previous morning in the market at Aix by Madame Cézanne. Can this really be Schopenhauer's view?

At first sight it seems that it must be. When he first introduces the Ideas in Book II he says the best summary of the Platonic doctrine of the Ideas is given by Diogenes Laertius: 'Plato teaches that the Ideas exist . . . so to speak, as patterns or prototypes, and that the remainder of things only resemble them, and exist as their copies' (WR I: 130). In another place Schopenhauer says that '[a]t bottom, even form and colour, which are what is immediate in the apprehension of the Idea through perception, do not belong to the Idea, but are only the medium of its expression; for, strictly speaking, space is as foreign to it as is time' (WR II: 364). So it seems that while Madame Cézanne buys a copy, Cézanne paints the 'prototype': while she buys something that is round and rosy, the apple he sees has neither colour nor shape.

In fact, however, this impossibly odd view of the objects of art is not Schopenhauer's position. In *On the Fourfold Root of the Principle of Sufficient Reason* he says that the Ideas function like 'normal intuitions' (FR: 206). And normal intuitions, he says, as intuitions, i.e. perceptual objects, are different from concepts in being 'determinate throughout'. (Concepts, remember (pp. 39–42 above) are supposed to be sketchy, undetailed, 'abstract'.) On the other hand they resemble concepts in that they 'have to do with many things' which enables them to function as 'representatives of concepts' (FR: 198–9). In *The World as Will* Schopenhauer explicitly attributes this combination of determinacy and universality to the 'Ideas'. Whatever Plato may have meant by the term, he says, as *he* uses it, the Ideas are not 'abstract, discursive, wholly undetermined within [their] . . . sphere' like concepts, but are, rather, 'absolutely perceptive and though representing an infinite number of individual things, . . . yet thoroughly definite' (WR I: 233–4; see, too, WR I: 262).

What Schopenhauer is getting at with the idea of a 'normal intuition' (he takes himself to be simply repeating Kant's theory of geometrical demonstration) is the way in which axioms of geometry can be demonstrated through the construction of figures. I draw a line, and then another parallel to it. The result is that you can simply *see* that parallel lines never meet. Of course the lines I draw have a particular length. But what you see is valid for all parallel lines because the particular length of the lines is irrelevant to the demonstration. The result is universally valid, that is, because I have made no use of, not paid any attention to, the particular length my lines happen to have.

This suggests that rather than being the exotic entities they at first seemed to be, the objects of aesthetic attention just are ordinary perceptual objects, objects perceived, however, in a special way: with one's attention focused on what is universal in them and away from what is idiosyncratic. And this, in fact, is precisely what Schopenhauer says when he comes to discussing the Ideas in Book III, specifically, that is, in the context of art:

to the brook which rolls downwards over the stones, the eddies,
waves, and foam forms exhibited by it are indifferent and
inessential: but that it follows gravity and behaves as an inelastic,
perfectly mobile, formless and transparent fluid, this is its essential
nature, this *if known through perception*, is the Idea

(WR I: 182).

I shall attend shortly to the force of the emphasis, here, on perception (as opposed to conception). For the moment the important
thing to notice is that perceiving the Idea is not perceiving something *other than* the brook but rather perceiving *the brook* with one's
attention focused on the 'essential' and away from the 'inessential'.
The following quotation makes it absolutely explicit that it is
indeed the individual perceptual object that is the object of aesthetic experience. 'Art', says Schopenhauer,

plucks the object of its contemplation from the stream of the
world's course, and holds it isolated before it. *This particular thing*,
which in that stream was an infinitesimal part, becomes for art, a
representative of the whole, an equivalent of the infinitely many in
space and time

(WR I: 185; emphasis added).

So it is not something *other than* the ordinary individual that is the
object of aesthetic experience, but rather, as in the case of the
geometrical diagram, the ordinary individual with one's attention
confined to what is universal in it. It is not something separate from
the individual that the artist sees, but rather 'the universal in the
particular' (WR II: 379; emphasis added). In poetry, for example,
though the poet always presents us with the particular he wants to
let us know the universal, which has the result that 'the type is
strongly marked'. This is why Shakespeare's lines are always appo-
site (WR: 427) — why he is, as the joke has it, so full of quotes.
The same is true of drama in general. Because it has the, so to speak,
hidden curriculum of disclosing the universal, its endeavour is

always to present 'significant characters in significant situations' (WR II: 432).

Though his admiration for Plato makes him generally want to de-emphasise the fact, Schopenhauer's use of the notion of the 'Idea' is actually, therefore, a long way removed from Plato's. For whereas the notion of individual things as 'copies' of the Ideas requires that the Ideas be *things*, Schopenhauer does not, in fact, treat them as things at all. 'Idea' is, in his aesthetic theory, a mere *façon de parler*, a merely nominal object. The best way of putting his view is to say that what is special about the artist is not that he perceives the Idea *instead* of the individual, but rather perceives the individual *as Idea*. To borrow a term from Nietzsche (who was, I believe, considerably influenced by Schopenhauer's talk of the Ideas) the artist 'idealises' the object: the artist, says Nietzsche, is governed by 'a tremendous drive to bring out the main features so that the others simply disappear in the process'. 'This process is called *idealising*' (*Twilight of the Idols*, 'Skirmishes of an untimely Man', section 8).

* * *

Quite apart from the fact that it turns his aesthetic theory into nonsense, another, decisive reason for rejecting the suggestion that what Schopenhauer imports into his philosophy are the Platonic Ideas conceived just as Plato conceived them, is that there is nowhere for them to go. According to Schopenhauer's version of Kantian idealism (we will go into this in greater detail in the next chapter) the thing in itself is 'one', beyond plurality, plurality being dependent of the forms of space and time, the *principium individuationis*. But the Ideas are many. So they cannot be located on the 'in itself' side of the 'in itself'–'mere representation' dichotomy. Hence they must be located on the representation side. Schopenhauer acknowledges this in the very title of Book III: the Ideas are said to present the 'Second Aspect' of 'The World as Representation'. But all that is to be found in the world as representation are individuals. So, ontologically speaking, the Ideas can only be normal individuals.

If, however, Schopenhauer's Ideas turn out to be so different from Plato's, what is the point of introducing his name and distinctive terminology at all?

In Book X of the *Republic*, pursuing what he calls 'the ancient quarrel between philosophy and poetry' (607b), Plato bans nearly all artists from the ideal state he is in the process of constructing. (Virtually the only artists that remain are the designers of abstract patterns for walls and the tellers of cautionary tales for children.) His claim is that though the poets have traditionally rivalled philosophy as a supposed source of profound wisdom, their pretensions are actually completely spurious. The argument for this, in a nutshell, is that whereas significant knowledge is always of the universal (Plato expresses this by saying that it is always knowledge of the 'Ideas' or 'essences' of things), art (like photography) only ever tells us about particular things. Knowledge, then, is the province of philosophy. Art is trivial; dangerously trivial, moreover, since dealing as it does in illusion and fantasy (television), it seduces us away from 'truth and reality'.

Schopenhauer calls this denigration of art 'one of the greatest . . . errors of that great man' (WR I: 212). Not that the identification of worthwhile knowledge with knowledge of the universal is a mistake. On the contrary, knowledge that is worth having is of universal essences; of *man* not *men*, of *life* not *my life*, of *existence* and not *existence in nineteenth-century Europe*.[1] Plato's mistake, rather, is to suppose that art – good art – cannot deliver the kind of knowledge in question. Art contains 'an acknowledged treasure of profound wisdom' (WR II: 407), and only Plato's radical mistake of supposing it to be concerned with the representation of the merely particular places him in opposition to this acknowledged fact. In reality, what is significant in art is never 'the particular . . . as such but always the universal in it' (WR I: 231).

* * *

Schopenhauer's insistence on the universal in art emerges in many ways. It leads him, for example, to attack the disdain of Dutch genre painting (the representation of everyday scenes from modest life, the master of which is Vermeer) based on the assumption that only events in world or biblical history are significant. This, he suggests, is quite mistaken. A painting whose significance is exhausted by the title 'Moses found by an Egyptian princess' is entirely trivial. The real 'inner' significance of such a work is never the particular historical event, but rather the universal embedded in it, the rescue of an orphan by a great lady through which is expressed a facet – compassion – of 'the many-sided Idea of humanity'. But that kind of significance can be expressed as well by humble as by grand painting since, from the point of view of expressing the universal, 'it is all the same whether ministers dispute about countries and nations over a map, or boors in a beer-house choose to wrangle over cards and dice' (WR I: 230–1).

* * *

It might be thought that portraiture would provide a stumbling block for the claim that the business of art is to present the universal. In fact, however, in some ways, it highlights the strengths of the theory.

What makes portraiture possible is that individual human beings express not only the 'Idea of the species' but also their own individual Idea.[2] This is expressed partly through permanent features of face and bodily form, and partly through fleeting but characteristic facial expression and body language. The individual Idea is the legitimate subject of portraiture. Yet individual character must never be treated as something 'quite peculiar to the man as a single individual', but rather as a side of the Idea of mankind specially appearing in this particular individual' (WR I: 221). If the artist fails to preserve this eye for the general, if the character of the individual 'abolishes' that of the species, then portraiture degenerates into the relative triviality of caricature (WR I: 225).

The strength of this theory is that it accounts for the fact that great portraiture reaches across the centuries, that – like Shakespeare – it is always contemporary. It accounts for the fact that a Rembrandt self-portrait is not just a picture of a seventeenth-century Dutchman with money worries and a bulbous nose but is also a portrait of *everyman*.

THE BEAUTIFUL

Art, then – good art – is for Schopenhauer, a cognitively important enterprise. It communicates knowledge to us, knowledge, moreover, of universal import. In this judgement he is, surely right and Plato wrong. Art does tell us about life and not just lives.

A further manifestation of Schopenhauer's strongly cognitivist view of art emerges in his account of beauty – beauty in the 'objective' rather than 'subjective' sense (see p. 113 above). In the 'objective' sense, an object's beauty consists simply in its expressing the Idea of the species to which it belongs (WR I: 210). To be aware of an object 'as Idea' and to be aware of it as beautiful are one and the same thing (WR I: 209).

A consequence of this is that since everything expresses an Idea, everything is to some degree, beautiful and so a proper subject for fine art – in German, to repeat, *die schönen Künste*, the beautiful arts. Yet objects may be more or less beautiful since, depending on how 'definite and distinct' their form is, 'the Ideas individualised in them more or less readily speak to us' (WR I: 200–1). In general, works of art are more beautiful than natural objects since the artist 'can express clearly what nature only stammers', articulate her only 'half-spoken' words (WR I: 222).[3]

A second variable on which beauty depends, claims Schopenhauer, is the importance of the Idea the object expresses. Since the metaphysical will is expressed most clearly in the Idea of humanity, it follows that it is more 'significant and suggestive' than any other Idea, and that humanity is the most beautiful of all natural objects (in the objective sense). The revelation of human nature is thus the highest aim of art (WR I: 210).

What we see in this account of the beautiful is a very tight connection between beauty and truth. Things are beautiful, the representations of art succeed, to the extent that, through the clarity and significance of their form, they direct our attention to the 'innermost being' (WR I: 210) of the world. They are the opposite when, through the proliferation of disorganised, irrelevant and distracting detail, they fail to communicate a coherent vision of the truth. In art, as Iris Murdoch puts it, beauty consists in 'the artful use of form to illuminate truth'.[4]

ART AND PHILOSOPHY

If one seeks to refute Plato's denigration of art by describing it in the terms which he reserves for philosophy one runs the risk of obliterating the distinction between art and philosophy.

One possible response would be to simply *accept* the obliteration of the distinction, to deny that there is any absolute distinction between art and philosophy. This, I think, in outline, is what a modern 'Continental' philosopher would say. Schopenhauer, however, at least when thinking explicitly about the nature of philosophy and its method, believes it vital to maintain the distinction between the two. Methodologically (though not in terms of content[5]), that is to say, he is what would now be called an 'Analytic' philosopher. Accordingly, he devotes a whole chapter of volume II, Chapter 34, to preserving and elucidating the distinction between art and philosophy.

He begins by making the problem seemingly worse. Great philosophy and great art both spring from the 'objective', will-free mode of contemplating the world, both overcome the 'mist of subjectivity' that envelops ordinary consciousness (WR II: 406–7).

Moreover both work towards the same goal. 'Not merely philosophy but also the fine arts work at bottom towards solving the
problem of existence'. Like philosophy, that is, 'every genuine and
successful work of art answers [the] . . . question' 'What is life?'
(WR II: 406).

So art and philosophy deal with the same question and may give
the same answer. They are, nonetheless, different, for while art
'speak[s] the naive and childlike language of *perception*', philosophy
speaks 'the abstract and serious language of *reflection*' (WR II: 406).
While philosophy is an essentially *conceptual* activity, art is fundamentally *perceptual*; so far as art is concerned, 'the concept is eternally
barren and unproductive' (WR I: 235).

What does this contrast between the conceptual and perceptual
amount to? The answer to this question consists in a number of
further distinctions Schopenhauer draws between art and philosophy, distinctions which are actually quite independent of Book
I's defective account of the conceptual/perceptual distinction
which was discussed in chapter 2.

* * *

Though both art and philosophy seek to uncover universal, Platonic
('mythic', one might say) truth about the nature of life, they seek to
communicate it in radically different ways. While philosophy seeks
the clear and unambiguous articulation of universal truth – 'the
world is my representation', 'the inner nature of everything is will',
'life is suffering' are presumably examples – art 'gives only a frag-
ment, an example instead of the rule'. It 'holds up to the questioner
an image of perception and say[s]: "Look here; this is life (*das ist das
Leben*)"' (WR II: 406).[6] 'Employing a distinction of Wittgenstein's,
we could say, then, that while a great and successful philosophy *says*
what life is like, art *shows* what it is like. So, for example, the turbulent rhythms running through a van Gogh cornfield-with-cypresses
or a starry sky might be said to *show* the Schopenhauerian truth that
the inner being of everything is will. And a Renaissance portrait of

the agonised yet serene martyrdom of St Sebastian, or an El Greco Crucifixion, might show what (Schopenhauer's) philosophy says: that though life is suffering there is a 'beyond' through which we can achieve a final homecoming, final 'salvation' (see, further, the discussion of tragedy pp. 142–5 below).[7]

It follows from this that while the knowledge of philosophy is always explicit, the knowledge of art is implicit WR II: 407). Note that Schopenhauer made essentially this distinction between philosophy and religion (see pp. 99–100 above). This might be seen as generating a further problem, namely, the problem of the difference between art and religion. Since art and religion have almost always been intimately connected, however, I am inclined to think that he would be happy to accept religious texts and ceremonies as kinds of artwork.

Another way Schopenhauer has of putting this contrast between the explicit and implicit is by saying that philosophy is related to art as wine is to grapes: philosophy provides actual wisdom, art potential wisdom. It follows that, in a unique way, art demands the 'cooperation of the beholder'. Since all that art does is to provide a 'purer repetition' of what lies before the eyes of all of us, it follows that the audience of art must be active in its contemplation: the spectator 'must . . . contribute from his own resources towards bringing that wisdom to light', must 'produce it afresh'. Consequently, he adds, the receiver of art 'grasps only so much of the work as his capacity and culture allow, just as every sailor in a deep sea lets down the sounding-lead as far as the line will reach' (WR II: 407).

This 'produc[ing] afresh' of the vision implicit in the work should not, however, be thought of as a burden. That the imagination is actively engaged in so doing is essential to the enjoyment of a work of art (WR II: 407). This is why the sketches of the masters are often more engaging than the finished work; they leave something over, 'indeed the final thing', for the beholder to do. The finished works often fall foul of Voltaire's remark that 'The secret of being dull and tedious is to say everything' (WR II: 407–8). One might think, here, of how much of the liveliness of the sketches disappears in John Constable's over-painted 'gallery' works.[8]

A final sub-contrast contained in the contrast between the perceptuality of art and the conceptuality of philosophy consists in the fact that whereas the content of the latter can be fully captured by paraphrase the content of the former cannot. Since the concept is something 'completely definable, hence something to be exhausted, something distinctly thought', it follows that philosophy 'can be, according to its whole content, communicated coldly and dispassionately in words'. Since the Idea, on the other hand, as perceptual, is something 'in its fuller determinations . . . inexhaustible', the content of art can never be fully captured in paraphrase. This is what accounts for the 'absurdity' of trying to 'reduce a poem of Shakespeare or Goethe to an abstract truth, the communication thereof would have been the aim of the poem'. A mark of the greatness of great art, that is, is that it 'always leaves behind something . . . we cannot bring down to the distinctness of a concept'. WR II: 408–9).

This contrast is, surely, a consequence of the previous one. Since great art requires that its audience should recreate the work within the terms of its own culture and experience, its content can never be 'reduced' to any final and definitive interpretation. All great art, that is to say, is, in a sense, a performance artwork. And just as there can be no definitive performance of a Beethoven symphony, so there can be no definitive interpretation of the 'meaning' of, say, Shakespeare's *Hamlet*. There is always more 'meaning' available to be disclosed by alternative interpretations.

* * *

By way of defending himself against the charge of having obliterated the distinction between art and philosophy, Schopenhauer offers, then, a sharp and seemingly compelling distinction between the two. The difference between them is that philosophy is conceptual while art is perceptual. That is to say: (1) while philosophy *says* art *shows*, which means that (2) while the knowledge provided by philosophy is explicit that provided by art is implicit, which in turn means that (3) the knowledge provided by the former is actual, that provided by the latter merely potential, which entails that (4) while the knowledge of philosophy comes ready-made that provided by art must be recreated by the beholder. Finally, (5) while the content of a work of philosophy can be fully captured by paraphrase that of a work of art cannot.

In his reflections 'On Philosophy and its Method' in his last major work, *Parerga and Paralipomena*, Schopenhauer reveals something of the background presuppositions that lie behind the above dichotomisation. The discussion (the crucial passage is at PP II: 9–11) concerns what he calls 'higher consciousness' or, alternatively, 'illuminism'.

Illuminism is knowledge that is incapable of articulation in literal language. Schopenhauer has no trouble at all in accepting that there is such knowledge. It is the basis of Eastern mysticism, indeed of all mysticism. Even great philosophy, he says, the philosophy of Plato and Spinoza – and, by implication, his own – is based on a 'concealed illuminism'. (Remember the early notebooks' record of Schopenhauer's own experience of a 'better consciousness' (see p. 100 above.)

The fact, however, that deliverances of illuminism are not literally 'communicable' means that they have no place in *philosophy*. Consequently, he says, 'at the end of my philosophy I have indicated a sphere of illuminism as something that exists, but have guarded against setting even one foot thereon'. (This will be discussed in chapter 8.)

Since Wittgenstein was, as we will see in chapter 9, a close reader of Schopenhauer, it is no accident, I think, that Schopenhauer's position here can be summed up in the final words of Wittgenstein's *Tractatus*:

There is indeed that which cannot be put into words. It *shows* itself
(*es zeigt sich*); it is the mystical . . . Whereof we cannot speak we
must remain silent

(propositions 6.522–7).

There are, Schopenhauer accepts, things that are accessible to the
mystics and even to philosophers during off-duty moments. Such
things 'show themselves' in the lives of the mystics and in great art
such as, perhaps, the El Greco *Crucifixion* mentioned earlier. 'We',
however, we *philosophers*, 'must remain silent' about them.

But why, exactly? Because, says Schopenhauer, philosophy is
'rationalism' (science). And the distinguishing mark of science is
that it seeks, not merely to persuade, but *to prove*, to 'demonstrate'.
The limits of the demonstrable are the limits of philosophy. But
only that which is capable of literal articulation is capable of demonstration. The trouble, therefore, with the non-'communicable' is
that it is indemonstrable. This is the reason why that which can
only be 'shown' has no place in philosophy.

Schopenhauer is, in my view, quite right that 'demonstration',
'rationalism', does mark a distinction between genuine works of
philosophy and what we usually think of as works of art. Actually,
however, why cannot philosophy *both* communicate by rational
'demonstration' *and* by 'showing'? Wittgenstein says that 'Whereof
we [philosophers] cannot speak, we [philosophers] must remain
silent. But why, instead of silence, should we not poeticise? Why
should we not 'show'? Why can't the philosopher *also* be an artist,
why can't he 'show' *at the same time as* 'saying'? After all, the first
philosophers, the Pre-Socratics, and even Plato himself were as
much poets as philosophers.

I shall return to this issue in the next chapter. For the moment let
me simply note that neither Schopenhauer not Wittgenstein offer
any answer to this question. They simply assume a dichotomy
between art and science ('rationalism') such that nothing is
allowed to belong on both sides of the divide. This, however, strikes

me as both arbitrary and a falsification of the nature of philosophy. (Elizabeth Lutyens, who set Wittgenstein's *Tractatus* to music, would also seem to be of this view.)

TRAGEDY AND THE VALUE OF ART

In this section I want to conclude the exposition of Schopenhauer's philosophy of the (non-musical) arts by indication how that philosophy fits into his wider metaphysical and existential concerns. This necessitates a brief return to the subjective side of art.

Art, we saw, seeks to answer the question 'What is life?'. But it does not do so as a 'winged angel-head' (see p. 61 above). Rather, as we have seen, it 'work[s] . . . towards a solution to the problem of existence' (WR II: 406), towards solving the 'ever-disquieting riddle' (WR II: 171), towards dealing with the existential concerns we all have as embodied, willing, suffering human beings. Given this, and given that he is a pessimist, it is not altogether surprising that Schopenhauer identifies tragedy as the highest of the literary arts (WR I: 252).

Like Aristotle before and Nietzsche after him, what interests Schopenhauer is the nature of the 'tragic effect'. Why do we willingly submit ourselves to depictions of 'the wailing and lamentation of mankind, the dominion of chance and error, the fall of the righteous, the triumph of the wicked (WR II: 433)? Presumably we must derive some kind of satisfaction from it. But what kind?

Schopenhauer answers that tragedy is the 'highest degree' (WR II: 433) of the feeling of the sublime. It exposes us to the 'bitterness and worthlessness of life' (WR II: 435), he says, in such a way as to makes us feel

urged to turn our will away from life, to give up willing and loving life. But precisely in this way we become aware that there is still left in us something different that we cannot possibly know positively, but only negatively as that which does *not* will life.[9] Just as the chord of the seventh demands the fundamental chord; just as a red colour

demands green, and even produces it in the eye; so every tragedy
demands an existence of an entirely different kind, a different world,
the knowledge of which can always be given to us only indirectly, as
here by such a demand. At the moment of the tragic catastrophe we
become convinced more clearly than ever that life is a bad dream
from which we have to awake

(WR II: 433).

Simultaneously, then, tragedy produces a feeling of 'resignation'
(WR II: 434) towards (or from) this life and an intimation of 'an
existence of a different kind, although wholly inconceivable to us'
(WR II: 435), an intimation, in other words, of a kind of
immortality, an aliveness to, in Kant's language, the 'supersensible'
side of our being (see p. 120 above). It produces the sense, to borrow an image from Rilke, of 'death and the realm of the dead' as
but the 'side' of life that, like the dark side of the moon, is averted
from us.

Schopenhauer suggests that resignation does not belong to the
content of Greek tragedy[10]. Its heroes display Stoic/heroism rather
than resignation in the face of their terrible fate. Nonetheless it
produces the 'spirit' of resignation in the spectator as an 'obscure
feeling' (WR II: 435). In tragedies written within the spirit of
Christianity, however, serene, even cheerful resignation is not
merely the effect of the tragedy but is depicted in it. The hero (or
just as frequently heroine), with a gaze fixed on some higher reality, seems hardly even to notice the terrors afflicting his this-
worldly life, 'stands before us with perfect virtue, holiness and
sublimity, yet in a state of supreme suffering' (WR I: 91). This
combination of the feeling of the sublime with a partial articulation
of its content produces an intensification of the effect, which is
why Schopenhauer says that tragedy is the highest form of the
feeling of the sublime. It is also the reason he says (in a bold
departure from the Graecophilia that has dominated German
thought since the eighteenth century) that, on the whole, modern

tragedies are superior to Greek, that Shakespeare is 'much greater' than Sophocles (WR II: 434).

Schopenhauer cites Bellini's opera *Norma* to illustrate what he has in mind (WR II: 436). I would add Puccini's *Madam Butterfly*. Superficially Butterfly, the Japanese innocent, is a fool; everyone can see that Pinkerton, the American sailor, is a bounder who will use and abandon her. But Butterfly is unmoved; in the right production, not because she is a fool but because, in the profundity of her love, she *already exists* in a realm that is above such petty calculations of the egoistic will. She is, that is to say, what Schopenhauer calls a 'sublime character' (WR I: 206).

* * *

As will appear in the discussion of Book IV, 'resignation' in favour of a different kind of existence 'beyond' the will is Schopenhauer's own solution to the 'riddle' of existence. Tragedy is therefore of the utmost value from his point of view as pointing us, at the level of feeling, towards the solution to the problem of life that his philosophy will seek to validate, towards, as he calls it, 'salvation'.

Does this then mean that no other art is of any value at all, that art that is untouched by the tragic sense of life is existentially worthless? Not so. For Schopenhauer says, remember, that if we properly appreciate *any* great artwork then we enter the aesthetic state in which we 'celebrate the Sabbath from the penal servitude of willing', experience the bliss of will-lessness. Towards the end of Book IV he reminds us of this and draws a connection between the aesthetic state and 'denial of the will' which we will see to constitute his final solution to the 'riddle' of life, his account of 'salvation'. From the aesthetic state, he says, 'we can infer how blessed must be the life of a man whose will is silenced not for a few moments, as in the enjoyment of the beautiful, but for ever, indeed completely extinguished, except for the last glimmering spark that maintains the body and is extinguished with it' (WR I: 390).

All art, then, not just tragedy, is, in its subjective aspect, valuable as a pointer to the final solution to the problem of life. The aesthetic is an intimation of the ascetic. As Nietzsche correctly puts it, all art, in Schopenhauer's representation, produces a 'thirst' for life-denial, a 'lure to eternal redemption' (*Twilight of the Idols*, 'Skirmishes of an Untimely Man', section 22).

But what does tragedy then do that the other poetic arts do not? Why is it the highest of the arts? Because, I think (though Schopenhauer is somewhat indistinct on this point), it offers us, at the level of feeling, the promise of a genuine 'salvation'. Without tragedy, without the experience of the sublime in general, will- and life-denial, 'resignation', would appear as an end in itself. The message of aesthetic experience would be to reject life, but there would be no question of rejecting it *in favour of anything else*. As an alternative to the life that is 'denied' there would be only the nothing – the *absolute* nothing. Yet, as we will see in chapter 8, Schopenhauer's philosophy affirms, at the end, not an absolute but only a 'relative' nothing – a something which is a 'nothing' in the sense of being 'nothing intelligible to us'. Without tragedy the message of art would be nihilism – there is nothing beyond life, but life is so appalling that this nothing is to be preferred. Tragedy, however, by pointing to a genuine 'beyond', overcomes nihilism. It is, I think, this pointing to something which genuinely deserves to be called 'salvation' that, for Schopenhauer, gives tragedy its unique value.

A CRITICISM OF SCHOPENHAUER'S PHILOSOPHY OF ART

Schopenhauer's philosophy of art is full of wonderful illuminations. Nonetheless it seems to me to be open to the following major criticism.

Let us return, for a moment, to his general theory of the aesthetic state. The transformation of the subject occurs, he says, when 'we devote the whole power of the mind to perception', when 'we lose ourselves in the object'. It occurs when the mind becomes the object's 'clear mirror, so that it is as though the object existed without anyone to perceive it', since 'the entire consciousness is filled and occupied by a single image of perception'. In this condition, since we have forgotten our will, the 'subjectivity', the will-mouldedness, of ordinary practical consciousness disappears. Perception becomes purely 'objective'. The 'why and whither' of things disappears, we apprehend 'simply and solely the what' (WR I: 178–9).

Suppose that Schopenhauer's account of aesthetic experience stopped at this point. And suppose we asked: in what, exactly, does the 'objectivity', the 'whatness'-disclosing character of aesthetic experience consist? The answer would be, in Schopenhauer's own words, that it consists in one's becoming a 'clear mirror': in other words, in one's entering a state of what we may call *pure phenomenological receptivity*. It consists specifically, one would say, in (a) the disappearance (or at least recession) of what ordinary consciousness adds to things – their equipmental 'being for us' – and (b) the restoration of all those qualities intrinsic to the object which get deleted in practical consciousness. In aesthetic experience, therefore, one would say, the object (a) appears in the fullness of its individual and unique 'in-itselfness'[11] and (b) in nothing but its 'in-itselfness'.

Yet as we have seen, this is, in fact, not what Schopenhauer means when he talks about confronting the pure 'whatness' of things. What he means is confronting the thing as Platonic Idea.

This transformation of the object of aesthetic consciousness from the individual grasped as individual to the individual grasped as Idea is, says Schopenhauer, 'simultaneously and inseparably' (WR I: 197) tied to the transformation of the subject. The two transformations happen 'at one stroke' (WR I: 179).

Now that we have understood what it is to perceive an object as Idea we can see how different this notion of 'objectivity' is from pure phenomenological receptivity. For, in its own way, *Schopenhauerian 'objectivity' itself involves forms of addition and subtraction* to and from the in-itselfness of the object. Additions are involved because, Schopenhauer holds, natural objects being always imperfect representatives of their Ideas, the artist is required to make imaginative additions to the object in order to articulate the universal truth it only 'stammers' (WR I: 222). And subtractions are involved because details that are distracting, confusing and irrelevant, details which hinder the disclosure of the universal, are allowed to 'withdraw into obscurity' (WR I: 194). It is this twofold (as Nietzsche calls it) 'idealising' of the object which, remember, made art in general more (objectively) beautiful than nature (see p. 135 above).

It seems to me that Schopenhauer is certainly mistaken in claiming that the transformation of the object into Idea is 'inseparable' from the transformation of the subject. The latter naturally leads to the pure phenomenological receptivity which Schopenhauer describes with, in fact, great insight and accuracy *and it may just stop there*. One can think, perhaps, of Japanese art. Here there is no 'idealising', no, as one might say, tarting up of the object. The tear in the leaf which makes it *that unique individual* may be precisely what it is focused upon.

So in so far as Schopenhauer wants to insist on the transformation of the object as an essential constituent of the aesthetic state, this is an *additional requirement* he places on a state of consciousness that he is willing to call genuinely 'aesthetic'.

* * *

Schopenhauer seems to be led to the inseparability thesis by the following line of reasoning. Spatio-temporal identification is egocentric. But the aesthetic subject has lost its identification with the embodied ego, and cannot, therefore, identify things as located in space or time. So the objects of his gaze are non-spatio-temporal and so non-individual entities, and so they must be the Ideas.

But this is badly flawed. The mistake lies in supposing that egocentric, or as we might say, pragmatic space is the only space. Things can be in space – for example, the tree in the landscape painting – without being in egocentric space, and things can be in time – the events in a play – without being in egocentric time.

Still, the requirement that the objective transformation accompany the subjective might still be a genuine requirement of the state that is productive and receptive of *great* art. Should we agree with Schopenhauer on this point? I think not. On the contrary, the requirement is, I believe, a serious mistake.

Let us recall Schopenhauer's *motivation* for the insistence – his desire to correct Plato's 'greatest error'. Effectively Plato argues that (a) only universal knowledge is worth having (b) there is no universal knowledge in art so (c) art is not worth having. Schopenhauer's defence of art consists in agreeing with (a) but rejecting (b).

Rejecting (b) is absolutely the right thing to do. Art does disclose universal truth – Schopenhauer is surely right about this. But because he accepts (a) he is forced to devalue all those aspects of art that have to do with the particular rather than universal. At best the particular is the mere medium for the communication of a universal message. As itself, it is never of value. Here, I think, we reach the heart of Schopenhauer's mistake.

Sometimes he sees, or nearly sees, that pure phenomenological receptivity can't be excluded from the attributes of artistic 'genius'. The already quoted 'clear mirror' passage is the most striking. But striking too is the contrast between the ordinary man's failure to 'linger' on things – his quickly reaching for instrumental concepts under which to pigeonhole them 'as a lazy man reaches for a chair' – with the 'dwelling' on things on the part of the genius (WR I: 188). In another striking passage Schopenhauer speaks of the genius's tremendous power of focused concentration so that 'the rest of the world vanishes for him' and the object 'fills all reality' (WR II: 389).[12]

These passages correctly emphasise the artist's tremendous powers of *focused attention*. What I want to argue against Schopenhauer's Platonist conception is, firstly, that in some indisputably genuine art it is attention focused precisely on the unique in-itselfness of things – not, or not exclusively, on their universal significance – that occurs, and, secondly, that, in its own way, such attention is as valuable as is attention to the universal.

Concerning the first point, I might mention again the Japanese flower painting where attention may be focused on the tear in the leaf precisely to highlight the uniqueness of what is actually present. (Since, for Zen, everything is a manifestation of Buddha's nature, focusing on the uniqueness of the individual has the character of an act of worship.[13]) Or, closer to home, I might mention Constable's Suffolk landscapes which, whatever else may be involved, can be nowhere but in Suffolk, or Cézanne's Mont Sainte-Victoire (see illustration on p. 205 below), which can be nowhere but in Provence.

Concerning the second point, it seems to me that in life, attention to the uniqueness of things, to precisely their *difference* from other things, is essential to avoiding what one might call 'the globalizing gaze' – the gaze that levels things down to the same. One cannot treat things as intrinsically valuable, as ends in themselves, unless one knows *what* they are in themselves. And if one is oblivious to that then, even with good intentions, one's kindness towards things will be the kindness that kills. (If one puts every old person into equiformed 'sheltered' accommodation most will be condemned to end their days in misery.) 'Pay attention', pay attention to the unique individuality of things, is an important moral imperative. From which follows the importance of training in the state of paying attention, in pure phenomenological receptivity, and of art which helps us to see the beauty of small and local things.

Strangely enough Schopenhauer sees precisely this point in his criticism, in Book I, of the 'moral pedant' (see pp. 42–3 above) who, because of his enslavement to universal rules, is blind to 'reality's fine shades of difference and innumerable modifications'. His preference for thinking over looking, his blindness to what is given to him by 'perceptual' consciousness, leads him, says Schopenhauer, into moral 'incompetence' (WR I: 60). His insistence on making art conform to Plato's criterion of respectability, however, prevents him carrying this insight over into Book III's discussion of art.

* * *

By no means do I wish to minimise the importance of Schopenhauer's emphasis on the universal in art. Certainly art which primarily reveals the 'universal in the particular' (Turner rather than Constable, for instance) is *one* type of great art. What needs to be removed, however, is the *tyranny* of this quasi-Platonic paradigm. We need to allow at least one other type of greatness – the greatness of 'small' art, of art that is concerned with the particularity of things.

And, importantly, we need to allow that the two can coexist, with different degrees of emphasis, in the wonderful complexity of the same work – the Rembrandt self-portrait, for example – and to allow *both* the universality of the work *and* its particularity to be of value.

MUSIC

Schopenhauer played the flute. He loved music and knew a great deal about it. He regularly attended the Frankfurt opera. His impact on composers has been greater than that of any other philosopher. Richard Wagner thought he had succeeded in defining 'the true nature of music' and, as we will see in chapter 9, profoundly altered the character of his *Ring* cycle after discovering Schopenhauer. Gustav Mahler thought he had written 'one of the profoundest' works ever written on music, and gave the famous conductor Bruno Walter a copy of *The World as Will* as a Christmas present. Prokofiev found some 'brilliant ideas' in *The World as Will*, while, for Schönberg, Schopenhauer 'says something really exhaustive about the essence of music in his wonderful thought'. Other composers who knew and esteemed Schopenhauer's philosophy include Brahms, Liszt, and Rimsky-Korsakov.[14] What, then, is this philosophy of music that has had such a deep impact?

As already noted, Schopenhauer regards music as lying beyond the scope of his general theory of art and as needing, therefore, a separate philosophical interpretation. For whereas the other arts represent the everyday world (as 'Idea'), music does not. There is, of course, the phenomenon of 'programme music', the imitative representation of birdsong and battle scenes (cannons in the 1812 Overture), but all this is to be 'entirely rejected' as incompatible with the true nature of music (WR I: 263–4).

So is music non-representational? Is this what makes it unique? This certainly was the opinion of Leibniz who, Schopenhauer reports, described music as 'An unconscious exercise in arithmetic in which the mind does not know it is counting' (WR I: 256); as, in other words, a system of sounds which, while no doubt pleasant, are without meaning, without reference to anything beyond themselves.

But this, says Schopenhauer, has to be wrong. Music is universally recognised as a 'language', as *saying* something, something, more-over, of the utmost profundity. It follows that it *must* be represen-tational, must be related to reality as a 'copy (*Abbild*)'. But since it is not a copy of the world of objects, the world as empirical represen-tation, there is, within the dualism of representation and will, only one thing left for it to be a representation of: the will. What music is about, then, is the will, the thing in itself (WR I: 257). (*Which* thing in itself, the Schopenhauerian or the Kantian thing in itself, will be a crucial question.)

Of course, the other arts represent the will, too. As bodily and facial gestures express a person's inner will, so the plastic and liter-ary arts, by representing, as it were, the physiognomy of nature, represent nature's inner will. But only music has *direct* access to the will, provides us with an '*immediate*. . . copy' of it (WR I: 257; emphasis added). It follows that music is the profoundest, the highest of all the arts. While the direct object of the other arts is the 'shadow', music takes us directly to the 'essence' of things (ibid.).

* * *

Music, then, copies the will. But so does the world of nature, the world whose fundamental pattern is represented by the Ideas. Hence there must be a 'parallelism' between music and nature, one which is revealed in the structure of musical harmony. The bass corresponds to the mineral, the tenor to the vegetable (can many tenors have taken kindly to this idea?), the alto to the animal and the soprano to the human (WR II: 447–8). So here is a partial confirmation of Schopenhauer's theory.

This is an idea of such unparalleled silliness that I shall discuss it no further. (Who says that either nature or harmony *has* to divide into exactly four levels? What would Schopenhauer say about the utterly different harmonic structure of Indian or Balinese music?) What is much more interesting is Schopenhauer's discussion of melody, his treatment of it as 'the secret history of the . . . will'. (WR I: 259).[15] For example, 'rapid melodies without great deviation' report the will in 'cheerful' mood (WR I: 260) – Beethoven's 'Ode to Joy' might be at the back of Schopenhauer's mind here.[16] 'Slow melodies that strike painful discords and wind back to the keynote only through many bars are sad.' Adagios in a minor key express the 'keenest pain'. Rapid dance music composed of short phrases 'speaks only of ordinary happiness which is easy of attainment. Dance music in the minor key seems to express the failure of . . . trifling happiness' (Ravel's *La Valse*, perhaps) and so on. (WR I: 260–1). In general, melody tells of the will in all its many modes of striving, satisfaction, boredom and dissatisfaction.

* * *

Music is, then, the language of the will. It represents the emotions. Not, however, 'particular and definite' emotions but rather their 'inner nature' divorced from all 'accessories and so also without any motives for them' (WR I: 261).

What is the 'inner nature' of an emotion? An emotion, Schopenhauer is suggesting, has two components: an object and an inner 'feeling' (WR II: 448) which possesses dimensions of intensity, duration, waxing/waning and others difficult or impossible to express in language[17], and which is closely connected to bodily sensations. The object determines what in the world the emotion is directed towards – what, for instance, one is angry *at*, what one is afraid *of*, what one hopes *for*. The feeling is what causes it to be that particular kind of emotion. A person who was hit and returned the blow, they claimed, in anger, yet clearly reported only feelings of warm, calm relaxation would be incomprehensible. So it is this object-less inner feeling which music represents.

That this is the nature of musical representation explains why, (to borrow Nietzsche's phrase) music 'gives birth'[18] to words. Since music, says Schopenhauer, gives the 'universal' aspect of an emotional sequence or narrative – that which is common to all instances of, for example, love, followed by loss, followed by grief, followed by acceptance of loss – we have a natural tendency to supply the music with a text which stands to the universal an 'example' (WR I: 263, WR II: 449). Hence, for example, we (not Beethoven) speak of the 'Moonlight' sonata and 'Pastoral' symphony. (The text of course may be visual rather than verbal as in Walt Disney's classic *Fantasia*.)

THE PROBLEM OF OPERA

Music, then, provides the secret history of the will; that is, the thing in itself. But, to repeat, *which* thing in itself? The Kantian thing in itself on the *other* side, or the Schopenhauerian thing in itself on *this* side of the appearance–reality distinction? If it is the former then we can say, as Schopenhauer often does, that music, while giving insight into the psychological, is also (inarticulate) metaphysics, that it expresses the nature of ultimate reality. The basis of this claim will be the view that ultimate reality *is*, in a broad sense psychological in nature, something of which the character is revealed in 'inner' experience. Parodying the remark of Leibniz quoted earlier, Schopenhauer says that 'Music is an unconscious exercise in metaphysics in which the mind does not know it is philosophizing' (WR I: 264). On the other hand if it is only the 'thing in itself in relation to appearances' (see pp. 96–8 above) then while music gives deep insight into *psychological* reality, it does not refer to the metaphysical (in the sense of the supra-natural.) The ambivalence between the two senses of 'thing in itself', between the inner–outer and the surface–depth metaphors, which, as we have seen, affects all of Schopenhauer's philosophy, affects his theory of music too.

The ambivalence comes to a head in Schopenhauer's discussion of the proper relation between music and words, a discussion which concerns, above all, the question of the status and value of opera.

If we interpret Schopenhauer as saying that music represents the *Kantian* thing in itself then it seems that, strictly speaking, opera is a degenerate form of music. For if music gives us direct access to the thing in itself, and if, as we have seen Schopenhauer to hold, the highest form of art is that with the highest cognitive value, then it would seem that the highest form of music is purely instrumental music – 'absolute' music, as Wagner called it. For if music gives us immediate knowledge of ultimate reality then the addition of words and action would seem at best an irrelevance, and at worst a serious distraction. In Platonic terms, if music takes us directly to the sunlit world of reality, what possible interest could one have in trying to decipher the nature of that world by looking at the flickering shadows in the cave?

Sometimes Schopenhauer treats his theory of music in this way, with the result that he appears to be extremely hostile to opera. It is, he says, 'strictly speaking, . . . an unmusical invention for the benefit of unmusical minds', something to seduce those who would otherwise never listen to music (the blue-rinse brigade) into doing so. A truly musical mind wishes only the 'pure language of tones'. Hence the mass is superior to opera since, through constant repetition, the words have been deprived of meaning, have become a mere 'solfeggio', mere sounds. (PP II: 432–6). Rossini's operatic music is great music, but only because 'it requires no words at all, and therefore produces its full effect even when rendered by instruments alone' (WR I: 262). (Or when sung in a language one does not understand: the battle over surtitles when they were first introduced into opera houses in the 1970s was in fact the battle we are discussing now.)

To be set against these remarks, however, is the fact that Schopenhauer loved opera. Bellini's *Norma* he describes as 'quite apart from its excellent music . . . and considered according to its motives and interior economy . . . a tragedy of extreme perfection' (WR II: 436). And Mozart's *Don Giovanni* he describes as one of the summits of art, a 'perfect masterpiece' by one of 'the very greatest of masters' (WR II: 410). In line with this love, Schopenhauer can be discovered making perfectly opera-friendly remarks. Provided the words are appropriate to the music and do not force it into unmusical contortions for the sake of the action, opera, he says, is a great art form. What makes it great is that the music gives 'secret information on the feelings expressed in the words' (WR II: 448) (Wagner's *Leitmotive* are the ultimate exploitation of this capacity). In other words, opera is just fine if it is properly done since music and words combine to give a stereoscopic view of the world, to give both its inner and outer reality.[19]

Notice, however, that this view requires that the thing in itself represented by music be a psychological *rather than* a metaphysical reality. If words (as words, rather than meaningless sounds) are going to have a legitimate role to play in musical artworks then, from the point of view of Schopenhauer's cognitivist approach to art, we must get rid of the reality–shadow account of the relation between the inner and the outer and establish a relative equality between them. This is actually the best way to read Schopenhauer's philosophy of music since, as we already know, his mature view is that the will is *not*, in fact, the Kantian thing in itself. Read in this way, what Schopenhauer provides is a compelling account of what makes opera good rather than an account of why it can never be any good at all. Since that latter position, the blanket condemnation of opera as such, is absurd, this provides us with one important reason (we will discover others) for preferring Schopenhauer's mature to his youthful account of the status of the will.

SUMMARY
The object of art in greater detail
The object of aesthetic apprehension is the individual perceived as 'Platonic Idea'. The point of introducing Plato's terminology is not to add a new layer to Schopenhauer's account of what there is, but rather to emphasise, contra Plato, that art, as well as philosophy, can provide valuable, that is universal, knowledge of existence. *Beauty* in art is bringing forth what is universal in the particular. But it only does so implicitly whereas philosophy does it explicitly. (This, it is suggested, is too absolute a distinction between art and philosophy.) *Tragedy* – the highest instance of the 'feeling of the sublime' – is the highest form of non-musical art since it gives us intuitive insight into a realm 'beyond the will', and hence into the possibility of genuine 'salvation'.

Criticism of the account of the object of art
The transformation of the object into 'Platonic Idea' is *not* 'simultaneously and inseparably' tied to the transformation of the everyday subject into the aesthetic subject. Moreover, valuable art *can* be art which attends to the particularity of the particular. Or it can be art which attends to *both* the universal and the particular in things.

Music
Since music does not represent the world of objects it cannot be accounted for in terms of the theory thus far discussed and requires its own special theory. According to this, music represents not objects but 'the will'; it represents the inner feeling of emotions divorced from their outer object. *The problem of opera.* Schopenhauer

says that, in representing the will, music represents the 'thing in itself'. The question is: which thing in itself – Kant's or Schopenhauer's? If it represents the former, opera, the addition of words to music, turns out to be a degenerate art form – which is what Schopenhauer sometimes says. If, however, it represents the latter then opera, as Schopenhauer also sometimes says, is a fine art form; the words describe the outer side of things the music the inner, so they combine – as in Wagner – to give a stereoscopic view of reality. Schopenhauer's ambivalence about the thing in itself is reflected in his ambivalence concerning opera.

FURTHER READING

P. Gardiner, *Schopenhauer*, chapter 5.

D. Jacquette (ed.), *Schopenhauer, Philosophy, and the Arts*.

C. Janaway, *Schopenhauer*, chapter 6.

I. Soll, 'Schopenhauer, Nietzsche, and the Redemption of Life through Art' in *Willing and Nothingness*, pp. 79–115.

Seven

Ethics

CAN PHILOSOPHY CHANGE YOUR LIFE?

The fourth and final book of the *World as Will*, at which we have now arrived, is concerned with what Schopenhauer calls 'the road to salvation' (WR II: 634). It describes a kind of pilgrim's progress from egoism, via altruism ('virtue') to mystical asceticism ('denial of the will'). So, as Schopenhauer notes, it would seem to be the most 'serious' (WR I: 271) part of the work, the place where it will culminate in the deduction, from all that has gone before, of how we ought to live our lives. In traditional philosophical jargon, it seems to be the place where Schopenhauer's philosophy is going to become explicitly 'practical', action-guiding.

It comes as a considerable shock, therefore, when, right at the beginning of the book, Schopenhauer says that philosophy can *never* be practical:

> In my opinion . . . all philosophy is always theoretical, since it is essential to it always to maintain a purely contemplative attitude, whatever the immediate object of investigation; to inquire, not to prescribe. But to become practical, to guide conduct, to transform character are old claims which with mature insight it [philosophy] ought finally to abandon. For here, where it is a question of worth or worthlessness of existence, of salvation or damnation, not the dead concepts of philosophy decide the matter, but the innermost nature of man himself, the daemon which guides him and has not chosen

him but has been chosen by him, as Plato would say; his intelligible
character as Kant puts it

(WR I: 271).

This dispiriting claim that philosophy can never 'guide conduct'
raises the question of why one should take the trouble to read Book
IV at all — or indeed any of Schopenhauer's philosophy. If it can't
make any difference to one's life why should one bother with it?
The only possible answer is curiosity, 'idle' curiosity as one might,
tendentiously, be inclined to put it. This, coupled with Schopenhauer's bleak description of the human condition and the fact that
he spent much of his time in the Frankfurt years in the bourgeois
comfort of a smart hotel, is what gives rise to Georg Lukács's disap-
proving description of Schopenhauer's philosophical construction
as

> like a modern luxury hotel on the brink of the abyss of nothingness
> and futility [with] . . . the daily sight of the abyss, between leisurely
> enjoyment of meals and works of art . . . only enhanc[ing] one's
> pleasure in this elegant comfort'.[1]

Given Schopenhauer's account of the human condition as one of
misery and death, the idea of studying our fate out of mere curiosity — studying us as one might study the death throws of an
unattractive species of beetle — seems to convict Schopenhauer of
the very heartlessness his mother was said to possess and of which
he accuses the 'optimists' such as Leibniz and Hegel (PP II: 304–5).

So we need to look rather carefully at what it is that leads Schopenhauer into this self-undermining position, at whether he really
gives himself a fair press. We need to look at whether Book IV is
really devoid of a capacity to make a difference to our lives.

* * *

Schopenhauer obviously allows that philosophy can, *in a sense*, be
'practical', 'guide conduct'. Action, we have seen, is a function of

character, what we fundamentally will, and 'motives', information
(see pp. 61–8 above). So, clearly, a change in 'motives' will produce
a change in action, and there is no reason why philosophy – some
philosophy at least – should not produce a change in the information we have about the world that is relevant to how we act. Schopenhauer says, for example, quite explicitly, that the attainment of a
general view of human nature, of, for instance, the egoism and
inflexibility of most human beings, will enable us to navigate our
way around the world with less stress and disappointment than
would otherwise be the case (WR I: 304).

What he means, then, is not that reading philosophy can't
change conduct but that it can't change *character*. And since he holds
(in the above quotation) that (a) the 'worth or worthlessness of
existence', i.e. one's moral status, and (b) 'salvation or damnation',
i.e. whether or not one will achieve 'salvation', depend on character, he concludes that reading philosophy can have no effect with
respect to these fundamental issues. His claim, in a nutshell, is,
then, that philosophy can only have a *superficial* effect on our lives.
Fundamental change is what it cannot achieve. Why not?

He seems to present two reasons. First, that nothing at all can
change character. This is the thesis we have already met in Book II –
that character is innate and immutable (see p. 66 above). Second,
that even if something could, *per impossible*, change character it could
never be the 'dead' words of philosophy. I shall begin by discussing
the first.

FREEDOM AND CHARACTER

Why does Schopenhauer think that nothing can ever change the
character of a human being? The thesis of the innateness and
immutability of character is, of course, essential to the project of
Book II, the project of completing the scientific image. For if our
knowledge of what it is, fundamentally, that makes human beings
'tick' is to provide the basis for deciphering the character of natural
forces, if my character is to be fundamentally homogeneous with

that of the rock, then the former must be as immutable as the latter. Since rocks cannot change their character Book II's systematic concerns demand that human beings cannot either.

What character needs to be like for the project of Book II to work, however, is one thing, whether character is really immutable another. So we need to ask: why does Schopenhauer think it is actually *true* that human character can never change? The answer, in a nutshell, is that he believes that Kant, at least in outline, has solved the ancient and tormenting problem of free will versus determinism.

* * *

Kant's fundamental project was to reconcile religion and morality with the new and dramatically successful science of Newtonian physics. The heart of the problem is freedom. For whereas Newtonian physics holds that *everything* is rigidly determined by causal laws, religion and morality demand that human action be free. If my actions are the inescapable consequence of events which happened aeons before my birth, then I cannot, surely, be held responsible for them, and a God who punished or rewarded me for those actions could not be a just God.

The solution Kant provides in the 'Third Antinomy' of the *Critique of Pure Reason* (A 532–38) is an application of transcendental idealism. Concerning the world of nature, he concedes, Newtonian science is absolutely correct. Everything is causally determined. With respect to every human being, in particular, there is in principle a discoverable set of laws covering all of its behaviour. Kant calls this set of laws one's 'empirical character'. Since, however, the embodied human being is, along with every natural object, a mere representation, there must be, he holds, some ground of empirical character in the real world of things in themselves. There must be some reason why just these laws and not others hold with respect to my behaviour. Kant calls this one's 'intelligible character'. And though, of course, we cannot *know* this (since, for Kant, of course, we cannot *know* anything about reality 'in itself'), it is at least *possible* that this intelligible ground of empirical character consists in a free choice made by my real, 'intelligible' self. As an article of *faith*, moreover, this possibility is one which we can hold to be the truth of the matter.

Kant never goes into the details of this picture of things, with the result that it remains obscure just how what he suggests is even possibly a resolution of the 'antinomy' between freedom and determinism. But it may be that what he has in mind is influenced by a memory of Plato. (Note that in the quotation on pp. 158–9 above Schopenhauer equates the 'daemon' which, according to Plato, one 'chooses' with Kant's notion of 'intelligible character'.)

At the end of the *Republic* Plato recounts what he calls the 'Myth of Er'. In outline, the myth suggests that at the end of each life, and before one is reincarnated, one surveys a number of options and then makes a fundamental, defining choice as to what one's next life is to be.

If one thinks about railway trains one can see how this might be turned into a resolution of the freedom/determinism problem. Where the trains go, what routes and how long they take, is entirely beyond my control. But which train I catch is entirely up to me. Similarly, Kant's idea may be that 'intelligible character' is a fundamental, life-defining choice as to which embodied human being I am to 'travel' around in – or as. As with every other natural object, all its actions are determined by factors entirely beyond my control. But that it is *me* is my own choice and responsibility.

This, at any rate, is how I think Schopenhauer reads Kant.

* * *

Schopenhauer says that the passage we have been discussing is the 'profoundest' part of Kant's whole philosophy (WR I: 505). And it is, he claims, the point at which 'Kant's philosophy leads to mine, or mine springs from his as its parent stem' (WR I: 501). Noting the sketchy obscurity of Kant's resolution of the antinomy, he asks rhetorically: does it not 'sound like a riddle to which my teaching is the solution' (WR I: 502)?

As we already know, human character is, for Schopenhauer, that which mediates between input and output, 'motive' and action. It can, he says, be thought of as 'a single maxim characterising what I will as a whole' (see pp. 66–7 above), can be thought of, in Sartre's language, as my 'fundamental project'.

When it comes specifically to addressing the freedom/determinism issue, however, it turns out that this is more than a mere mode of representation. The 'intelligible' ground of my empirical character, Schopenhauer holds, is a single act of fundamental choice. So although the natural world is exceptionlessly governed by causal laws, it is my choice which attaches me to a particular empirical character, makes it my character. Given, however, that causality only applies to empirical reality it follows that my life-defining, intelligible choice is uncaused, and in that sense free.

Schopenhauer sums all this up in the following passage:

> freedom is . . . transcendental, i.e. it does not occur in appearance. It is present only insofar as we abstract from the appearance and from all its forms in order to reach that which, since it is outside of all time, must be thought of as the inner being of man in himself. By virtue of this freedom all acts of man are of his own making, no matter how necessarily they proceed from the empirical character when it encounters the motives. This is so because the empirical character is only the appearance of the intelligible character in our cognitive faculty as bound to time, space and causality – i.e. the manner in which the essence in itself of our own self presents itself to this faculty. Accordingly, the will is of course free, but only in itself and outside of appearance. In appearance, on the contrary, it presents itself already with a definite character, with which all of its actions are in conformity and therefore, when further determined by the supervening motives, must turn out so and not otherwise
>
> (FW: 97: see, too, WR I: 113, 155–6; WR II: 319–321).

Schopenhauer represents his resolution of the freedom/ determinism problem as a mere clarification of Kant's. In fact, however, there is an important difference. For whereas Kant represents free, 'intelligible' choice as a merely *possible* solution, Schopenhauer – much of the time at least – represents it as the truth of the matter. The truth of universal causation is an inescapable datum. But so too is 'the wholly clear and certain feeling of *responsibility* for what we do'. Since the 'Kantian' accommodation of both these facts is the only possible accommodation, we have no option but to accept it as the truth of the matter (FW: 94; see, too, WR II: 184).

* * *

And hence, to return to the matter at hand, we have to accept that character cannot be changed by anything that happens in the empirical world such as, for instance, the reading of a philosophy book. But should we really accept this conclusion? For at least three reasons I think that the answer is that we should not.

The first is that the supposed only possible solution to the problem of freedom and determinism is, it seems to me, basically incomprehensible and so not really a solution at all. Since according to any normal conception, a free choice or act of will is an *event*, and since events require *time*, the idea of 'intelligible' choice, an act of choice as occurring in the atemporal domain of the Kantian thing in itself, cannot really be made comprehensible.

The second reason is that though the affirmation of universal causality may have seemed inescapable in the regimented days of Newtonian science, in our present, more relaxed age of quantum indeterminacy it is not so obvious that we cannot escape the dilemma simply by denying universal causation.

The third reason is that since we have seen the mature Schopenhauer finally accept Kant's thesis of the unknowability of the (Kantian) thing in itself, even if the idea made sense, we could not know, from his mature point of view, that reality in itself contains such items as free acts of will.

IS PHILOSOPHY 'DEAD'?

As noted earlier, however, Schopenhauer has a second reason for making the claim that philosophy cannot make a fundamental difference to one's life. Even if, *per impossibile, something* could change character, it would not be the 'dead' concepts of philosophy (WR I: 271). Why not?

One argument is this:

> virtue is as little taught as is genius; indeed, the concept is just as unfruitful for it as it is for art . . . We should therefore be just as foolish to expect that our moral systems and ethics would create virtuous, noble and holy men, as that our aesthetics would produce poets, painters, and musicians
>
> (WR I: 271).

And, of course, there is an obvious truth here: reading Kant's *Foundations of the Metaphysics of Morals* or Mill's *Utilitarianism* will not turn one into a virtuous person (though it might help if one already has a disposition that way) any more than reading *Teach Yourself Composing* is going to turn you into a great composer (though, again, it might help develop a pre-existing talent). The average level of virtue among professors of moral philosophy is, in my observation, not noticeably higher than among any other professional group.

The fact is, however, that philosophy isn't just 'moral systems', normative ethics. It is also, in particular, metaphysics. What gives point to this observation is that Schopenhauer himself says that 'to be just, noble, and benevolent is nothing but to translate my metaphysics into action' (WR II: 600). (As we will see, the metaphysical vision outlined in Book IV discloses the distinction between self and others as illusory, which turns out to be precisely the insight in which virtue – that is to say, altruism – is grounded.) So if virtue is grounded in Schopenhauerian metaphysics, the question becomes acute: why can't one gain the requisite insight and become virtuous by reading Schopenhauer's philosophy?

With an eye, one suspects, on the gap between his own comfort-able existence and that of the saintly ascetic, Schopenhauer says that it is 'just as little necessary for a saint to be a philosopher as for a philosopher to be a saint' (WR I: 383). Though the saint 'knows' the truth of otherness-overcoming metaphysics, it turns out, she knows it inarticulately, 'intuitively' (WR II: 600). The philosopher, on the other hand, knows things only articulately, has 'conceptual', 'theoretical' knowledge. The saint, as we could put it, knows 'in the heart'; the philosopher only 'in the head'.

But why can't 'head' knowledge *become* 'heart' knowledge? Why can't at least *a* route to acquiring the kind of knowledge the saint has be through the head?

Because, says Schopenhauer, knowledge acquired through read-ing philosophy books cannot *motivate*. Its concepts are 'dead'. But why so? Why *must* the language of philosophy be like this?

Schopenhauer writes, to repeat:

> In my opinion . . . all philosophy is always theoretical, since it is essential always to maintain a purely contemplative attitude, whatever the immediate object of explanation; to inquire not to prescribe
>
> (WR I: 271).

As it stands, this passage seems to me self-contradictory. For pre-cisely what it is doing is *prescribing*, prescribing how philosophy should be done.

What underlies the prescription, I think, is the 'rationalistic' or, as I called it, 'Analytic' conception of philosophy as a science which we saw also to underlie Schopenhauer's absolute distinction between philosophy and art (pp. 136–42 above). What underlies the prescription, that is, is the ideal of philosophy as a science together with the familiar notion that science must be entirely 'value-free', must be free of all rhetorical, poetic and emotive language. As long, at least, as he is thinking explicitly about the nature and method of philosophy, Schopenhauer thinks that the conceptual language of philosophy must be 'dead' (WR I: 271), 'cold[ly] dispassionate' (WR II: 409), because otherwise it *doesn't count as philosophy*.

In fact, however, as I have already indicated, I see no reason to believe this. There is no reason to believe philosophy must be 'value-free' science save for an historical prejudice grounded in nothing more than academic compartmentalisation. There is no reason to believe that the two activities are exclusive, that philosophy can't be theoretical *and* motivating, can't address head *and* heart, at one and the same time. The first philosophers, the Pre-Socratics, as I observed, are as easily classifiable as poets as philosophers. And in modern times, a salient case is Martin Heidegger, who expounds his account of modernity's 'forgetfulness of Being' in prose which is simultaneously the vehicle of a 'rational' demonstration that the consciousness of modernity is engulfed by a deep metaphysical error, and a poetic recollection which allows us again to experience the magic and mystery of that which has been forgotten as a result of this error. In fact, though, it seems to me that not only *can* philosophy be analytic and motivating at the same time, 'thinking' and 'poeticising', but that it *always is*, at least surreptitiously – even the most seemingly 'dry' works of 'Analytic' philosophy.

Thus, for example, W. V. Quine, who takes as the motto of his famous book *Word and Object* Otto Neurath's saying that human beings are like sailors who must repair their boat while at sea, and so can do so only plank by plank, uses his considerable rhetorical skills to create a certain feeling of community, the feeling – Nietzsche often seeks to create the same feeling – that we are all part of the scientific, but essentially pragmatic, enterprise of voyaging and conquest.

So philosophy can prescribe as it describes, move as it observes, argues and analyses, and of course Book IV does all of these things. By describing the life of the saint it employs, in fact, a classic way of offering a certain form of life as something to be emulated. The misalignment between Schopenhauer's philosophy of philosophy and his actual philosophy emerges very clearly when we juxtapose the claim that business of philosophy is 'to inquire not to prescribe' with, for example, the statement that we only have to see, with the help of great art, 'that peace which is higher than all reason, that ocean-like calmness of the spirit, that deep tranquillity and unshakeable confidence and serenity' on the countenance of the saint in whom 'the will has turned and denied itself' to experience a 'deep and painful yearning' (WR I: 411).

DEATH AND IMMORTALITY

Since Book IV is supposed to be concerned with 'ethics', it is something of a surprise to discover that the first substantive topic to be discussed is that of death and immortality. In fact, however, there is a strategic purpose to this starting point: overcoming the fear of death is a matter of attaining part – though not all – of the metaphysical knowledge that is the basis of virtue.

* * *

The first thing Schopenhauer does with the topic of death is to use it to confirm his account of the human essence. Fear of death, he suggests, is a universal human trait. And it is man's *worst* fear, the greatest of all evils, his greatest anxiety. But this is just the 'reverse side' of the will to live. Since ordinary human beings regard life as the highest good, death has to be the worst of all evils.

Regarding death as the worst evil is obviously not, says Schopenhauer, the product of rational reflection. If it were – the argument, here, is borrowed from the Roman philosopher Lucretius – we would regard prenatal non-existence with the same horror as we regard death. And, moreover, rational consideration of the character of life (here Schopenhauer's pessimism is obviously presupposed) would convince us that death ought to be welcomed as a friend rather than feared as an enemy. What we must conclude, then, is that fear of death, i.e. the will to live, is just a 'blind instinct' – not a rational choice that is the product of a consideration of life in terms of some higher value such as happiness, but simply something programmed into us from birth (WR II: 464–8).

Nonetheless, that abhorrence of death is a universal instinct, that it belongs to our natural consciousness, does not mean that we lack the power to overcome it, to face death with composure. The 'triumph of knowledge over the blind will to live which is nevertheless the kernel of our being' (WR II: 466) through religious faith or philosophical knowledge is possible – though, Schopenhauer insightfully adds, however much we achieve equanimity in the face of death we can never completely immunise ourselves from attacks of blind panic (WR I: 283).

* * *

To provide a 'consolation' in the face of death, to find an 'antidote' to it, is the principal task of all religions, says Schopenhauer. And it is the principal task of philosophy, too, which is the reason Socrates defined philosophy as 'a preparation for death' (WR II: 463; see, too, p. 161). (Notice that since this applies, presumably, to Schopenhauer's own philosophy, he has already contradicted his official position that philosophy cannot make any fundamental difference to our lives.)

Schopenhauer observes, as we have seen (pp. 99–100 above), that God, in nineteenth-century Europe is 'dead'. A belief in the existence of God has become impossible (among the educated classes) on account of the widespread awareness of the inner absurdities and contradictions of Christian metaphysics. We are, therefore, deprived of the consolation provided by traditional Christianity. Or rather, we vacillate between two falsehoods; the belief in resurrection together 'so to speak, with skin and hair' and the belief that death is total annihilation (WR II: 464). Because of the dominance of the latter, however, the dominance, that is to say, of 'the absolutely physical viewpoint', we see the rise an attitude of 'eat and drink for after death there is no more fun', an attitude which can be described as a descent into 'bestiality'; a condition in which, quite literally, there is nothing which elevates the human being above the animal (WR II: 464).

Schopenhauer says that the only consolation that can be offered in the face of death is the assurance of some kind of immortality. The insect that prepares a nest, lays its eggs and then simply dies with the calmness of someone laying out his clothes and breakfast for the following morning, couldn't do so without the obscure certainty that the one who dies is in its inner essence identical with the one that is born (WR II: 477). Only immortality provides equanimity.

This is a striking thought: the idea of what Schopenhauer calls the 'dark . . . nothing' (WR I: 411–12), of total annihilation, of becoming absolutely nothing, is one we cannot face with equanimity. If it is right, then whatever he may say, one who believes that death is his utter extinction (Michel Foucault, for example) cannot but inhabit a mood of fundamental anxiety. Of course, as Lucretius suggests, the thought of having been nothing does not strike us with the same horror as that of becoming nothing. But perhaps the point is just that there has first to be an 'I' for anything bad to happen to it.

Even, however, from a purely materialistic point of view, Schopenhauer suggests, we do not have to regard death as annihilation. The endless cycle of death and birth (or better, rebirth) is 'nature's great doctrine of immortality' (WR II: 477). Even from this point of view, fear of death is like the foolish leaf about to fall in autumn refusing to recognise its inner being in the tree (WR II: 477–8). We live on, that is to say, in our children and in the species – in, as we might want, these days, to put it, our genes.

So the antidote to fear of death discoverable even within a completely materialistic outlook consists in the transcendence of individuality, attaining to a point of view from which the extinction of the individual is a matter of complete triviality. 'Only small and narrow minds', says Schopenhauer, are unable to grasp the triviality of death, unable to ascend, at least at times, to the eternal, supra-individual point of view.

Schopenhauer says that since we are all, in fact, 'nature', the world-will[2] (WR I: 281) – according to Book II, remember, we are all 'objectifications' of the unitary world-will – a man 'may certainly and justly console himself for his own death and for that of his friends by looking back on the immortal life of nature which he himself is' (WR I: 276). Yet in Book II, as we saw (pp. 79–82 above), nature's lack of care for the individual made it an object of horror. The world-will, remember, was condemned as fundamental and ultimate evil. It is, therefore, hard to see how, from a Schopenhauerian point of view, the thought of one's own fundamental identity with it could possibly be a source of comfort.

This shows, it seems to me, that, given Schopenhauer's pessimistically moral[3] mode of thinking, a natural supra-individual entity cannot in fact do the job of providing a 'consolation' in the face of death. Earlier I argued that radical – as Schopenhauer understands it, Kantian – idealism does not play a genuine role in Book II, that only partial idealism is genuinely active. Now, however, we see radical idealism to be really required. It is when Schopenhauer turns to the 'practical' topics of Book IV that it comes genuinely into force.[4]

* * *

The consideration of 'nature's great doctrine of immortality' raises, from a materialist and therefore provisional perspective, the possibility of self-transcendence, of identifying one's self with, or as, something other than the embodied individual which does indeed face absolute annihilation. (The possibility of, as it were, parachuting out of the plane that is about to crash.) It points to the possibility of identifying oneself with something eternal. But of course – here Schopenhauer makes the transition to his own 'metaphysical' viewpoint – the real answer to the question of immortality lies, he says, not in identifying oneself as something eternal but rather as something timeless.

The matter depends on the reference of the 'equivocal' word 'I'. At first glance, the only candidate for its referent seems to be something given in experience, the bodily individual. But really this identification is quite unwarranted since 'the I or ego is the dark point in consciousness, just as on the retina the precise point of entry of the optic nerve is blind' (WR II: 491). Much influenced by Schopenhauer's reflections, Wittgenstein puts the point by saying (in proposition 5.6331 of the *Tractatus*) that the form of the visual field (and by implication consciousness in general) is not like this:

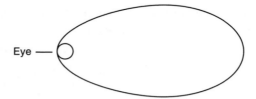

Figure 7.1

What, then, is the form of the field of consciousness? According to radical idealism it is like this:

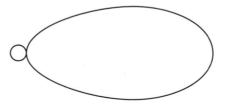

Figure 7.2

Just as dreams need a dreamer outside the dream, so the ideal status of consciousness requires a non-ideal subject (WR II: 492).

In speaking of the immortality he takes to be implicit in Kant's idealism, Schopenhauer emphasises particularly, the ideality of time: the 'most complete answer' to the question of immortality is 'Kant's great doctrine of the *ideality of time*' (WR II: 493). Fear of death is, Schopenhauer suggests, dread of losing the present, dread of, as we might put it, 'becoming history'. But this is as mistaken as it would be for the sun to lament in the evening: 'woe is me! I am going down into eternal night' (WR I: 280). Really, we are not on the revolving sphere of time, but are the fixed point before which the sphere rotates. The real self does not move through time, rather time moves before it. It inhabits eternity, something to be conceived not as 'succession without beginning or end' but rather as a *nunc stans*, a 'permanent now' (WR I: 280).

This, then, is Schopenhauer's real antidote to fear of death. It is a metaphysical truth that is most closely approximated to by Hinduism and Buddhism 'which teaches man to regard himself as Brahman, the original being himself, to whom all arising and passing away are essentially foreign' (WR II: 463). It is also, to repeat, the metaphysical truth that is intimated by the sublime in art (see p. 120 above).

<h2>EGOISM</h2>

The discussion of death introduces into Book IV the idea of the real self as something outside space and time. But there is more to Schopenhauer's account of the real self than this. Not only, he holds, is the real self a transcendent entity, it is also the case that *there is only one* real self. In other words, everyone's real self is identical with everyone and everything else's real self: *tat tvam asi* (this art thou) as the *Upanishads* puts it, is a formula Schopenhauer never tires of repeating. To see the point of this aspect of his metaphysics we need to turn to his moral philosophy.

* * *

Schopenhauer thinks of moral philosophy as confined to one issue: the explanation of virtue and the correlative explanation of vice. So he views moral philosophy as a branch of psychology. It turns out, however, that at a deep level psychology crosses over into metaphysics, so that the explanation of virtue becomes a 'metaphysical explanation' (BM: 199). It turns out, that is, that while the vicious are deeply enmeshed in metaphysical *illusion*, the virtuous possess profound (if inarticulate) insight into the fundamental nature of reality. For this reason virtue is not only explained but also (at least partially) justified. Virtue is based on insight; viciousness is based on error, on a kind of blindness.

* * *

The discussion begins with the topic of 'egoism', that condition in which a person 'makes himself the centre of the world and considers his own existence and well-being before everything else, [i]n fact . . . is ready for this to sacrifice everything else . . . to annihilate the world in order to maintain his own self' (WR I: 332). Egoism, in other words, is the condition in which the only interests that count for anything are my own. The egoist elevates his own interests to 'colossal proportions' (BM: 132–3), prefers, in Hume's words (which are surely at the back of Schopenhauer's mind here), the destruction of the Indian subcontinent to the scratching of his little finger.

Schopenhauer says that egoism is 'the natural standpoint' (ibid.). The reason is that everyone finds 'the whole will' in himself (ibid.), in other words finds himself alone to be a 'phenomenon of the will' (WR I: 104). What he means here is that the only will I know about directly is my own. Though I may have intellectual reasons for attributing the capacity for feeling, suffering, desiring and intending to you, according to the way the world is presented in naive experience, the only desires, and hence interests, that exist are my own. It is natural, that is to say, to assume that only I am a 'real person' (WR I: 104).

In other words, Schopenhauer is saying, there is a natural disposition to see and treat others as mere things: to treat them as mere pieces of equipment to be manipulated without scruple in whatever way suits one's own interests. There is a natural disposition to treat them, in Kant's language, merely as 'means', never as 'ends'.[5]

That egoism is the natural state explains why 'war all against all' is also the natural condition of human beings. You are naturally disposed to treat me as a mere thing, I am naturally disposed to do the same to you, and we are each disposed violently to object. This is what gives rise to the necessity for the state and provides it with its sole justification. The state, that is, is the product of rational egoism. Its sole task is to ameliorate the harm we do to one another, to prevent, so far as possible, my pursuit of my interests from damaging the interests of others, to take the edge off the 'war all against all' (WR I: sections 61–2).

* * *

Schopenhauer regards 'normative ethics', the attempt to establish the fundamental principle or principles of morality over which Kant laboured so long and hard, as a non-discipline since it is simple common sense. The supreme principle of morality, as everyone knows, is just 'harm no one; on the contrary help everyone as much as you can' (BM: 69).[6]

Schopenhauer says that egoistic action is not always 'wrong (Unrecht)'. Provided it does not cause harm to others it is 'right'.[7] On the other hand, given the competitive situation in which we find ourselves, egoistic action is, inevitably, very often wrong. It is, indeed, the sole source of wrongdoing. The sole source of wrongdoing, in other words, is the inflicting of harm on others, 'denying' their wills, in the course of 'asserting' one's own (WR I: 334).

MALICE

Sometimes Schopenhauer appears to identify another source of wrongdoing, namely 'malice (Bosheit)', which is closely related to (there is no exact English translation) Schadenfreude – literally 'harm-joy' – the taking of pleasure in the discomfort and suffering of others. Sometimes, that is, he describes malice as 'disinterested cruelty', cases where the suffering of others, rather than being collateral damage caused by the unconstrained pursuit of one's own interests, is pursued as an 'end in itself' (BM: 133–6). In On the Basis of Morality he says that all possible motives can be classified under three headings: egoism (the desire for one's own 'weal'), compassion (the desire for another's 'weal'), and malice (the desire for another's 'woe') (BM: 145).[8] In the *World as Will*, however, malice, it seems to me, is treated as an unobvious species of egoism.

It is true that in the main work, too, malice is described as something which

> has not sprung from egoism, but is disinterested; this is wickedness proper and rises to the pitch of *cruelty*. For this the suffering of another is no longer a means of attaining an end of one's own will, but an end in itself
>
> (WR I: 363).

Schopenhauer continues, however, by providing a 'more detailed explanation' of malice. People of powerfully egoistic wills, he says, suffer very intensely. (Since pain is unsatisfied or frustrated desire, the more powerful the desire the more intense the pain.) And this, he says, creates envy and hatred of the apparently happy. So the malicious person targets them and seeks to cause them intense pain. The reason for this is that the sight of another whose suffering is even greater than ours alleviates our own suffering. Even if you are sick the sight of a terminally sick person makes you feel better about your lot, gives you the 'there-but-for-the-grace-of-God-go-I' feeling, makes you count your blessings – few though they may be. So, says Schopenhauer, an extremely wicked person

> seeks indirectly the alleviation of which he is incapable directly, in other words, he tries to mitigate his own sufferings by the sight of another's; the suffering of another becomes for him an end in itself: it is a spectacle over which he gloats
>
> (WR I: 364).

I think it is obvious that 'end in itself' here can't mean what one would expect it to – otherwise the passage simply contradicts itself.[9] Schopenhauer's point consists in a contrast between, for example, someone who tortures someone else because he wants to obtain information and someone who tortures simply because he is a very wicked and unhappy person. For the unhappy sadist, the pain of the other is an 'end in itself' in the sense that there is no further change in the outer world to which it is a means. The intended change, rather, is a purely internal one.

This is a plausible explanation of malice. It should be accepted as Schopenhauer's considered view (a view abbreviated rather than contradicted in *On the Basis of Morality*) since otherwise he has no explanation of the phenomenon at all. It does, however, generate a problem. For if one is to mitigate one's own pain by seeing someone else in even greater pain one must be *aware* of the suffering of others. Yet the egoist is supposed to be someone who is desensitised to the sufferings of others, experiences them as 'mere things'.

One of Schopenhauer's strengths as a psychologist is his awareness of the complexity of the human psyche. Every human being, we have seen him suggesting (chapter 6, note 2), has a touch of every human attribute, even if only as an undertone, an 'obscure feeling'. So even the extreme egoist has a touch of sensitivity to the sufferings of others.[10] But only a touch. What follows is that his strategy is not likely to be very successful. It also follows that the sadist is liable to ever more horrible acts in the attempt to break through the barrier of desensitisation.

* * *

Egoistic action, we have seen, is the norm of human behaviour. And we have seen, too, that it is not necessarily 'wrong'. Indeed, through hope for reward or fear of punishment, a thoroughgoing egoist might never perform a single wrong action:

> It is conceivable that a perfect state, or even perhaps a complete dogma of rewards and punishments after death firmly believed in, might prevent every crime. Politically much would be gained in this way; morally, absolutely nothing . . .

> (WR I: 369).

The reason that nothing would be gained morally − that there would be no increase in 'moral worth', as Schopenhauer calls it − is that he agrees with Kant's famous assertion that nothing is good save the 'good will': 'In ethics the question is not one of action and result, but of *willing*' (WR II: 591). It concerns, in other words, 'character'.[11] Since all action motivated by self-interest lacks 'moral worth', what follows is that virtue is simply action which has as its 'ultimate object' the welfare of someone *else* (BM: 142−3). In a word, virtue is simply altruism.

ALTRUISM

Schopenhauer is quite clear that, though rare, there are genuinely altruistic actions and genuinely altruistic people; those

> whose character induces them generally not to hinder another's efforts of will as such, but rather to promote them and who are therefore consistently helpful
>
> (WR I: 360).

What he wants us to grasp is the extra-ordinariness of altruism. As art is an extraordinary transcendence of ordinary consciousness so virtue, too, is a transcendence of the 'natural standpoint'. As art is a matter of 'genius' so, in its own way, is altruism. It is an 'astonishing, indeed mysterious phenomenon' (BM: 144).

The question that interests Schopenhauer is: how is altruism possible? How can we make the phenomenon intelligible to ourselves? How is it possible 'for *another's* weal and woe to move my will immediately, that is to say, in the same way as it is usually moved only by my own?'.

What it requires, Schopenhauer decides, is that I feel the other's 'woe' just as I ordinarily feel my own, that 'I am in some way *identified with him*' (BM: 243−4). Virtue is, therefore, 'sympathy (*Sympathie*)' − or, as we would say, 'empathy'. Combined, however, with Schopenhauer's pessimism − there is a very great deal of suffering and very little joy in life[12] − a more specific description of the virtuous character can be given. Virtue is, says Schopenhauer, 'compassion (*Mitleid*)' (WR I: 375–6, WR II: 601). 'All love (*agape, caritas*) is compassion' (WR I: 374).

But what is the basis of sympathy and compassion? David Hume, who also identified sympathy – 'humanity', 'fellow feeling' – as fundamental to virtue, holds that no further explanation is necessary:

> It is needless to push our researches so far as to ask, why we have humanity or fellow-feeling with others. It is sufficient that this is experienced to be a principle of human nature. We must stop somewhere in our examination of causes
>
> *(Enquiries:* 219–20).

The reason, I think, for this disinclination to probe any further is that the benign Hume does not see human nature as tilted particularly strongly towards egoism – so he just itemises the impulses he finds to be there. But for Schopenhauer, with egoism as it were mandated by the human epistemological situation, altruism presents itself as an *übermenschlich* transcendence of the human situation as astonishing as that of the artistic genius. It is, therefore, something that *demands* an explanation.

Only metaphysics can provide one. What happens when 'to a certain extent the non-ego has become the ego' (BM: 144) is that the virtuous person has, to a degree, seen through the 'veil of Maya'. She has intuitively realised that since space and time, which are the *principium individuationis*, characterise the realm of appearance merely, it follows that individuality, plurality and otherness are foreign to reality as it is in itself, that the distinction between ego and non-ego is an illusion. To one degree or another, therefore, the virtuous person realises the truth of Eastern wisdom that 'this art thou (*tat tvam asi*)' (BM: 210). Virtue is, says Schopenhauer, 'practical mysticism' in that it 'springs from the same knowledge that constitutes the essence of all mysticism' (BM: 212). The just person – the person who lives by the first half of the 'harm no one; on the contrary help everyone as much as you can' principle – shows a certain degree of insight, the person of positive philanthropy (*Menschenliebe*) – one who lives, too, by the second part – a higher degree (WR I: 375, WR II: 602). This is why Schopenhauer says that virtue is nothing but 'my metaphysics translated into action', that it precedes from 'the immediate and *intuitive* knowledge of the metaphysical identity of all beings' (WR II: 600–1).[13]

THE METAPHYSICS OF VIRTUE

With this explanation and justification of virtue as consisting in the dissolution of the I–you dichotomy one has the sense of finally seeing at least some of the point of Schopenhauer's monistic metaphysics. And this is how Schopenhauer himself sees it: in *Parerga and Paralipomena* he speaks of his whole philosophy as directed towards a final culmination in 'a higher metaphysical-ethical standpoint' (PP I: 313).

Let us call the doctrine that the real self is non-empirical, not an object in the world of experience, and that it is identical with all other real selves, 'metaphysical solipsism'.[14] Metaphysical solipsism is, then, the explanation of altruism. But it also explains several other phenomena to do with the moral life.

It explains, firstly (at least part of) the pain of the bad conscience: remorse for harm inflicted on another is a faint glimmering of the knowledge that the will that is harmed is really none other than one's own will, so that the harm is a self-harming. Such knowledge presences, says Schopenhauer, as an 'obscure feeling' (WR I: 335).

And metaphysical solipsism explains, secondly, the phenomenon of 'eternal justice' (WR I: section 63 *passim*). Since the time of Socrates, claims Schopenhauer, 'the problem of philosophy has been . . . to demonstrate a *moral* world-order as the basis of the *physical* (WR II: 590), to show that the world is an ultimately just place. If the only kind of justice that existed were ordinary, human, "temporal" justice this could never be the case, since the very clever or very powerful are always beyond its reach. What makes ordinary justice fallible is the gap, the logical and temporal interval, between crime and punishment. If, then, there is to be an inescapable, an infallible kind of justice there must be no such gap. "Punishment", rather, "must be so linked to the offence that the two are one" (WR I: 351).

And in fact, since metaphysical solipsism is true, crime and punishment are the same. Since there is no self–other distinction it follows that 'tormentor and tormented are one' (WR I: 354), a metaphysical truth intimated in temporal – and therefore mythological – terms in the Eastern myth of reincarnation and karma (WR I: 355–6, WR II: 600). It follows that 'the tormentor . . . is mistaken in thinking he does not share the torment, the [tormented] . . . in thinking he does not share the guilt (WR I: 354).

The world is, then, a just place: 'If we could lay all the misery of the world in one pan of the scales [of justice], and all its guilt in the other, the pointer would certainly show them to be in equilibrium (WR I: 352). Monistic metaphysics, which is really just an articulation of Indian wisdom (WR I: 356–7), proves its worth by solving 'the problem of [Western] philosophy'.

CRITICISM OF SCHOPENHAUER'S MORAL PHILOSOPHY

What are we to make of this 'higher metaphysical-ethical standpoint'?

Schopenhauer says that a consequence of his doctrine of eternal justice is that

a happy life . . . given by chance or won from it by shrewdness, amid the sufferings of innumerable others, is only a beggar's dream in which he is king[15] but from which he must awake to realise that only a fleeting illusion had separated him from the suffering of his life

(WR I: 353).

One cannot be a happy king in a kingdom of beggars. This, it seems to me, has the ring of truth to it, a truth that is, as Schopenhauer says, somewhat 'mysterious'. Nonetheless, there seem to me at least two serious criticisms that have to be made of Schopenhauer's 'metaphysical explanation' of virtue.

The first is that, given the momentous weight his doctrine of metaphysical solipsism is required to bear, the argument for it seems just too fragile.

Intuitively, first of all, the argument − space and time are the conditions of plurality, they characterise only appearance, there-fore reality in itself in 'one' − is just too *short*, trite even, to carry much conviction. And once it is considered at all critically the following problems emerge. First, we have never really been con-vinced that space and time characterise *merely* appearances − remember the Magritte possibility (p. 24 above). Second, even if they do, it is disputable that they constitute the *only* way of making sense of plurality (numbers, for example, are a plurality but are not in space or time. Third, even if space and time do characterise appearances, merely, and are the only way we can make sense of plurality, it does not follow that the thing in itself is 'one', since that treats what is supposed to be beyond the realm of objects as itself an object. And fourth, even if reality in itself were to be 'one' it doesn't follow that it is any kind of a *self*. In sum, therefore, the argument for metaphysical solipsism is as full of holes as a piece of Gruyère cheese.

The second major problem with metaphysical solipsism is this. Schopenhauer asserts, first, that the difference between the egoist and the altruist is that while the former acts for his own interests the latter acts for the sake of another's. This is why the latter's actions possess 'moral worth' while those of the former do not. As the discussion proceeds, however, it becomes clear that, after all, the altruist *does* act for the sake of his own interest, the only differ-ence between him and the egoist being that he acts for the sake of the interests of his *metaphysical* rather than his empirical self. So, as we might put it, the empirical altruist turns out to be a metaphysical egoist. And given that egoism excludes 'moral worth', it is entirely unclear why his moral status should be any different from that of the common-or-garden egoist.

* * *

In spite of these defects, however, it still seems to me that both Schopenhauer's psychology of virtue and his doctrine of eternal justice contain, as Iris Murdoch puts it, a depth of 'humane wisdom'.[16] What I want to suggest, however, is that the insight they contain is, in reality, phenomenological rather than metaphysical. I want to suggest that, gripped by the will to create a grand metaphysical system which he shares with all his nineteenth-century German contemporaries, Schopenhauer forces what is essentially a non-metaphysical insight into ill-fitting metaphysical clothing.

Let me start by returning to the second of the above criticisms. What makes it look as though Schopenhauer's account of altruism just reduces it to a weird kind of egoism is that he seems to represent the altruist as reasoning ('intuitively'):

I love me.
I see that you = me (*tat twam asi*).
Therefore, I must love you.

But suppose that what really moves the altruist is that she loves us, and is therefore moved to care equally for all members of the 'us', for self and others. On this representation of the altruist, no egoism of any sort is involved since the fundamental object of love is a non-ego. Notice that an 'us', a community, is a natural entity a plurality of individuals. No appeal to metaphysics, to a non-spatio-temporal unity, is required to explain its existence.

Sometimes Schopenhauer does describe the egoism/altruism contrast in this way rather than in terms of metaphysical solipsism. On WR II: 599–600 for example, he compares the '*particular* viewpoint' from which the individual is 'all in all' with the '*universal* viewpoint' (the 'us' viewpoint) from which the individual is 'nothing'. This suggests that his real insight is that, rather than being a matter of the dutiful following of rules, as Kant thought, ethics, virtue, is fundamentally a matter of vision, of, in Wittgenstein's phrase, 'see[ing] the world aright' (*Tractatus*, proposition 6.54).

* * *

But why is adopting the universal rather than individual point of view seeing the world '*aright*'? Why is the universal in some sense the *right* point of view?

In proposition 6.422 of the *Tractatus* (a proposition I shall discuss in greater detail in chapter 9), Wittgenstein writes − in what is very clearly a meditation on Schopenhauer's doctrine of 'eternal justice' − that

> When an ethical law of the form 'Thou shalt . . .' is laid down ones
> first thought is: And what if I don't do it? It is clear, however, that
> ethics has nothing to do with punishment and reward in the usual
> sense of the term.

'Ethics', in other words, has nothing to do with, in Schopenhauer's terminology, 'temporal justice' − for, we may presume, the reasons given by Schopenhauer. Wittgenstein goes on to say, however, that though 'there must indeed be some kind of ethical reward and punishment', these should not be 'consequences' of actions, at least not in the sense of 'events'. Rather they must 'reside in the action itself'. In explanation of this he adds that the 'good . . . exercise of the will' results in a 'happy' world, the 'bad exercise of the will' in an 'unhappy' world (proposition 6.43).

This passage, it seems to me, is partially (though not, I shall argue in chapter 9 completely) a précis of one of the most insightful of the ways in which Schopenhauer draws the egoism/altruism contrast. By altruism, he says, 'the heart feels itself enlarged, just as by egoism it feels contracted'. For while egoism

> concentrates our interest on the particular phenomenon of our own
> individuality, and then knowledge always presents us with the
> innumerable perils that continually threaten this phenomenon,
> whereby anxiety and care become the keynote of our disposition

altruism

> extends our interest to all that lives . . . [so that] through the
> reduced interest in our own self, the anxious care for that self is
> attacked and restricted at its root; hence the calm and confident
> serenity afforded by a virtuous disposition and a good conscience.

Schopenhauer concludes the passage by saying that 'the good person lives in world of friendly phenomena: the well-being of any of
these is his own well-being'. The egoist, on the other hand, 'feels
himself surrounded by strange and hostile phenomena' (WR I:
373–4).

What, with Wittgenstein's help, we can extract from these passages is the insight that 'eternal justice' exists, that there is a 'moral
order' to the world, that moral punishment and reward *are* infallible
on account of the identity of crime and punishment. The demonstration of this identity does not, however, demand anything as
grand as the doctrine of metaphysical solipsism. Rather, all it
requires is the insight that the wrongdoing and the unhappiness of
alienation have a common cause – the inability to transcend the
individual standpoint – and that the same is true of virtue and the
happiness of solidarity: they both arise from viewing the world
from the universal standpoint. Hence, Schopenhauer is, I think,
right. The wicked are *inescapably* unhappy while the good *necessarily*
achieve a certain kind of happiness.

There is, then, great insight, Iris Murdoch's 'humane wisdom',
contained in Schopenhauer's moral philosophy. But it is insight
which is, as Wittgenstein helps us to see, entirely independent of
the shaky mechanism of metaphysical solipsism. What Schopenhauer shows is that the difference between the vicious and the

virtuous is that they live in different 'worlds'. The egoist (and the neo-liberal) lives in a world of 'atomic individualism', a world in which one of the 'atoms' – the one he calls 'me' – is privileged as the sole object of care. The altruist, on the other hand, inhabits a world in which the atoms congregate into a whole, a community, which is the object of his primary identification and care. These different worlds are, however, different *phenomenal* worlds. They are simply different ways of seeing the everyday world of individuals. And since this difference in phenomenal worlds is sufficient to explain the difference between the egoist and the altruist, there is no need to look for a difference in *metaphysical* worlds. The excursion into Kantian metaphysics is superfluous. Moreover, it lands Schopenhauer in a serious metaphysical confusion.

* * *

Schopenhauer claims, as we saw, that altruism is 'practical mysticism' in that it 'springs from the same knowledge that constitutes the essence of all mysticism' (BM: 212), the knowledge of metaphysical solipsism. Yet for the person of virtue the unitary essence of all things is the will, the 'world-will' as I called it: he realises that in harming another he is harming that will which is their common essence, realises, in Schopenhauer's image (see p. 82 above), that harming another is a case of the bulldog ant's tail stinging its head.

The world-will, however, is evil. Yet mysticism, as we are about to see, is a state of beatitude. So the realm into which the mystic gains insight cannot be the will but must be 'beyond' it. So, as we have observed before, the (Kantian) thing in itself cannot be the will. In sum, then, the representation of the altruist as possessing *ultimate* metaphysical insight, as possessing the *same* order of insight as the mystic, is inconsistent with the possibility of 'salvation', a topic to which I now turn.

SUMMARY

Schopenhauer denies that philosophy can change your life (a) on the grounds that character is innate and unalterable and (b) on the grounds that philosophy is a value-free inquiry. Both grounds are criticised.

Death and Immortality

The task of philosophy is to provide 'consolation' in the face of death. The true source of such consolation is radical idealism: since time is merely ideal, the true self is beyond time and beyond mortality.

Ethics

Since it is beyond space and time the true self is also beyond individuality and plurality. It is 'one'. This 'otherness'-abolishing metaphysics is the basis of virtue, i.e. altruism. An intuitive grasping of it is what overcomes the egoism that is written into everyday consciousness of the world. Though as a metaphysical thesis this radical monism is unconvincing, it is argued, it contains, nonetheless, great insight into the psychology of altruism.

FURTHER READING

J. Atwell, *Schopenhauer: the human Character*, Part II.

D. Cartwright, 'Schopenhauer's narrower sense of Morality' in *The Cambridge Companion to Schopenhauer*, pp. 252–92.

P. Gardiner, *Schopenhauer*, chapter 6.

C. Janaway, *Schopenhauer*, chapter 7.

Eight

Salvation

DENIAL OF THE WILL

Schopenhauer might have made himself more acceptable to, as he calls it, 'the spirit of philosophical ethics prevailing in Protestant Europe' (WR II: 607), if he had ended *The World as Will* with complete altruism – universal love – offered at the end of the story, the final human ideal. As it turns out, however, virtue is not the final but only the penultimate step (WR II: 608) on the 'road' to the final goal of 'salvation' (WR II: 634). This, which Schopenhauer describes as the '*summum bonum*', the 'highest good' (WR I: 362), consists in something he calls 'denial of the will'.

Let us return to the description of the 'friendly' world of the altruist (pp. 184–5 above) for a moment. Though the altruist experiences a sense of trust and solidarity with his fellows, nonetheless, says Schopenhauer, 'his knowledge of the lot of man in general does not make his disposition a cheerful one' (WR I: 374). In fact, in a certain way, the altruist's disposition is *even less* cheerful than that of the egoist.

The egoist suffers. Yet, deeply enveloped as he is, in the veil of Maya, the illusion of separateness, he thinks that suffering is just *his* problem, and a temporary one at that. The virtuous, by contrast, take to themselves the suffering of others. At the highest level, the saintly, Christ-like figure takes to himself the suffering of the whole world, past present and future. This means that

If we compare life to a circular path of red-hot coals having a few cool places, a path that we have to run over incessantly, then [the egoist] . . . is comforted by the cool place on which he is just now standing, or which he sees near him, and sets out to run over the path.

The saint, by contrast, who sees through the principium individuationis,

sees himself in all places simultaneously and withdraws. . . . In other words it is no longer enough for him to love others as himself, and to do as much for them as for himself.

Rather, his will 'turns about' and 'denies' itself: 'he ceases to will anything' (WR I: 380) including the works of love, the attempt to alleviate the suffering of others.

What happens, at a very high pitch of altruism, Schopenhauer suggests, is that the saint has a moment of sudden and piercing insight.[1] What he (or she – many of Schopenhauer's example of sainthood are women) sees in this moment of insight is the futility of the works of love. He realises that to alleviate an individual's material want only opens him up to the suffering of boredom (see pp. 210–13 below). And he realises that at the very moment of relieving one individual's suffering, another suffering being has come crying into the world; that as soon as pain is extinguished in one shape or place it breaks out in another. What he realises, in short, is the truth of the general principle that 'the ceaseless efforts to banish suffering achieve nothing more than a change in its form' (WR I: 315) (we might call this the 'conservation of pain' principle). In a word, the saint comes to an intuitive realisation of the truth of philosophical pessimism: that 'life is suffering', and hence 'existence . . . an error' (WR II: 605), is not just a temporary or localised truth but is true of all life at all times and all places.

With this realisation one develops a 'strong aversion' to – one 'shudders at' and 'withdraws' from – life and the world (WR I: 379–80). One undergoes a kind of 'conversion' (WR II: 612) experience, a radical 'turning (Wendung)' (WR I: 410). Knowledge of the whole, escape from the egoist's illusion of the transitoriness of pain, becomes the 'quieter of the will' (WR I: 379), leads to a 'resignation' (ibid.) from life. 'Affirmation' of the will changes into 'denial', to, that is, a 'ceas[ing] to will anything' (WR I: 380), including the works of love. One undergoes what Schopenhauer calls the 'transition from virtue to *asceticism*' (WR I: 380).

The saint, then, enters a state of will-lessness. Of course, he is still an embodied human being with the normal range of human instincts and desires. So it is hard to maintain the life of true asceticism. Discipline – self-discipline – is required. This means, according to Volume I, that the life of the ascetic will be character- ised by 'fasting, and even . . . self-castigation and self-torture, in order that, by constant privation and suffering, he may more and more break down and kill the will that he recognises and abhors as the source of his own suffering existence and of the world's' (WR I: 382).

In Volume II, however – by the time of whose writing Schopen- hauer had considerably deepened his knowledge and admiration of Buddhism[2] – he observes that deliberate self-mortification is absent from Buddhism[3], 'and perhaps rightly so [since] justice itself is the hairy garment that causes its owner constant hardship, and philan- thropy that gives away what is necessary provides us with constant fasting' (WR II: 607).[4] On this account the 'transition from virtue to asceticism' is a more subtle one. Outwardly, there will be no change at all. All that will have changed is the motive: the works of extreme altruism are no longer performed out of love but out of the desire for personal hardship. (One might think, here, perhaps, of Mahatma Ghandi, in whom love and asceticism seem to have been curiously mixed.)

* * *

Schopenhauer's ultimate hero is, then, the ascetic, the will- and world-'denier'. Since will is the human essence it is appropriate to call him, as one who overcomes human nature, Schopenhauer's ultimate '*Übermensch*', his 'overman'.[5] This account of ultimate wisdom as the insight that 'existence is an error', that 'it would be better for us not to exist' (WR II: 605), this view of life- and world-'denial' as the 'highest good', might well be found shocking, even offensive. Anticipating howls of protest from life-affirmers, Schopenhauer points out that the idea that life is something we need 'salvation' from is the essence not just of his philosophy but of Christianity, Hinduism and Buddhism – in other words, of all the world's great religions (WR II: 628, WR I: 383). (Islam Schopenhauer does not consider to be a great religion.[6])

It is, nonetheless, fairly obvious that we need to ask some serious questions about Schopenhauer's advocacy of 'denial of the will'. Specifically, at least the following:

1   Is not the idea of a 'transition' from virtue to asceticism inconsistent with the assertion that character is innate and unalterable (see p. 66 above)?

2   If life is as terrible as Schopenhauer makes out, why should we bother with asceticism when suicide presents itself as a speedier, more decisive alternative?

3   What is the *point* of the whole exercise? What actually *is* the 'salvation' that is supposed to be attained through 'denial of the will', and why is it the 'highest *good*'? Moreover (an issue we have already touched upon), how can Schopenhauer allow even the possibility of salvation given that the 'thing in itself' might well seem to be evil incarnate, the world-creating 'will'? And just how is the *ascetic* state supposed to be related to the *aesthetic* state which, as we have seen (pp. 111–13 above), also involves escape from the will?

And finally,

4   Is life really as terrible as Schopenhauer asserts? Is pessimism really true? Do we *need* 'saving'?

I shall look at Schopenhauer's answers to these questions in the order in which I have raised them.

DENIAL OF THE WILL AND THE UNALTERABILITY OF CHARACTER

What we have learnt so far about character is that the will to live is the essence of all human beings, and the will to live in a particular way (e.g. as a saint or a sinner) is my individual character. According to Schopenhauer, this character is both innate and unalterable. We have been told, moreover, that the actions I perform are an absolutely determined function of my character together with the 'motives' that come my way in just the way in which the stone's behaviour is an absolutely determined function of its unalterable nature together with the causes that act upon it.

Schopenhauer himself admits that 'denial of the will' seems to be clearly excluded on this account of things. There seems, he says, to be a clear

> contradiction between our assertions on the one hand, of the necessity of the will's determination through motives according to the [unalterable] character, and our assertions, on the other, of the possibility of the whole suppression of the will, whereby motives become powerless
>
> (WR I: 403).

In fact, though, he suggests, the contradiction is apparent rather than real. By way of removing the appearance, he makes two points.

The first is that denial of the will 'does not proceed directly from the will but from a changed form of knowledge'. So long, he says, as 'knowledge . . . follows the principle of sufficient reason' (attends to 'the where, the when, the why and the whither' in things (see p. 112 above)) 'the power of motives is irresistible'. In the ascetic state, however, 'knowledge is withdrawn from the power of motives' (WR I: 403). What this means is that entry into the ascetic state 'is not a . . . change, but a . . . suppression of character' (WR I: 403). That is, it remains true of me, now as before, that *were I to be* presented with 'motives' X Y and Z I *would* acts in ways A, B, and C. So my *character* is in fact unaltered. It is just that I am now no longer presented with motives.

Schopenhauer's second point is that the life-transformation involved in entry into the ascetic state is not a transformation that lies within my own power. The change in 'knowledge', that is, is something I cannot *make* happen but rather *receive*. It 'comes, suddenly, as if flying in from without'; it is a product, not of 'works', but an *'effect of grace'* (WR I: 404). So it remains true that I can produce no radical change in my life. If the transition to asceticism happens at all, it happens *to* me rather than *through* me.

Technically, the distinction between character change and character suppression saves the inalterability of character thesis. But only at the expense of destroying the whole deterministic structure of the empirical world set up in Book II, according to which human behaviour is as completely subject to causal laws as is the behaviour of rocks and is in principle as predictable. If human beings can, for unaccountable reasons, suddenly be withdrawn from the 'power of motives', if the laws governing their behaviour can be suspended in cases where there is a turn to asceticism then there can be no such predictability.

Effectively Schopenhauer admits this. Denial of the will represents an exception, a *'real* contradiction', to the thesis of universal determinism. It represents a 'transcendental change' which arises 'from the direct encroachment of the [thing] . . . in itself, knowing no necessity, on the necessity of the phenomenon' (WR I: 403). The turn to asceticism is (to borrow a term from Stephen Jay Gould) a 'skyhook' which occasionally descends from the noumenal into the phenomenal and disrupts the causal order of things. So Schopenhauer admits that the previous affirmation of universal causal determinism is now suspended to accommodate denial of the will. He admits, in other words, that his 'Kantian' reconciliation of the supposed presuppositions of science with the facts of human life (see pp. 160–5 above) is inadequate. (Note that by allowing that we sometimes enter the aesthetic state Schopenhauer has, in fact, already allowed for skyhooks, miracles, for the suspension of 'the power of motives'. I shall return shortly to the question of the relationship between the aesthetic and ascetic states.)

SUICIDE

Our second question concerned suicide. If life is really as terrible as Schopenhauer says it is, we asked, why should we bother with asceticism when suicide presents itself as a more decisive alternative?

At the beginning of *The Myth of Sisyphus* (p. 11) Albert Camus famously claims that

> [t]here is but one truly serious philosophical problem and that is suicide. Judging whether life is or is not worth living amounts to answering the fundamental question of philosophy.

Surprisingly though, Schopenhauer thinks it incumbent on any 'ethical system' to condemn suicide.[7] Stoicism's inability to do so, its recommendation of suicide in cases where pain becomes intolerable, he takes to be a proof of its ultimate bankruptcy (WR I: 90–1). But how can Schopenhauer himself satisfy this condition? Surely the saint, on realising the horrendous nature of existence and the futility of trying to do anything about it, will commit suicide – or at least ought to?

Not so, says Schopenhauer. Far from being the product of the saint's insight into the truth about the world, suicide is actually a 'masterpiece of Maya' (WR I: 399), the product of deep metaphysical illusion. How so?

The central fact about the suicide – the suicide of despair – suggests Schopenhauer, is that, paradoxical as it may seem, he actually wills life. What he is dissatisfied with is merely 'the conditions in which it comes to him' (WR I: 398). He thinks everyone else is having a grand party from which he alone is excluded. It is this sense of 'accidentality' of being specially and uniquely selected for pain, which 'gives suffering its sting', since 'we are not usually distressed at evils that are inescapably necessary and quite universal such as old age and death' (WR I: 315). A trouble shared is a trouble halved; unshared, it is doubled.

So one difference between the saint and the suicide is that the latter is ignorant of what the former knows, the truth of philo-sophical pessimism.

But why would realising the universality of pain make any dif-ference? Because to do so, to do so 'intuitively', with heart and not just head, is to 'identify' with the sufferings of all sentient beings past, present and in the infinite future. Hence to realise pessimism in the heart is to see that suicide is (like virtue) 'futile' (WR I: 399); as futile as removing a toe in the hope of curing a cancer that afflicts the whole body. In other words, suicide is an act of extreme ego-ism, the most extreme failure of emotional identification with others, extreme lack of empathy. If I care equally about me and you and you . . . then my suicide is a complete irrelevance to solving the problem.

Schopenhauer allows, as a partial exception to this characterisa-tion of the suicide, the terrible but recurrent case of the father who kills the children of whom he is extremely fond and then kills himself. Though still deluded, this type of suicide shows a partial intimation of the truth that the problem is not my life but rather life as such (WR I: 400).

There seems to me something insightful about this picture of the suicide as exceptionally self-obsessed; as someone who has become so isolated from the rest of the world that it seems to them that only their own pain matters, indeed that only their own pain exists. This is, I think, particularly true of men who commit suicide on account of business failures. The relative triviality of the motive requires that the suicide has become absolutely insensible to the vastly greater suffering of millions of others.

SALVATION

The third question, or set of questions, I raised at the beginning of this chapter concerns 'salvation (Erlösung)'. What is the point of the whole exercise? What *is* salvation, and why is it the 'highest *good*', indeed any kind of a 'good'? Why, having once achieved the state of will-lessness, is the saint so keen to maintain or regain it? Moreover, how can Schopenhauer allow it to be even possible given that the thing in itself is the evil will? And finally, just how is the ascetic state is related to the aesthetic state which, as we saw in chapter 5, is also a state of will-lessness?

Schopenhauer says of one who has become so complete an ascetic that the regime of self-discipline is no longer necessary that

> such a man who, after many bitter struggles with his own nature
> has at last completely conquered, is then left only as pure knowing
> being, as the unclouded (*ungetrübter*) mirror of the world. Nothing
> can alarm or distress him any more; nothing can any longer move
> him; for he has cut all the thousand threads of willing which hold us
> bound to the world, and which, as craving, fear, envy, and anger
> drag us here and there in constant pain
>
> (WR I: 390).

This is a thought we have met before. Since pain consists in a disjunction between the will and the world, to give up willing is to achieve equanimity, immunity to pain and hence to anxiety. What, in short, the ascetic is doing is celebrating just that 'Sabbath from the penal servitude of willing' (WR I: 196) we saw to constitute the nature of aesthetic delight (p. 112 above). As already noted, Schopenhauer makes explicit this continuity between the aesthetic and ascetic states: recalling Book III's discussion of aesthetic delight, he says in Book IV that anyone who has ever experienced the briefly blissful will-lessness of the aesthetic state will be able to infer how delightful must be the state of one in whom the will is silenced for ever (WR I: 390).

But is this all there is to 'salvation'? Is salvation *just* equanimity, *ataraxia*, as the Greeks called it (WR II: 159)? The answer is that it is not since Schopenhauer continues by saying that, having cut the 'thousand threads of willing', the ascetic

now looks back calmly and with a smile on the deceptive images
(*Gaukelbilder*) of this world which were once able to move and
agonise even his mind, but now stand before him as indifferently as
chessmen at the end of a game, or as fancy dress cast off in the
morning, the form and figure of which taunted and disquieted us on
the carnival night. Life and its figures (*Gestalten*) merely float before
him as a fleeting appearance, as a light morning dream to one half-
awake, through which reality (*Wirklichkeit*) already gleams
(*durchschimmert*), and which can no longer deceive; and, like this
morning dream, they too finally vanish without any violent
transition

(WR I: 390–1).

What this passage asserts is a natural transition from extreme asceticism to mysticism, to an encounter with supra-natural reality.
Everyday, objectual consciousness, the 'veil of Maya', is, we know,
the product of the practical, will-serving intellect. It is 'the life-
dream of the man who wills' (WR I: 411). So the weaker the will,
Schopenhauer suggests, the 'thinner' the veil between us and
reality itself. When there is a *complete* 'abolition' of the will, the
veil of Maya, too, is completely abolished, becomes 'nothing' (WR
I: 412).

What, then, the ascetic achieves is a dissolution of the opacity of
the 'veil of Maya'. It becomes translucent, vouchsafing him or her a
mystical vision of 'reality'. Salvation is more than equanimity since
it involves a cognitive content.

But what actually is this supposed 'reality' accessed by the mystic? Is it not just an 'empty nothingness' (WR I: 408), the mere
hallucination of a stressed body? Of course, Schopenhauer replies,
to us willers the mystic's vision is an empty nothingness. 'Nothing',
that is to say, is simply the absence of being. And being, for willers,
is just the world of the *principium individuationis*. So of course, to us,
there is nothing at all beyond the world of objects.[8] But to one who
has achieved the will-less state, it is the world of the willer that has

been disclosed as 'nothing'. Its hold over us, its seeming reality, has been 'abolished' so that it now stands before us as nothing but a bad dream from which we are, thankfully, awaking. So, as Schopenhauer puts in the concluding sentence of the whole work,

> what remains after the complete abolition of the will is, for all those who are still full of will, assuredly nothing. But also conversely, to those in whom the will has turned and denied itself, this very real world of ours with all its suns and galaxies, is – nothing
>
> (WR I: 411–12).

Is there, then, just a stand-off between competing accounts of what is real and what hallucination, what is real and what is 'nothing'? Can philosophy not adjudicate between the reality-claims of the will-full and the will-less?

Well, of course, it can and does. For we know from Kant, Schopenhauer believes, that the world of objects *is* mere appearance, *is*, ultimately, a 'dream'. So of course (Schopenhauer seems to take this point to be too obvious to be worth making explicit) the ascetic is right and the realist about empirical objects wrong. What, however, is the *character* of the 'reality' to which the ascetic gains access?

Common to all forms of mysticism, says Schopenhauer, is 'consciousness of the identity of one's own inner being with that of all things or with the kernel of the world' (WR II: 613).[9] But common, too, is pantheism: 'pantheistic consciousness is essential to all mysticism' (WR II: 613). So, for example, Meister Eckhart's spiritual daughter cries out to him after her conversion: 'Sir, rejoice with me, I have become God' (WR II: 612). In sum, therefore, the mystic's vision is one of the *holiness* of the ultimately real, a reality with which she, like all things, is in truth identical.

But how do we know the mystics are *right*? Does philosophy have anything to say, here? Can it do anything by way of validating the claims of mysticism?

Conceptual thought, as we know, is dependent on sense-experience for its meaningfulness. So that in trying to discuss the 'transcendent', in trying to discuss the character of that which lies beyond nature, it runs up against its limits 'as against the walls of our prison' (WR II: 641). And as we have seen, philosophy is, according to Schopenhauer, essentially 'rationalism', an exercise in conceptual thinking. So, he says, at its 'highest point', his philosophy has to assume a 'negative character'. It can speak of what, in denial of the will, is abandoned, but never of what is 'laid hold of' (WR II: 612). It 'indicates', as we have already seen, a sphere of 'illuminism . . . higher consciousness' but 'guard[s] against setting even one foot thereon' (PP II: 9–11). Though the mystics 'precede positively' (WR II: 612) where philosophy comes to an end, we must not fool ourselves into thinking that their talk of 'reabsorption into *Brahman*' or '*nirvana*' satisfies the conditions of literal meaningfulness (WR I: 411).

So philosophy cannot 'demonstrate' there to be a *nirvana*. At least, there is nothing philosophy can do to *directly* validate mysticism as insight rather than illusion. Yet indirectly, suggests Schopenhauer, it can support the claims of the mystics. For one thing, we may observe that they do not form a 'sect'. In spite of the 'inner agreement' of their reports on the character of ultimate reality they come from a widely different array of religious and cultural backgrounds and generally do not know one another. There is, that is to say, no collusion between them. And when a number of independent witnesses report, as it were, 'sightings' of the same thing, the most likely explanation, surely, is that what they have 'seen' is, in fact, 'there' (WR II: 614).

Another point is this. We know from Kant that the world of space and time is ideal. But since – so, at least, Schopenhauer has argued – space and time constitute the only possible *principium individuationis*, it follows that reality itself is 'beyond plurality'. But suffering, indeed willing of any kind, requires plurality, requires a distinction between willing subject and recalcitrant object.[10] So reality itself *has* to be beyond suffering.

In the privacy of the early notebooks, it will be remembered, Schopenhauer records his occasional vision that reality is indeed like this: his habitation of that 'better consciousness' which, as he puts it, 'lifts me up into a world where neither personality, nor subject not object, exist any more' (see p. 7 above). In *The World as Will*, of course, since private mystical experience is supposed to have no legitimate place in a work of philosophy, he makes no mention of this. But it is, presumably, the 'concealed illuminism' which, he says, is the ultimate inspiration of his philosophy (PP II: 11).

Indirectly, then, Schopenhauer concludes, philosophy can lead us towards accepting the 'indubitable' 'reality (*Wirklichkeit*)' (WR II: 614) of the claims of mysticism. Beyond empirical reality there is indeed 'nothing' – nothing comprehensible to the rational mind, no-thing. But it is not an 'empty' nothing. It is a 'relative', not an 'absolute' nothing (WR I: 409). To put the point in philosopher's jargon, that which transcends empirical reality is an *epistemological* but not a *ontological* nothing.

Philosophical reasoning leads us to this point. But so, too, does the reason of the heart. When, perhaps with the aid of great art such as that of Raphael of Correggio, we compare 'the ocean-like calmness of the spirit' of the mystic with 'the miserable and desperate nature of our own condition', we are provided with 'complete and certain gospel'. Who, that is, would *want* to question the promise of salvation contained in mystical revelation? For both head and heart we have, therefore, adequate grounds 'to banish the dark impression of that nothingness, which as the final goal hovers behind all . . . holiness, and which we fear as [in Francis Bacon's borrowed words] children fear to go into the dark' (WR II: 411).

* * *

Fear of death, fear of the 'nothing', is, then, something we do not need to have. Contrary to Dylan Thomas's demand that we 'Rage, rage against the dying of the [this-worldly] light', Schopenhauer

suggests, we *can* 'go gentle into that good night'. This conclusion
makes clear, I believe, the real character of Schopenhauer's doctrine
of salvation and, in fact, of his entire philosophy; it is a 'consolation' in the face of death.

We saw in the discussion of death and immortality in the last
chapter that to provide such a consolation, to provide an 'antidote'
to fear of death, is the principle task of philosophy (see p. 169
above). The discussion there, showed us that we should not fear
death as extinction, that 'immortality' is guaranteed to us by Kantian idealism, immortality as timeless rather than eternal existence.
What the discussion of mysticism adds – within the limits inseparable from philosophy as 'rationalism' – is an assurance that
immortality is a blessing rather than a curse, something to be welcomed rather than feared; that Dylan Thomas's 'good night' is not
just a farewell, but that what awaits us really is a *good* night. When
we put these assurances together with Schopenhauer's pessimism,
his account of this-worldly existence as a painful 'error', we can see
that Socrates' definition of philosophy as 'a preparation of death',
which he endorses (WR II: 463), is one that really does describe
the fundamental character of his own work. Schopenhauer's philosophy is a prolonged and ultimately consoling meditation on the
inevitability of death.

* * *

The discussion of mysticism is, as Iris Murdoch says (op. cit.: 62),
a sincere and moving exercise in 'religious' thinking. Nonetheless,
two questions, at least, need to be asked about his doctrine of
salvation. The first concerns the joyfulness of mystical insight.

The mystic's vision of ultimate reality, we have seen, is a
'pantheistic' vision of the unified divinity of all things. But – the
reader of the preceding nine-tenths of volume I is likely to object –
haven't we already learnt that ultimate reality, for Schopenhauer,
is the 'will', a will that is the personification of *absolute evil*?
Hasn't Schopenhauer indeed picked out pantheism for particular

criticism, on the grounds that, far from meriting the title 'God' – which would turn the empirical world into a 'theophany' (visible manifestation of God) – the essence of things is 'not divine but demonic' (WR II: 349)? And if that is the case, how could an authentic confrontation with ultimate reality produce anything but disgust and despair? Is it not, then, Schopenhauer himself who is in fact committed to dismissing mystical beatitude as mere hallucination?

In chapter 4 we saw how, towards the end of his life, Schopen- hauer deals with this problem: by explicitly distinguishing two senses of 'thing in itself', 'the Kantian thing in itself which is ultim- ate reality, and his own, new sense of the word in which the thing in itself, the 'will', though providing a deeper insight into the world of nature than everyday experience of objects, still, in the final analysis, belongs to the realm of 'appearance'. I called this 'the Schopenhauerian thing in itself' as distinct from 'the Kantian thing in itself'. The distinction between the two allows Schopen- hauer to say that, as a 'deciphering' of the dream from which the mystic finally awakes, the will, too, has, in the end, no reality beyond the dream. Though, to be sure, a deeper account of empir- ical reality than that provided by objectual experience, Book II of *The World as Will*, like all philosophy books, is merely a 'rung of the ladder' on which one climbs to 'insight', a rung one 'leaves behind as soon as it has raised [one] . . . one step' (WR II: 80).[11]

As already noted, in Volume I Schopenhauer has not yet made the distinction between the two senses of thing in itself. But it is, I suggest, already implicitly present in the work, for otherwise, at its 'highest point' it becomes not 'negative' but rather massively and obviously self-contradictory. So what Schopenhauer does, in effect, is unconsciously to 'morph' from one conception of the thing in itself to the other. In Book IV he transmutes what in Book II[12] had been regarded as the Kantian thing in itself into the Schopenhauerian thing in itself.

In Volume II, though he still has not become completely explicit about the distinction between the two senses of 'thing in itself', he in effect deploys it in confronting the question of how, from his point of view, mystical beatitude is possible. Since the 'theme' of philosophy 'must restrict itself to the world' to expressing 'from every aspect what this world is, what it may be in its innermost nature' (WR II: 612; emphasis added; Schopenhauer's emphases omitted), the question of what lies 'beyond the world' ('beyond the world *and consequently beyond the will*' he says quite explicitly at one point (WR II: 642)) is beyond its competence. Philosophy, that is, 'must remain cosmology and cannot become theology' (WR II: 612).[13] Since philosophy, in other words, is restricted to 'deciphering' the fundamental character of the dream, nothing it says can conflict with the claims of the mystic, can provide grounds for dismissing mystical vision as hallucination.

Sometimes, as in the bad-tempered letters quoted in chapter 4 (p. 97 above), Schopenhauer seems to diminish the transcendent by calling it 'cloud-cuckoo-land'. The suggestion contained in such positivistic rhetoric might be that while it perhaps exists, it is uninteresting. But in the seriousness of the meditation on death in the closing pages of the main work there is no such derision. The transcendent is the saving grace, the place of salvation.

* * *

The second question I raised is that of the relationship between the ascetic and aesthetic states. As we have noted, Schopenhauer suggests that, on the subjective side, there is a strong similarity between them. The will-less bliss that is aesthetic delight is a brief anticipation of the perfect equanimity of the ascetic state (WR I: 390). What, however, of the objective side of the two states?

In the ascetic state one becomes free of the will. So, says Schopenhauer, one becomes a 'pure knowing being', an 'unclouded mirror of the world' (WR I: 390). But as we saw in chapter 5, in the aesthetic state, too, one becomes the 'pure . . . subject of knowledge', the 'clear mirror of the object' (WR II: 178). So, one would think, the object of ascetic vision ought to be the same as the object of the (serendipitously same-sounding in both English and German) aesthetic vision. Yet, actually, it seems to be quite different. Whereas the object of aesthetic vision is the *whatness*[14] of the phenomenal world, the ascetic sees through the 'veil of Maya' to an ecstatic vision of transcendent holiness. So why on earth should the two will-free mirrors reflect such different things?

In Schopenhauer himself there is no attempt at all to answer, or even pose, this question. (Like most great storytellers, he often becomes so absorbed in the current phase of the plot as to be completely oblivious to the question of whether what he is currently telling is consistent with what has been told earlier.) The only remark I have to make that bears on the issue is to point out that the two accounts of the state of pure-mirroring are not actually *incompatible* with each other, that they can in fact be combined in an unexpected and fascinating way.

Consider, for example, one of Cézanne's magnificent late studies of Mont Sainte-Victoire (Figure 8.1).

The mountain unmistakably appears free of the distortions of will-ful consciousness. It is no ski slope, no piece of developer's real estate and neither is it a miner's store of bauxite. Appalled by the destruction wrought by the advance of the industrial revolution, Cézanne in creating the work was partly motivated by a desire to record the beauty of this area of the French countryside before it was finally destroyed. The mountain appears in the splendour of its individual whatness, its own unique being-in-itselfness. At the same time, though, as an object, it is to some degree dissolved, 'deconstructed'. (Cézanne is of course the father of cubism and of 'semi-abstract' painting in general.) The brush strokes allow the mountain to become partially translucent so that one sees through the object to the infinite blue depths beyond. In Schopenhauerian terms, the 'veil of Maya' becomes transparent allowing one to see through to the holiness of the (non-'empty') 'nothing' beyond.

Figure 8.1 *Cézanne's Mont Sainte-Victoire*

Following the poet Friedrich Hölderlin, Martin Heidegger speaks of great art as that which, while allowing beings to appear in their unique 'ownness', at the same time 'founds the holy' by allowing objects to become translucent to it.[15] And he finds Cézanne to be a great artist for the reasons I have outlined. Remarkably, the effort to reconcile Schopenhauer's account of the ascetic with his account of the aesthetic generates a new, and partially mystical conception of the latter which comes very close indeed to the Heideggerian conception of greatness in art.

PESSIMISM

The last of the four questions I raised concerning Schopenhauer's doctrine of salvation was the question of pessimism. Is life *really* as terrible as he makes out? Do we really *need* 'saving' from it? In a word, is pessimism really true?

First of all, exactly what *is* Schopenhauer's pessimism? Though he does not clearly distinguish them it actually contains two components, one descriptive the other evaluative.

The descriptive claim is that 'All life is suffering' (WR I: 310). (*Alles Leben ist Leiden* – for short and for the sake of a neat alliteration, *Leben ist Leiden*). In making this claim Schopenhauer does not of course mean that moments of pleasure, happiness, joy *never* occur. His point rather is that when they do they are *exceptions*, that life contains *on balance* (WR II: 576) more – overwhelmingly more – suffering than happiness.

The evaluative inference from this descriptive claim is that life and the world are things which 'ought not to be': 'existence is . . . an error or mistake', 'it would be better for us not to be' (WR II: 605). Life, says Schopenhauer, drawing as he often does on his background in commerce, is 'a business that does not cover the costs' (WR II: 574), something not worth investing in. Though it might seem that the evaluative claim (Schopenhauer's life-'denial') follows from the descriptive as night the day, this is not in fact the case. For there might be reasons for valuing life other than those provided by a calculus of 'satisfactions' and 'dissatisfactions'.[16] Life, that is to say, might be something other than a 'business', a point to which I shall return.

* * *

Why should we believe in Schopenhauer's (descriptive) pessimism? He offers us a large number of arguments. Part of his strategy, it seems, is the shotgun principle – to overwhelm with quantity. Here is a sample.

(A) 'Life is a constantly prevented dying, an ever-deferred death' (just as 'alertness and activity of our mind are a continuously postponed boredom') (WR I: 311).

> At the same time dangers of the most varied kinds threaten [a person] . . . from all sides, and to escape from them calls for constant vigilance. With cautious step and anxious glance around he pursues his path, for a thousand accidents and a thousand enemies lie in wait for him. Thus he went in the savage state, and thus he goes in civilised life; there is no security for him
>
> (WR I: 312).

'Care' (WR I: 197) – anxiety, in other words – is the inescapable undertone to all our existence.

Well, possibly it is. But that doesn't establish that on balance there is more suffering than happiness in our lives, still less does it suggest that non-existence is preferable to existence. Some philosophers – Camus, for example – have even suggested that the sense of living on the edge of the abyss of death actually *increases* life's joys. Others, such as Heidegger, have suggested that it increases the sense of the *meaningfulness* of one's life.

(B) Human beings always live

> in the expectation of better things . . . On the other hand the present is accepted only for the time being, is set at naught, and looked upon merely as the path to the goal. Thus when at the end of their

> lives most men look back, they will find that they have lived
> throughout *ad interim*; they will be surprised to see that the very
> thing they allowed to slip by unappreciated and unenjoyed was just
> their life, precisely that in the expectation of which they lived
>
> (PP II: 285–6).

For we humans, that is to say, 'happiness lies always in the future, or else in the past, and the present may be compared to a small dark cloud driven by the wind over a sunny plain; in front of and behind the cloud everything is bright, only it itself always casts a shadow' (WR II: 573).

Unmistakeable words of wisdom. But they do not, surely, constitute an argument that life is suffering – only that foolish lives are. What Schopenhauer does here is to identify a trap – into which, admittedly, we all too easily fall – a failure in what he calls 'Lebens-weisheit' (literally 'life's wisdom' but better, I think, 'the art of living'). But from the identification of this trap we can learn. Schopenhauer here teaches us something about how to live, not that life is to be rejected.

(C) 'Homo homini lupus,' 'man is a wolf for man,' Schopenhauer tirelessly repeats:

> the chief source of the most serious evils affecting man is man
> himself. . ... He who keeps this . . . clearly in view beholds the world
> as a hell, surpassing that of Dante, by the fact that one man must be
> the devil of another
>
> (WR II: 578).

'Hell', as that latter-day Schopenhauerian Jean-Paul Sartre puts it, 'is other people'.[17]

Well yes, telling words, one feels inclined to say. The human being is indeed a questionable creature. But this is surely only one side of the picture. Relations of loyalty, trust, friendship and love exist too.

* * *

The above arguments are, however, no more than skirmishes, mood-setters, observations designed to make one more receptive to Schopenhauer's real argument for descriptive pessimism. This is an argument rooted in Book II's metaphysics of will, in the claim that the human essence, along with the essence of everything else, is will. I shall call it the 'stress-or-boredom' argument.[18]

The stress-or-boredom argument is made up of three ideas: that willing is suffering, that if willing stops for any length of time the result is boredom, and that if willing stops for a short time the result is a neutral state that cannot make up for the suffering involved in the other two states. I shall now look at the interplay of these ideas in detail.

'All willing springs from lack, from deficiency, and thus from suffering' (WR I: 196), 'from dissatisfaction with one's own state or condition' (WR I: 309; see too 312). It seems that the basic idea here is the logical point that you cannot will what you already have. You can, of course, *desire* or *want* what you already have. (The house cleaner might ask of one of one's possessions 'Can I throw this away?', to which 'No, I want it,' would be a perfectly sensible reply.) But you cannot *strive* for what you already have, and Schopenhauer consistently identifies willing with *action*, with *striving* to achieve a goal; acts of will, remember, are *identical* with actions (see pp. 78–9 above). One can, it is true, strive to *maintain* what one has – good health, for example – but that implies that *security* of possession is something one does not have and is striving to achieve. It seems to me, therefore, that, so far, Schopenhauer is right: the possibility of willing does require the 'lack' of what it is that one wills.

It might be said that dissatisfaction is not the same as suffering, but that misses the point. Schopenhauer's point is that if one is looking for positive value in one's life one will not find it in the state of willing. It is time therefore to turn to the alternative state: the state where one has attained one's goal and consequently is no longer willing. This is where Schopenhauer delivers his second blow to the idea that a happy life is possible:

> The basis of all willing is need, lack, and hence pain, and by its very
> nature and origin it is therefore destined to pain. If, on the other
> hand, it lacks objects of willing, because it is at once deprived of
> them again by too easy a satisfaction, a fearful emptiness and
> boredom comes over it; in other words, its being and its existence
> itself becomes an intolerable burden for it. Hence its life swings like
> a pendulum to and fro between pain and boredom, and these two
> are in fact its ultimate constituents
>
> (WR I: 312).

So the alternative to the suffering of willing is boredom. But boredom is itself a form of suffering, 'anything but an evil to be thought
of lightly: ultimately it depicts the countenance of real despair'
(WR I: 313). If we lived in a 'Utopia' where 'pigeons flew about
ready roasted', says Schopenhauer (putting his finger on the problem with fast food), 'people would die of boredom or else hang
themselves' (PP II: 293).

* * *

What is 'boredom' (or 'depression' as we would likely call it these
days), and why is it as bad as or worse than the suffering of
unrequited willing? Schopenhauer discussed the condition in some
detail, which makes him the first, and almost the last, philosopher
to pay serious attention to a condition fear of which is surely a
major driving force in human life.

As he describes it, boredom has three important features. The
first is perceptual: to the bored, the world shows up as grey, flat,
'dreary' (WR I: 314), 'dead' (WR I: 164). Nothing attracts our
attention, nothing 'interests' us, everything is indifferent, of equal
– which is to say of no – value.

The second feature is what philosophers (Sartre and Camus)
were later to call 'the absurd'. Since nothing has any value, and no
action, therefore, any point, the world and life shows up as a 'game'
(WR I: 164) which, because it is pointless, cannot engage our

interest. Schopenhauer says that in this state existence itself becomes a 'burden'. The result is that we seek to 'kill time' (WR I: 313). We adopt 'trivial motives' which 'are related to real and natural ones as paper money to silver, for their value is arbitrarily assumed' (PP I: 331–2): motives such as card playing, cigar smoking, in general 'rattling and drumming with anything we can get hold of' – for example, drumming on the table with one's thumbs.

In calling such motives 'arbitrary' Schopenhauer's point, I think, is that they are not *genuine* motives. Just as you cannot *choose* to believe that 2+2 = 5 so you cannot *choose* to want to do something. If I choose to interest myself in bridge because I am bored and need to fill up the time, then the fact that it is chosen undermines its capacity to hold my attention. Like beliefs, genuine, interest-holding desires are not things that I choose. Rather, they choose – 'grab' – me. Genuine, wholehearted desires, like genuine beliefs, are things I *discover* rather than invent.

Since nothing genuinely engages one's interest the third feature of boredom is a feeling of – eventually acute – frustration. One experiences the 'pressure of the will', but since it has no 'motive' on which to fix, an 'inner torment' results, the 'pain of longing without any definite object' (WR I: 364).

This is the essential point. When nothing engages one's will it is not the case that one enters a state of will-lessness. The 'pressure' of the will persists. In other words, though there is no state of affairs in the world we will to achieve, we wish that there were such a state of affairs. We experience, in other words (to borrow a phrase from Heidegger), 'the will to will'. Though no first-order willing occurs (willing directed to objects other than the will itself) there is, still, a second-order willing.

This is the crucial – and highly insightful – point in Schopenhauer's analysis of boredom. For several reasons. First, it provides a kind of indirect proof of his foundational claim that the human 'kernel' is will (even when you are not willing you are), that the human essence is 'doing' rather than 'being'. This is surely correct[19] given the truth of Schopenhauer's account of the human mind as something evolved as a thoroughly 'practical' organ (see pp. 28–32 above). For beings such as ourselves, non-action is bound to be a problem. Schopenhauer remarks on the carving of graffiti on famous monuments and the teasing of wild animals in captivity as a sign of this (WR I: 314). One might add recreational fishing. Just *being* on the water is impossible. We need to be killing something too.

The second reason the presence of the 'will to will' as a constituent of boredom is important is that it distinguishes it from the state of aesthetic contemplation into which it would otherwise collapse: in other words, it distinguishes uninterested from disinterested contemplation, distinguishes 'I'd like to manipulate things around but nothing grabs me' from 'I'm interested in the scene before me but have no desire to change anything'.[20]

The third reason the persistence of willing (albeit in a second- rather than first-order form) in the state of boredom is crucial to Schopenhauer's overall argument is that it explains just why boredom is suffering: it is suffering for exactly the same reason that willing is suffering, namely, it is a state in which there is a deep dissatisfaction of the will. Paradoxically, the pain of satisfied willing is of *exactly the same nature* as the pain of unsatisfied willing. Schopenhauer explains that when the pain of boredom becomes extremely intense it leads to acts of hideous cruelty such as those of Nero and Robespierre (WR I: 364). (As we saw in the discussion of malice, there is a strong connection between suffering and cruelty (see pp. 175–8 above).)

Life, then, swings between the two pains. Partly this is a claim about individual psychology. But it is also a sociological claim. On the whole, says Schopenhauer, while 'need and want' are the 'scourge of the people', boredom is the scourge of 'the world of fashion' (WR I: 313; see, too, PP I: 329). Translated into contemporary terms, this amounts to a distinction between the modern West and the fifty per cent of the world's population who live on less than two dollars a day, between the 'first' and the 'third' world. So, if Schopenhauer is right, boredom (under the title of 'depression') is a 'disease of affluence'. That we have become a consumer society, a society given over to 'trivial motives' that do not really grip us, might suggest that he is. (Schopenhauer suggests that the inner vacuity of boredom leads to a craze for society, diversion, amusement and luxury of every kind (PP I: 329). As in the decaying days of the Roman Empire, it leads to the demand for '*panem et circenses* (bread and circuses)' (WR I: 313), a demand which might well seem characteristic of the modern age.[21])

* * *

But of course, as Schopenhauer recognises, want and boredom aren't really the only states available to us. They are just the 'poles'. Surely, then, we can find a way between them, between the Scylla of want and the Charybdis of boredom?

Schopenhauer agrees that we can. Indeed, he thinks that many (middle-class) people do: 'they will, they know what they will, and they strive after this with enough success to protect them from despair and enough failure to protect them from boredom and its consequences' (WR I: 327). The 'happiest life', that is to say, is when 'desire and satisfaction follow each other at not too short and not too long intervals, [which] reduces the suffering occasioned by both to the smallest amount' (WR I: 314).

In other words, if we live wisely we will try to make sure our desires are capable of satisfaction, but will do our best to make sure that we don't stay satisfied for too long before another life-shaping desire comes along.

There are, in short, at least two alternatives to the state of willing: (a) the state in which the satisfaction of all one's major life-shaping desires lasts a long time and becomes boredom and (b) the state in which it lasts a relatively short time on account of the fact that some new project has swept us once more into action. If then we can fill our lives with (b)-type states, states which Schopenhauer calls states of '*satisfaction*, well-being, happiness' (WR I: 309), then, surely, we can live reasonably contented, pleasurable lives. They might be briefer than the states of unsatisfied willing which precede them, but, one might suggest, their intensity may well make up for the pain involved in their pursuit.

* * *

Schopenhauer responds to this suggestion with what I shall call the 'negativity of happiness' thesis. 'Pain', he claims, 'is something *positive* that automatically makes itself known: satisfaction and pleasures are something *negative*, the mere elimination of the former' (BM: 146; see too WR I: 319–20, WR II: 575), a mere 'painless state' (PP II: 287). In other words, even if we are *never* bored and if the periods of painful willing are brief, so-called pleasure can never make up for it since it has no positive value whatever. The 'happi*est*' life is still, on balance, an unhappy one.

Why should we believe the negativity of happiness thesis?

The thesis comes, as Schopenhauer acknowledges (BM: 146), from Plato. But he defends it with a number of observations that are uniquely his own. Possession, he points out, quickly takes away the charm of the possessed (WR I: 146). That to which we are accustomed is no longer felt as a pleasure. The shiny red sports car for which one has scrimped and saved becomes, after a couple of weeks, just 'the car'. Such disillusionment, Schopenhauer observes, is particularly marked in the case of sex: 'everyone who is in love will experience an extraordinary disillusionment after the pleasure he finally attains' (WR II: 540).[22] Experience shows that with the achievement of a long awaited goal (one's first book contract, perhaps) one actually doesn't feel much better than before (WR I: 316).[23] Moreover, since positive happiness does not exist it cannot be a subject of art. This is why, in literature the author presents 'only a strife, an effort, and struggle for happiness, never enduring and complete happiness itself', and why the work 'conducts its heroes to their goal through a thousand difficulties and dangers;

but as soon as the goal is reached it quickly lets the curtain fall'
(WR I: 320). Jane Austen, for example.

Of course, Schopenhauer doesn't really believe that *all* satisfaction of the will is *purely* negative. Though possession of the desired
object, the shiny red sports car, 'quickly begets satiety' (WR I: 313–
14), there is a brief honeymoon period in which positive pleasure is
experienced. His response to this point is fairy clearly: yes, but not
much, not nearly enough to make up for the pain of the corresponding willing.

But then Schopenhauer mentions, with Plato, pleasures which
come 'by themselves':

> All satisfaction, or *what is commonly called* happiness is really
> and essentially always negative only and never positive. It is not a
> gratification which comes to us originally and by itself (*von selbst
> auf uns*)
>
> (WR I: 319; emphasis added).

Following Plato, he cites the pleasures of smell – the sudden scent
of jasmine on the night air, perhaps. And, again in Plato's company,
he explicitly exempts intellectual pleasures from the negativity
thesis (BM: 146).[24]

It seems, therefore, that whereas the negativity of happiness
thesis suggests that we experience just three states – the pain of
willing, the pain of boredom and a neutral state which as such
cannot compensate for the others – Schopenhauer actually acknowledges four: the previous three plus a third state composed, relatively insignificantly, of those 'satisfactions' (as we may call them)
which do establish a little positive credit, but mainly of the pleasures which do not presuppose any preceding state of willing. The
question now is: doesn't the existence of this fourth state, on Schopenhauer's own showing, blow the case for pessimism out of the
water?

* * *

Schopenhauer's reply is that

> What might otherwise be called the finest part of life, its purest joy,
> just because it lifts us out of real existence and transforms us into
> disinterested spectators of it, is pure knowledge which remains
> foreign to all willing, pleasure in the beautiful, genuine delight in
> art[25] [and in intellectual ideas]. But because this requires rare
> talents it is granted only to extremely few, and even to those only as
> a fleeting dream
>
> (WR I: 314).

This looks weak and anecdotal. As Schopenhauer himself points out, the case for pessimism has to be made 'a priori', i.e. rooted in fundamental principles, otherwise 'it might easily be regarded as a mere declamation on human misery . . . and as such . . . charged with one-sidedness' (WR I: 323). It would, that is to say, be vulnerable to the 'beer-glass' objection: the glass the pessimist sees as half-empty the optimist sees as half full. There is no fact of the matter, only 'seeing as', only interpretation, interpretation which tells us something about the interpreter but nothing about the world.

In fact, however, the point about the scarcity of pleasures which come 'by themselves' is not merely anecdotal but is rooted in Schopenhauer's account of the human essence as will and in his evolutionary account of the human brain as *essentially* a 'medium of motives', *essentially* a 'tool' in the service of that will. It follows, as we have seen (pp. 125–7 above), that the person of 'genius' *has* to be, to one degree or another, a freak, 'against nature', a '*monstr*[um]' (WR II: 377). Even in the genius the state of pure knowing has to be an exceptional state rather than the norm – merely a 'fleeting dream'. It is, in other words, a biological necessity that, for most of us most of the time, such minimal happiness as we may achieve is something we have – in the words of the American Constitution – 'pursued', something which comes as a satisfaction of the will (WR II: 634).

Schopenhauer describes the pleasures which come by themselves, the 'pure pleasures' (WR I: 314), as the 'effects of grace' (WR I: 404). They are, in other words, pleasures which we *receive* rather than achieve. Receptivity is a necessary condition of the higher pleasures – and of creativity. But most of us are cut off from them by the irresistible urge to action. Biology forces us to conceive of the *summum bonum* in terms of the satisfaction of willing.

* * *

So should we then accept Schopenhauer's case for (descriptive) pessimism, accept that the human condition is essentially one of suffering? I think not. For right at the beginning the argument contains a fatal flaw.

The basic shape of the argument, to recapitulate, is simply this: willing is suffering, not willing is boredom, so life is suffering. But why does willing have to be suffering?

Schopenhauer argues, we saw, that 'all willing springs from lack' (WR I: 196), i.e. from 'dissatisfaction with one's state' (WR I: 309). Earlier on I defended the first of these statements. I argued that willing really does presuppose a lack, i.e. a non-satisfaction of the will. But is *non*-satisfaction the same as *dis*-satisfaction? Not necessarily.

Suppose I am writing a book, this one for example. I have written eight chapters, but there is one more to go. I am striving to complete the book. But does that require that I am 'dissatisfied' with my present condition? No. On the contrary, I am highly pleased to have (nearly) completed eight chapters.

But, it may be said, you would, surely, *rather* have completed the book and so you *must* be to a degree dissatisfied that you have not yet done so. Well, even if I were somewhat dissatisfied, that would by no means outweigh the satisfaction of having got as far as I have. That is, my state might well still be, overall, one of satisfaction. Actually though, it is not necessary that I experience any dissatisfaction at all. Not perhaps knowing what I will do with my life when I

have finished (and standing, perhaps, in mortal dread of Schopenhauerian boredom) I may well value very highly the state of being
en route to, rather than at, the end. It is better, I may well feel, to travel
than to arrive. So the fatal flaw in the stress-or-boredom argument
is the confusion between non-satisfaction and dis-satisfaction.

Yet in a way, it seems to me, this hardly matters. There is such a
wealth of insight into the human condition contained within its
framework that the question of whether or not the argument is
completely watertight pales into insignificance. Schopenhauer's
failed argument, it seems to me, is worth a thousand successful
arguments by lesser philosophers.

* * *

One final matter. As I mentioned at the beginning of the discussion
(pp. 206–7 above), Schopenhauer's pessimism does not just consist
in the descriptive claim that life is, on balance, suffering, that the
human will is far more often 'dissatisfied' than 'satisfied'. It consists, further, in the inference to the evaluative judgement that life is
an 'error', something it would have been better never to have had,
something to be 'denied'.

If we ask what it is that justifies the inference the answer is that it
is a rather stark form of hedonism: the view that the only thing of
value is pleasure. Schopenhauer's pessimism would then be, in full,
this: life contains much more pain than pleasure; the only thing of
value is pleasure; therefore, life is not worth living. Certainly his
'business' image – 'life is a business that does not cover the costs'
(see p. 206 above) – presents his rejection of life as the result of a
hedonistic calculation, the result of totting up life's pleasures
('profits') and its pains ('costs') and calculating that since the
former outweigh the latter it is worth 'investing' in.

One might well feel doubtful that life can be treated in this way
as a kind of 'business', feel that it is just not possible to assign
numerical values to all of life's experiences. (How, for example, do
you evaluate a brief but very intense pleasure against a long but

very mild pain?) A greater difficulty with Schopenhauer's evaluative pessimism, however, is the hedonistic assumption that the *only* thing we value is pleasure. For there might be other things which we not only value but value more highly than pleasure.

According to Nietzsche, for example, our highest value (at least if we are healthy in spirit) is *meaning*; personal growth or, as he calls it, 'power'.[26] Taking a swipe at Bentham's hedonism – but it could equally well have been Schopenhauer's – Nietzsche says: 'Man does not seek pleasure, only the Englishman does.' What 'man' seeks, rather, is 'meaning'. I shall pursue Nietzsche's critique of Schopenhauer in the next chapter.

SUMMARY

Schopenhauer's pessimism asserts that in this world of pain 'denial' of the will to life, which expresses itself in a 'transition from virtue to [mystical] asceticism', is the 'highest good'. Denial of the will is the path to 'salvation'.

Issues surrounding this thesis

1   By allowing the possibility of denial of the will Schopenhauer contradicts the previously affirmed thesis of universal causal determinism by allowing the occurrence of a kind of miracle.
2   Surprisingly, but in a compelling way, Schopenhauer rejects suicide. It is the product of illusion.
3   What *is* 'salvation'?
    (a) Is it just the equanimity of will-lessness which is anticipated by the will-lessness of the aesthetic state? It is argued to be more than this, since Schopenhauer attributes cognitive insight into a transcendent domain, the 'better consciousness' of his early notebooks, to the mystical ascetic. The mystic is vouchsafed a vision of ultimate reality, something that while 'nothing' to us is not an 'empty' nothing.
    (b) This reveals the fundamental character of Schopenhauer's

entire philosophy: it is, as he says philosophy must be, a 'consolation' in the face of death.

(c) Schopenhauer's doctrine of 'salvation' presupposes, of course, that the 'thing in itself' is not the (evil) will.

(d) The ascetic state looks very like the aesthetic state. Yet while the ascetic sees *through* the 'veil of Maya', aesthetic consciousness dwells on the richness of the 'veil'. These two accounts of the perception which accompanies 'denial of the will' can be combined in a way that anticipates Heidegger's account of greatness in art.

4   Is pessimism true? Is life something we need 'saving' from? Schopenhauer's central argument that life is a choice between the suffering of want and the suffering of boredom, though flawed, is full of human wisdom.

FURTHER READING

J. Atwell, *Schopenhauer on the Character of the World*, chapter 7.

P. Gardiner, *Schopenhauer*, chapter 7.

C. Janaway, *Schopenhauer*, chapter 8.

I. Murdoch, 'Schopenhauer' in *Metaphysics as a Guide to Morals*, pp. 57–79.

Nine

Schopenhauer's Influence and Legacy

Is Schopenhauer a 'great' philosopher? How long a shadow does he cast? I shall try to answer this question by looking at his influence on philosophers, on artists, on Freud and psychoanalysis, and at his influence on currently fashionable, evolutionary approaches to mind and behaviour. Finally, I shall attempt a general remark about what we modern (or postmodern) individuals in general owe to Schopenhauer.

SCHOPENHAUER AND THE PHILOSOPHERS

Schopenhauer never had a paid university post. Moreover, the academy has never really forgiven him for his disrespectful remarks about the 'professors of philosophy'. In not awarding him the prize for his competition essay *On the Basis of Morality* (even though it was the only entry) the Royal Danish Society found itself unable 'to pass over in silence the fact that several distinguished philosophers of recent times [i.e. Hegel – the society was packed with Hegelians] are mentioned in a manner so unseemly as to cause just and grave offence' (BM: 215–6). And so it has continued. There has never been a Schopenhauerian school of philosophers. Until recent years it would have been the exception rather than the rule to find him on the teaching curriculum. Even in the 1980s (as I know from personal experience) it was difficult to find anyone willing to publish a book on Schopenhauer. And even during the writing of this book a distinguished German philosopher (who shall remain nameless) told me, with a slightly rueful grin, that he had never properly studied Schopenhauer (a) because he was too difficult and (b) because he had done a lot of work on Hegel and – well, you know, all those remarks about Hegel. . . .

So Schopenhauer was an academic outsider. It is not surprising, therefore, that those philosophers of significant status on whom he had a direct influence were themselves, in one way and another, outsiders. Friedrich Nietzsche abandoned his professorship of Greek literature at Basle to become a lonely wanderer from one cheap pension to another, Ludwig Wittgenstein was disposed to disappear into remote huts in Norway and obscure primary schools in Austria, and Max Horkheimer was a Jew in Nazi Germany. I shall discuss in turn the relationship in which each of these philosophers stood to Schopenhauer. Since Nietzsche and Wittgenstein have been regularly referred to in preceding chapters, what I shall be concerned to do in their cases is to situate the earlier, isolated comparisons within an overall picture of their relationship to Schopenhauer.

* * *

In 1865 Nietzsche, then a twenty-one-year-old student, discovered *The World as Will* in a second-hand bookshop in Leipzig. As he put it in his *Schopenhauer as Educator*, he found it to be a book 'written especially for me'. A shared reverence for Schopenhauer is what initiated his friendship with Richard Wagner (of whom more anon).

Nietzsche knew Schopenhauer more intimately than any other philosopher. Throughout his career Schopenhauer is his guiding star, first as, in his own words, his 'sole educator' and later as his 'antipode'. In the latter role he is even more important than in the former, since, as Nietzsche himself repeatedly emphasises, it is only in the 'against' that one can discover the 'for', only in fraternal strife with the 'enemy' that one can discover oneself.

Nietzsche's first book *The Birth of Tragedy* (1872) is, like *The World as Will*, preoccupied with the problem of suffering and the question of life's worth it inevitably brings with it. Its subtitle, *Hellenism and Pessimism*, indicates how much Schopenhauer was on his mind.

Like Book II of *The World as Will*, Nietzsche sees the world as the product of a 'primordial unity' or 'will'. But since, as both Schopenhauer and the ancient Greeks agree, the world is a world of suffering (the Greeks, observes Nietzsche, were as alive as Schopenhauer to the 'terror and horror of existence'), what seems to follow is that the world-creating will is essentially evil. How can we possibly live with this knowledge? (Nietzsche confronts this question by asking how the Greeks confronted it.)

As we saw in chapters 4 and 8, Schopenhauer's response to the question is, in the end, to abandon the identification of the will with the (Kantian) thing in itself. The evil will is not ultimate but only, as it were, penultimate reality. Nietzsche, however, has a different idea. What we must do is to abandon, not the identification of the will with the thing in itself but rather the moral point of view from which the will is judged to be evil. We must, that is, as the title of a later book puts it, get 'beyond good and evil'. We must understand the primordial will – which is what we all really are, given that the world of the *principium individuationis* is mere appearance – to be neither good nor evil but rather 'an entirely reckless and amoral artist-god' which creates this world for its diversion and entertainment – a kind of hyper-epic war movie. This is its sole point and justification: 'only as aesthetic [i.e. non-moral] phenomenon is existence and the world . . . justified' (*The Birth of Tragedy*, sections 5 and 24).

What has all this to do with the Greeks? (While writing the book Nietzsche was still a professor of Greek literature and was supposed to be producing a scholarly study of Greek culture.) The answer, he thinks, is that the amoral view of ultimate reality is the Greek view. Thus the 'dark Heraclitus' compared the 'world-building force' to 'a child at play who places stones here and there and builds sandcastles only to overthrow them again' (BT 24) when the whim takes it.[1] And what all this has to do with Greek tragedy, according to Nietzsche, is that though we empathise to some degree with the tragic hero as he undergoes his inexorable destruction, our primary identification is with the Greek chorus whose ecstatic chanting allows us to experience our true identity with the 'primal unity' — think of the Liverpool football terraces singing 'You'll never walk alone'. Tragedy, in other words (Nietzsche argues that the musical dramas of Richard Wagner are a rebirth of Greek tragedy so this applies to them, too), enables us to cope with the 'terror and horror' of life in the world of individuals because it allows us to experience ourselves as the other-worldly *spectator* rather than the this-worldly *bearer* of life's pain.

Schopenhauer's error, then, was neither his bleak description of human existence, nor his attribution of responsibility for the bleakness to a world-creating will. These ideas Nietzsche accepts completely. Schopenhauer's error, as Nietzsche sees it, was his residual Christianity, the fact that for all his rejection of Christian metaphysics, he remained enslaved by the outlook of Christian morality. As Nietzsche puts it later on:

> Against the theory that the 'in itself' must necessarily be good, blessed, true and one, Schopenhauer's interpretation of the 'in itself' as will was an essential step; but he did not understand how to *deify* this will; he remained entangled in the moral-Christian ideal . . . see[ing] it as bad, stupid and absolutely reprehensible
> (*The Will to Power*, section 1005).

The early Nietzsche's solution to the problem of pain and the question of life's worth is in a word, therefore, 'back to the Greeks'. We need to abandon the 'moral-Christian' perspective, to abandon the connection between the divine and (what we take to be) the good.

* * *

This is all very well, and might, perhaps, enable us to avoid condemning the world as ultimately evil. But it still does nothing at all to show that *life as an individual* is worth living. If salvation lies is recognising one's identity with the 'primal unity' then one might as well join it as soon as possible. Life may be justified (though there is surely a big question mark to be set against the idea that we are capable of abandoning the moral point of view) but not my (individual) life.

It is not surprising, therefore, that later Nietzsche adopts a different approach. (Since he had, by this time, abandoned the Kantian–Schopenhauerian idealism on which The Birth of Tragedy is based in favour of an entirely naturalistic outlook, this was mandated on other grounds, too.) As with his earlier philosophy, the central problem is still the Schopenhauerian problem of evil. 'Pessimism' as a description of human life remains true. But this doesn't mean that 'evaluative' pessimism as I called it (p. 206 above) – the judgement that life isn't worth living – follows. For the weak, for those suffering from an 'impoverishment of life', of physical energy (The Gay Science, section 370), it of course does. Being incapable of anything creative, of leading anything but a passive and reactive life, they cannot cope with pain and adversity. But for the healthy, the strong, those 'overflowing with energy that is pregnant with future' (ibid.), pain and adversity are positively welcomed as opportunities for growth and self-development. For the healthy, in other words, something other than pleasure and the avoidance of pain, is the highest value. Nietzsche calls it 'the will to power' or, alternatively, 'growth'. The healthy understand, in other words, that 'whatever does not kill me makes me stronger.'

Nietzsche refers to the evaluative pessimist – his prime examples are Schopenhauer and Wagner – as the 'romantic pessimist'. The person, on the other hand, who unreservedly welcomes life's pain as an occasion for self-overcoming and growth he calls the 'Dionysian pessimist'; that is, the 'Dionysian god and man' (The Gay Science, section 370). Another, more famous, name he uses is 'Übermensch' – 'superman' or 'overman'. When he says, therefore, that Schopenhauer is his 'antipode' what he means is that his Übermensch is the direct opposite of Schopenhauer's – the will- and life-denying ascetic. Without the latter it is unlikely that the former would ever have been born.

* * *

Nietzsche's most fateful legacy is the doctrine he called 'perspectivism' – fateful because (as Alan Bloom argues in *The Closing of the American Mind*) it is the foundational idea of the phenomenon known as 'postmodernism'. In *The Gay Science*, where the term is first introduced, Nietzsche defines it as the view that 'owing to the nature of *animal* [note the biological term] *consciousness*, the world of which we can become conscious is only a surface- and sign-world' (section 354). Perspectivism, that is to say, is the view that 'all existence is . . . essentially actively engaged in *interpretation*', which has the consequence that our human interpretation – which we can never step outside of – is only one of a potential infinity of interpretations (section 374).

The doctrine of perspectivism is, as I say, first introduced in *The Gay Science*. In the same work – and in spite of having come by now to regard him as his 'antipode' – Nietzsche refers to Schopenhauer's 'immortal doctrines of the intellectuality of intuition [and] . . . the instrumental character of the intellect' (section 99). The reference is to what I called Schopenhauer's 'evolutionary idealism' (pp. 28–32 above), his view that the way we perceive the world in ordinary consciousness is determined by the need to survive rather than the desire to know. We see in things what we need for their practical manipulation and no more. As we saw in chapter 5, Schopenhauer himself only considers one alternative perspective to everyday practical consciousness – that of the artist. But fairly clearly, implicit in the idea that need determines world-interpretation is the idea of a potential infinity of such interpretations. Since the needs of a pilot, a farmer and a hunter (not to mention a bat or a gnat) are different, they can, on the basis of Schopenhauer's insight, be expected to lead to world-interpretations that are also, to one degree or another, different. Full-blown, Nietzschean perspectivism is, that is to say, implicit in evolutionary idealism, and can be plausibly assumed to have grown out of it.

A few words about the later history of perspectivism. Nietzsche infers from the phenomenon of multiple interpretations that 'facts are . . . what there is not, only interpretations' (*The Will to Power*, section 481). But this is a mistake. That there are alternative interpretations of reality does not entail that we cannot grasp the *truth* about the world, only that we can't grasp *all* of the truth. That a building is a house of worship *as well as* an architectural monument does not entail that it is *not* an architectural monument – the religious and aesthetic 'perspectives' can *both* reveal a truth about the world. It is this simple mistake which Nietzsche builds – quite unnecessarily – into the doctrine of perspectivism that is really fateful, for in it lie the relativism and nihilism that make postmodernism, as it seems to me, such an intellectually and spiritually destitute phenomenon.

* * *

Nietzsche is generally regarded as the father of 'existentialism', that style of philosophising most commonly associated with Parisian cafés and the figures of Jean-Paul Sartre and Albert Camus. There are various ways of defining existentialism, but the simplest is to say that its concern is with 'existential' issues, issues that arise in and through ordinary life, the most pressing of which is the question of whether life is worth living at all, and if so why. Camus, after all, as already noted (p. 194 above), claims that the question of suicide is the *only* 'serious' question of philosophy.

Nietzsche, to be sure, was concerned with this question above all others. But it was not he but rather Schopenhauer who first placed the issue of the 'ever-disquieting riddle' (WR II: 171) on the philosophical agenda. It is, therefore, it seems to me, not Nietzsche but rather Schopenhauer, who deserves to be regarded as the first existentialist.

* * *

At the end of the first of his two great works, the *Tractatus Logico-Philosophicus*, Ludwig Wittgenstein turns – rather surprisingly, since up to this point we seem to have been reading a book devoted exclusively in issues in logic, metaphysics and the philosophy of language – to existential concerns. The focus of his attention is something he calls 'ethics' (propositions 6.42–6.43). In the pre-paratory notebooks for the work[2] he makes the claim that 'the happy life . . . is the only right life' (NB: 78) which makes it reason-ably clear that that by 'ethics' he means the study of the right i.e. happy way to live. What seems to follow is that being ethical in the more familiar sense of acting properly towards other people will belong to the 'ethical' life in Wittgenstein's sense to, but only to, the extent that behaving well towards others contributes to per-sonal happiness.

Like Freud (of whom more in a moment) Wittgenstein grew up in early twentieth-century Vienna, where Schopenhauer's thought formed part of the background of virtually every cultivated person. Though he does not always reach exactly the same conclusions as Schopenhauer, it is *The World as Will* that provides the medium for Wittgenstein's reflections on 'ethics'.

In what, as earlier noted, is very clearly a meditation on Scho-penhauer's doctrine of 'eternal justice' (pp. 180–1 above) Wittgen-stein writes that

> [w]hen an ethical law of the form 'Thou shalt . . .' is laid down one's first thought is: And what if I don't do it? It is clear, however, that ethics has nothing to do with punishment and reward in the usual sense of the term [It has nothing to do with, in Schopenhauer's terminology, 'temporal justice']. So our question about the *consequences* of an action must be unimportant. – At least those

consequences should not be events. For there must be something right about the question we posed. There must indeed be some kind of ethical reward and punishment, but these must reside in the action itself.

(And it is also clear that the reward must be something pleasant and the punishment something unpleasant.)

(Tractatus proposition 6.422)

What are these rewards and punishments that are not 'consequences' but reside — as Schopenhauer's doctrine of the identity of tormentor and tormented holds — 'in the action itself'? The only relevant comment Wittgenstein makes is the somewhat mysterious

If the good or bad exercise of the will does alter the world, it can alter only the limits of the world, not the facts . . . In short the effect must be that it becomes an altogether different world. It must, so to speak, wax and wane as a whole.

The world of the happy man is a different one from that of the unhappy man

(Tractatus proposition 6.43).

This waxing/waning metaphor irresistibly recalls the expansion/ contraction metaphor Schopenhauer uses to contrast the world of the altruist with that of the egoist. Schopenhauer says, to repeat, that while egoism

concentrates out interest on the particular phenomenon of our own individuality, and then knowledge always presents us with the innumerable perils that continually threaten this phenomenon, whereby anxiety and care become the keynote of our disposition,

altruism

extends our interest to all that lives. . . . [so that] through the reduced interest in our own self, the anxious care for that self is

attacked and restricted at its root; hence the calm and confident
serenity afforded by a virtuous disposition and a good conscience.

The altruist, Schopenhauer says, lives 'in a world of friendly phenomena' while the egoist 'feels himself surrounded by strange and
hostile phenomena (WR I: 373–4).

That Wittgenstein's waxing/waning metaphor so strongly
recalls Schopenhauer's expansion/contraction metaphor makes
it look as though Wittgenstein's person of 'good will' is the
Schopenhauerian altruist and the person of 'bad will' is the
Schopenhauerian egoist. In fact, though, I think, only the second
half of this equation holds. What Wittgenstein really means by the
'good exercise of the will' is a version of asceticism, of Schopenhauer's 'denial of the will'.

Reflecting that 'there is no logical connexion between the will
and the world which would guarantee it', Wittgenstein concludes
that '[e]ven if all that we wish for were to happen, still this would
only be a favour granted by fate, so to speak' (*Tractatus* proposition
6.374). Nothing guarantees us against frustration and pain, nothing guarantees that what we will to happen will actually happen. So
the life of willing is likely to be a life of suffering, from which it
follows that the 'ethical', i.e. 'right', i.e. 'happy', life must in some
way represent an escape from the will: 'I can only make myself
independent of the world – and so in a certain sense master it – by
renouncing any influence on happenings' (NB: 73). And only such
independence guarantees happiness: 'The only life that is happy is
the life that can renounce the amenities of the world. To it the
amenities of the world are so many graces of fate' (NB: 81).

What, then, is happiness? Happiness implies 'living in the present' (NB: 74), that is, living 'without fear or hope' (NB: 76). But
what is achieved by such a life? In a later work, the 'Lecture on
Ethics', Wittgenstein mentions the state of mind in which one is
inclined to say 'I am safe, nothing can injure me whatever happens'
as that to which he is disposed to attribute 'absolute or ethical

value'. What he has in mind, in other words, is precisely the absolute equanimity, the immunity to fear and anxiety, the 'ocean-like calmness of the spirit' that is achieved by the Schopenhauerian will-denier (see p. 200 above).

In a word, then, Wittgenstein's account of 'the good exercise of the will' consists not in the life of willing led by the Schopenhauerian altruist but in the transcendence of willing achieved by the Schopenhauerian ascetic. It consists in the renunciation of willing, the renunciation, that is to say, of *striving*. Wittgenstein allows that the happy person can 'want' things (and presumably act with the aim of fulfilling those wants) provided he will 'not be unhappy if the want does not attain fulfilment' (NB: 77). The crucial point, here, seems to be detachment. The 'ethical' person wants and acts, but preserves, always, a 'non-attachment' to those wants.

Wittgenstein's identification of the good will (or 'attitude' (NB: 86)) with the abandonment of willing in the sense of striving explains the *Tractatus*' oracular pronouncement that 'Ethics and aesthetics are one and the same' (proposition 6.421). The *Notebooks* reveal this remark to be the condensation of

> The work of art is the object seen *sub specie aeternitatis* [from the eternal point of view]; and the good life is the world seen *sub specie aeternitatis*. This is the connection between art and ethics. The normal way of looking at things sees objects as it were from the midst of them, the view *sub specie aeternitatis*, from the outside.

This account of art is, of course, a direct repetition of Schopenhauer's account of aesthetic perception as perceiving things not from the ordinary, 'interested' point of view but rather '*sub aeternitatis specie*' (WR I: 179).[3] Schopenhauer, as we saw, regards the aesthetic state as a brief intimation of 'how blessed must be the life of a man whose will is silenced not for a few moments, as in the enjoyment of the beautiful, but for ever' in the life of one who has achieved complete 'denial of the will' (WR I: 390; see pp. 111–12 above).

Following Schopenhauer's line of thought, Wittgenstein has simply identified the two, will-free states.

A final comment on the Schopenhauer–Wittgenstein connection. Most scholars would agree that the metaphysical outlook of the *Tractatus* is thoroughly naturalistic. There is no relegation of the material world to the domain of appearance and hence no affirmation of a metaphysically transcendent domain. This means that Wittgenstein's asceticism cannot be of the mystical, other-worldly type that Schopenhauer admires. It must rather be a this-worldly asceticism, an asceticism of the type which Schopenhauer describes (and rejects) as 'entirely lacking a metaphysical tendency and transcendent end' (WR II: 159). What Schopenhauer is referring to here is Stoicism. So it seems that Wittgensteinian 'denial of the will' amounts to something like Stoicism. It is not a preliminary to one's translation to *another* world but rather a prescription for living a halfway acceptable life in *this* one.

It may be remembered that one of Schopenhauer's sharp-eyed criticisms of Stoicism is that in teaching mere detachment from, rather than the abandonment of, desire it forgets that things to which we become accustomed usually become a necessity. For this reason he prefers the genuine poverty preached by the Stoics' predecessors, the Cynics, and regards Stoicism as a bourgeois debasement of Cynicism (WR II: 155–6; see pp. 35–6 above).

In later life Wittgenstein was inclined to minimise the value of Schopenhauer's philosophy – and hence its value to him. But as is well known, his own life was of a strongly ascetic character: he gave away the fortune he inherited from his industrialist father, and his room in Trinity College, Cambridge is said to have been furnished with nothing but a tin trunk and a deckchair. Given his close acquaintance with *The World as Will* it is entirely possible that he took Schopenhauer's criticism of Stoicism to heart and, in practising what he preached, in attempting to live the 'ethical' life, committed himself to the life of the Cynic.

In theoretical matters, Wittgenstein's later philosophy of the

Philosophical Investigations is very different from – according to many an explicit rejection of – the philosophy of the *Tractatus*. But since his personal life was rather clearly an attempt to live the 'ethical' life as conceived in the *Tractatus*, it seems that in existential matters he did not change his mind. Given that this conception of the ethical life is so strongly influenced by Schopenhauer, it may be said that, in a way, Schopenhauer stayed with him all his life.

* * *

Together with Theodor Adorno, Max Horkheimer (1895–1973) founded the so-called Frankfurt School. As was the case with all members of the school, Horkheimer's 'critical theory' was strongly informed by Marxism, in particular by Marx's critique of capitalist society as a class system that enslaves the masses to the owners of capital. Yet Horkheimer also observed that in spite of the good intentions of figures such as Lenin, attempts to put Marxist theory into practice have always ended up in 'a terroristic totalitarian bureaucracy'.[4] The cause he attributed to Marxist optimism. Marx (following Hegel) was a 'prophet of secular salvation'. He believed in the perfectibility of human society through the institution of a communist state. Since the pot of gold at the end of the rainbow shines so gloriously, all measures of subjection and cruelty towards present individuals carried out in the interests of furthering the 'end of history', seem, to the Marxist optimist, to be justified. Against such crazed 'fanaticism', finds Horkheimer, Schopenhauer's demolition of the Hegelian idea of the possibility of an end of history, his demonstration that suffering will always be with us, that it is inseparable from human existence as such, is a vital corrective. Schopenhauer's 'doctrine of blind will as an eternal [and directionless] force', observes Horkheimer, removes from the world the treacherous gold foil which the old [in particular, Hegelian] metaphysics had given it.' And by doing this, he concludes, he 'exposes the motive for solidarity shared by men and all beings: no need is ever compensated in any Beyond'. Solidarity –

the need for Schopenhauer's ethics of justice (human rights) and compassion – Horkheimer concludes, is grounded in Schopenhauer's therapeutic 'hopelessness'. (Schopenhauer himself makes the explicit observation that whereas optimistic theories which view human beings as the potential 'incarnation of a god' are liable to savage intolerance towards the frailties of actual individuals, pessimistic theories which view sadness and sin as written into the structure of human nature are more liable to lead to compassion towards actual individuals (PP II: 304–5.))

SCHOPENHAUER AND THE ARTISTS

The clarity and beauty of his prose, his unerring sense for the concrete example that is worth a thousand words, his abhorrence of jargon (so important to establishing the mystique of a priestly 'in-group') and his zestful abuse of the great and good in the professorial firmament, have, as observed, placed Schopenhauer beyond the academic pale. On the other hand, these same qualities have made him highly accessible to lay people and in particular to artists. It has been plausibly assessed that Schopenhauer's influence on creative artists of 'the very front rank' surpasses that of any other philosopher since the Greeks.[5] Thus, among major artists who not only praised Schopenhauer but also exhibit a clear debt to him are, to name but a representative selection, Wagner, Tolstoy, Turgenev, Zola, Maupassant, Proust, Hardy, Conrad, Mann, Samuel Beckett and Jorge Louis Borges. The question I should like to pose is: why? Why is it that Schopenhauer's philosophy that has produced such a deep resonance among creative artists?

* * *

Richard Wagner discovered *The World as Will* in 1854 and was, of course, particularly affected by Schopenhauer's philosophy of music. This he clearly read in what I earlier (pp. 153–6 above) called the 'metaphysical' rather than the 'psychological' way, the latter being very much in line with his own earlier theory as expressed in his book *Opera and Drama*. The discovery took place in the middle of writing the music for the *Ring* cycle (the text for the whole cycle had been completed much earlier) and it produced a profound change in the character of the work. Whereas in the earlier part of the *Ring*, in, specifically, *Das Rheingold* and the first act of *Die Walkyrie*, the music is strictly subordinate to the words, in the post-Schopenhauerian part the orchestra becomes the dominant force. In the second and third acts of *Die Walkyrie*, in *Siegfried* and *Götterdämmerung*, there are long passages in which the words become mere vehicles for the music, pure, meaningless sounds – the 'sofeggio' Schopenhauer admired in religious music (see pp. 154–5 above).

Wagner was, however, also powerfully affected by Schopenhauer's general philosophy. Speaking with particular reference to *Tristan and Isolde*, the first opera entirely created after his discovery of *The World as Will*, he writes in a letter to a friend that Schopenhauer's philosophy came to him 'like a gift from heaven'. Its chief idea, he explains,

> the final negation of the desire for life, is terribly serious, but it shows the only salvation possible. To me of course that thought was not new, and it can indeed be conceived by no one in whom it did not pre-exist, but this philosopher was the first to place it clearly before me . . . longing for death, for absolute unconsciousness, total non-existence . . . [f]reedom from all dreams is our only final salvation.

And, of course, the star-crossed lovers in *Tristan* sing at great length of their longing for a return to 'the land of the night', for 'godlike, eternal, pristine oblivion'.

* * *

Tolstoy, who had a portrait of Schopenhauer in his study, began his intensive reading of *The World as Will* after the completion of *War and Peace* in 1869. He was tremendously impressed. To his friend A. A. Fet, whom he persuaded to make the first Russian translation of the work, he wrote:

> You say that he [Schopenhauer] wrote something or other on
> philosophical subjects. What do you mean, something or other? It's
> the whole world in an incredibly clear and beautiful reflection.

A few years later he underwent a major spiritual crisis which
resulted in a turn to asceticism; he abandoned the life of a wealthy
nobleman and landowner, gave up sex, made over his fortune to his
wife (with whom he produced thirteen children), and for the
remainder of his life lived the impoverished existence of the Russian peasant. Like Wittgenstein, in other words, he turned to 'denial
of the will'. It seems unlikely that this was unconnected with his
study of The World as Will.

Turgenev's works are full of Schopenhauerian themes such as the
negativity of happiness and the idea of stress and boredom as the
poles between which life's pendulum swings. Proust, too,
emphasises the idea that happiness is nothing positive but only a
release from pain, while one only has to recall Thomas Hardy's
looming Wessex skies to see how strong is his affinity for Schopenhauerian pessimism.

In the introduction to Joseph Conrad's Letters to R. B. Cunninghame
Graham, C. T. Watts writes: 'Conrad argues that reform is ultimately
futile because human nature is selfish and brutal . . . and because
humanity is in any case destined to perish of cold amidst a mech-
anistic and soulless universe'. And he adds that 'possibly the most
direct literary contribution to Conrad's pessimism was made by
Schopenhauer'. Another of Schopenhauer's admirers, Thomas
Mann, much in Horkheimer's spirit, praises his 'pessimistic
humanity', while Borges, asked by Brian Magee (op. cit.: 389)
why he did not articulate his fundamental vision of the world
replied that Schopenhauer had already done it. If we ask, finally,
what it was that drew Samuel Beckett to Schopenhauer, we need, I
think, look no further than the title of his most famous work,
Waiting for Godot.

Though of course different artists have been attracted to different aspects of Schopenhauer's philosophy the most common theme is what is obviously its most salient feature – pessimism and life-denial. This raises the question of why it should it be that the finest artistic minds of our time have, by and large, found themselves in agreement with such a philosophy. One answer – essentially Schopenhauer's own, as we have seen – is that the artistic 'genius' is a profound seer who (like himself) grasps the timeless essence of the human condition. Another – suggested perhaps by Adlerian psychology – would be that artists are life's cripples, that only those who are wounded and defeated by life turn to art, so that woundedness, desolation, *Weltschmerz*, is the condition out of which art is generally produced. A third answer would view the artist as neither seer nor cripple but as, rather, a kind of barometer of the underlying mood of his or her times. On this view, desolation would be the mood not of the artist as such but of, rather, the post-death-of-God age – the age of waiting for Godot – that we all inhabit. The artist of the present age, it holds, discovers authenticity in a philosophy of pessimism because, as Friedrich Hölderlin puts it, the age of God's 'default' is an age of 'destitution'.

Since this is by no means an exhaustive list of the possible explanations of the modern artist's affinity for pessimism no definitive decision as to the correct explanation can be given. For myself, however, I am inclined to reject the 'seer' view on the grounds, ultimately, that pessimism is a mood rather than a truth, and the 'cripple' view on the grounds that it is based on too narrow a selection of examples. (Though Byron had a club foot, Beethoven was deaf and bad-tempered, van Gogh cut off his ear, Hölderlin went mad and Coleridge was a drug addict, so far as one can tell Chaucer, Haydn and Jane Austen were of ultimately sunny dispositions, while Shakespeare's greatness, surely, is that he is beyond both optimism and pessimism.) This leaves the 'barometer' view; that the *Weltschmerz* of so many artists of modernity (the sense, Carl Gustav Jung admired Schopenhauer for articulating, that 'the ground of the world is somehow not in the best of conditions'[6]) is an indication of the underlying, but mostly unnoticed – repressed – mood of the times.

SCHOPENHAUER AND FREUD

The fundamental themes of Freudianism are sex, repression and the unconscious. Each of these themes, as I will now try to show, figure prominently in Schopenhauer and are treated in a way identical with, or at least somewhat similar to, the way they are treated by Freud.

As we know (p. 66 above), one of Schopenhauer's more challenging theses is that character is innate and unalterable. That does not mean, however, that our lives are always 'in character'. On the contrary, he observes, they are mostly of a 'zigzag' character, lacking grace, coherence and 'solidity'. The reason for this is that, mostly, we don't know what our characters are. We attempt tasks that are, for example, 'too noble' for our characters, we allow our self-image to be determined by others and so commit ourselves to projects for which we have no real aptitude or taste (WR I: 303–5).

The reason most lives are like this is that self-knowledge is very difficult to acquire. And a major reason for this is the need for self-esteem, a need (here Schopenhauer quotes La Rochefoucauld) that is 'cleverer than the cleverest man of the world' (WR II: 210). Because we need to think well of ourselves – because, in Freudian terms, of the 'superego' implanted in us by parental and social training – ignoble desires are repressed, denied admission into 'clear consciousness': 'the intellect is not to know anything about [them] . . . since the good opinion we have of ourselves would inevitably suffer' (WR II: 209–10). This means that we often only discover quite accidentally and belatedly what we really desire and fear. It may, for example, only be a feeling of 'joy not unmixed with shame' on hearing of the death of a relative whose heir we are that acquaints us with a desire we have unconsciously harboured for years (WR I: 210). And it may only be thoughtful reflection on the fact that our accountancy errors are predominantly in our own favour which acquaints us with, not conscious dishonesty, but rather 'an unconscious tendency to diminish one's *debit* and increase one's *credit* (WR II: 218). And it may be only an awareness that seemingly precipitate events are really 'secretly considered actions' ('Freudian slips') which reveals one to have acted on a motive one has refused to acknowledge (WR I: 296).

These passages show that the Freudian idea of repression, together with the correlative ideas of the unconscious as the receptacle of repressed desires and of the superego as creating the need for repression, are all clearly anticipated by Schopenhauer. And so too is the idea that seeming accidents can actually be intentional actions with unconscious purposes.

Another area in Schopenhauer's examination of mental life in which he deploys repression in a manner that anticipates Freud, is his discussion of madness. Madness, he says, is a disease of the memory. The mind, suffering some terrible trauma – sexual abuse by a father, perhaps – eradicates its occurrence from the memory and then, in order to create a convincing continuity, invents fictions to fill the resulting gaps (WR I: 192–3). (In a mild way, Schopenhauer suggests, this process is familiar to all of us. We are all disposed to divert our attention from things that are too painful or humiliating to face. We are all familiar with the 'violent casting out of one's mind' and even with the 'putting into one's head' (WR II: 400–1) that is involved. Madness, in the sense of the term introduced by Hannah Arendt, is 'banal', just an extreme version of what we all do a bit.)

Schopenhauer's final anticipation of Freud concerns sex. Just as Freud holds the real motive for an enormous amount of human action to be unacknowledged sexual desire, so Schopenhauer holds that

> Next to the love of life . . . [sexual desire] shows itself . . . as the strongest and most active of all motives, and incessantly lays claim to half the powers and thoughts of the younger portion of mankind.

It is the ultimate goal of almost all human effort; it has an
unfavourable influence on the most important affairs, interrupts
every hour the most serious occupations, and sometimes perplexes
for a while even the greatest minds. It does not hesitate to intrude
with its trash and to interfere with the negotiations of statesmen
[Monica Lewinsky?] and the investigations of the learned. It knows
how to slip its love-notes and ringlets even into ministerial
portfolios and philosophical manuscripts

(WR II: 533).

Freud acknowledges that all his major ideas had been anticipated by
Schopenhauer but denied that he was in any way influenced. He
asserts, for example, that

The theory of repression I certainly worked out independently [of
Schopenhauer]. I knew of no influence that directed me in any way
to it, and I long considered this idea to be original until O. Rank
showed us the passage in Schopenhauer's *The World as Will and
Representation* where the philosopher is struggling for an
explanation for insanity. What he states there concerning the
striving against the acceptance of a painful piece of reality agrees
so completely with the content of my theory of repression that
once again I must be grateful for the possibility of making a
discovery to my not being well read. To be sure, others have read
this passage and overlooked it without making this discovery, and
perhaps the same would have happened to me if, in former years,
I had taken more pleasure in reading philosophical authors. In
later years I denied myself the great pleasure of reading
Nietzsche's works with the conscious motive of not wishing to
be hindered in the working out of my psychoanalytic impressions
by any preconceived ideas. I have, therefore, to be prepared –
and am so gladly – to renounce all claim to priority in those many
cases in which the laborious psychoanalytic investigations can
only confirm the insights intuitively won by the philosophers.
The theory of repression is the pillar upon which the edifice

of psychoanalysis rests. It is really the most essential part
of it . . .'.

Elsewhere Freud writes that 'Schopenhauer's unconscious "will" is
equivalent to the psychological drives of psychoanalysis' and
praises him for 'reminding human beings in unforgettable words
of the still under-valued significance of their sexual drives.'[8]

Though this seems generous it is in fact almost certainly
disingenuous.

The first point is that in the Vienna in which, like Wittgenstein,
Freud grew up, *everybody*, as already noted, had an at least second-
hand knowledge of Schopenhauer's philosophy and in particular of
his ideas on sex. Partly this was so because people read Schopenhauer, but partly, too, on account of Eduard von Hartmann's *Philosophy of the Unconscious*. Now forgotten, this book by someone who
took himself to be a disciple of Schopenhauer, enjoyed enormous
celebrity in the last quarter of the nineteenth century and contrib-
uted to the process of making Schopenhauer's ideas widely known.

The second point is that in order to 'deny himself the pleasure'
of reading philosophers such as Nietzsche so as to come to psychoanalysis without preconceptions, Freud must have known, at some
level, which philosophers to avoid.[9] In the above passage, in other
words, Freud is repressing his prior acquaintance with philosophy
with the unconscious motive, no doubt, of increasing his own
originality. This psychoanalysing of the psychoanalyst is supported
by F. J. Sulloway's book on Freud[10], which points out that, as a
young man Freud actually attended a seminar in Vienna devoted to
the philosophy of Schopenhauer and Nietzsche.

SCHOPENHAUER AND EVOLUTIONARY VIEWS OF MAN

Forty odd years before the publication of Darwin's *Origin of the Species*
as we have seen (pp. 28–32 above), Schopenhauer identified the
human 'intellect' – i.e. brain – as the 'one great tool' by which a
relatively weak and defenceless animal has managed to survive in a

competitive environment. It follows, he says, that the brain does not present things to consciousness as they are in themselves. Rather, it is 'thoroughly practical in tendency', 'designed exclusively for practical ends', designed, that is, to present things to consciousness in the way that is most efficient for the attainment of 'those ends on the attainment of which depends individual life and its propagation' (WR II: 284–6). So, for example, the bridge over the Rhine appears to the traveller in a hurry as little more than a dash intersecting with a stroke, the chess pieces appear to the absorbed chess player as mere Xs which fulfil a certain role in the game (pp. 108–10 above). In general the representation of things in ordinary consciousness is determined by considerations of utility, not verisimilitude.

Recently this approach to the mind has been revived under the name of 'evolutionary psychology' and has been popularised and presented as something new and revolutionary by Steven Pinker. In his book *How the Mind Works*, Pinker makes the general claim that 'The mind is a system of organs of computation designed [sic] by natural selection to solve the problems faced by our ancestors in their foraging way of life'. And as an example of how this affects our perception of the world he points to the fact that while human beings are very good at distinguishing objectively very similar faces, crumpled balls of paper that are in fact very different in size and structure look the same. Since the general claim is exactly Schopenhauer's and the example one that it would be unsurprising to find in *The World as Will*, it is regrettable that there is no mention at all of Schopenhauer in Pinker's book.

Schopenhauer's pioneering status with respect to the biological study of humanity is, however, even more striking with respect to so-called 'sociobiology'. (The difference, I take it, between sociobiology and evolutionary psychology is that while the former seeks to exhibit various facets of human behaviour as 'adaptive', survival-promoting, the former is interested in the mental structures that explain adaptive behaviour.)

In his book *The Selfish Gene* Richard Dawkins paints a general picture of human beings as 'survival machines' driven around in by their genes. At the fundamental level the competitors in the Darwinian struggle for survival are genes and they control our behaviour so as to maximise their chances of survival. One of Dawkins's celebrated examples of how this affects our behaviour is the alleged contrast between male promiscuity and female fidelity. The explanation is that whereas the genes in the male can propagate themselves every day and can therefore work on the shotgun principle of self-preservation, the genes in the woman can only propagate themselves once every nine months. She/they, therefore, having all their eggs in one basket and needing a defender of the basket, follow and seek to enforce a culture of fidelity.

In his discussion of sex in chapter 44 of volume II (a discussion which is actually much closer to Dawkins than to Freud since it focuses on reproduction in a way Freud does not) Schopenhauer paints a general picture of the sexual urge as the triumph of what he calls the 'will to live of the species' over the self-interest of the individual. Why so much fuss about sex, asks Schopenhauer? Why do we sacrifice wealth, liberty and happiness for the sake of a sudden passion which, with our rational minds, we know will rapidly cool once its object has been gained? The answer is that we are driven by instinct rather than by rational reflection. But what is this instinct? It is, says Schopenhauer, the will of the species performing a 'meditat[ion] on the composition of the future generations'. From this point of view the mysteriousness of sexual attraction – why it is directed to one individual rather than another – becomes explicable. The primary interest of the will of the species, that is, is the health, strength and beauty of the child that will result. So, for example, claims Schopenhauer, short men tend to be attracted to tall women, and on men in general 'a full female bosom exerts an exceptional charm' since 'it promises the new-born child abundant nourishment'.

And then Schopenhauer comes to the promiscuity issue. Here is what he says:

> by nature man is inclined to inconstancy in love, woman to constancy. The man's love diminishes perceptibly from the moment it has obtained satisfaction; almost every other woman charms him more than the one he already possesses; he longs for variety. On the other hand, the woman's love increases from that very moment. This is a consequence of nature's aim, which is directed to the maintenance, and thus to the greatest possible increase, of the species. The man can easily beget over a hundred children in a year, if there are that number of women available; on the other hand, no matter with how many men, the woman could bring into the world only one child in a year (apart from twin births). The man, therefore, always looks around for other women; the woman, on the contrary, cleaves firmly to the one man; for nature urges her, instinctively and without reflection, to retain the nourisher and supporter of future offspring. Accordingly, conjugal fidelity for the man is artificial, for the woman natural
>
> (WR II: 542).[11]

It is really something of a scandal that, as with Pinker's book, *The Selfish Gene* makes no reference at all to Schopenhauer. Dawkins, of course, is no more guilty of plagiarism than is Pinker. But neither did he invent the evolutionary explanation of the alleged fidelity/infidelity contrast. Rather, it was something that had been for a long time 'in the air'. But the person who put it there in the first place, together with the idea of human consciousness as a product of evolution, was Schopenhauer. We can, therefore, speak of him as exerting a seminal, if unconscious, influence on both evolutionary psychology and on sociobiology and as, if not the father, certainly the grandfather of the two disciplines.

SCHOPENHAUER AND US

Greatness is a metaphor of size. Given the extraordinary breadth of Schopenhauer's influence – on, *inter alios*, philosophers, writers, composers, psychoanalysts, sociologists and psychologists – there can be, I think, notwithstanding his academic neglect, no doubting his 'greatness'. Moreover, though I have so far confined my attention to his influence on gifted individuals, it needs to be recognised that, through them, a great deal of his thinking has become part of the natural consciousness of the present age. That there are many interpretations of reality, that God is dead, that life or history has no purpose, that we are members of the *animal* realm (and should accord more rights to our fellow animals), that we are biological organisms so that the human psyche and human behaviour are moulded by evolution, that we are often governed by instincts and by motives which we do not know and of which we would not approve, are all ideas which belong to the taken-for-granted background to our lives. In assessing his stature we need to recognise that a – and usually the – primary source of all these ideas is to be found in Schopenhauer's philosophy.

SUMMARY
Influence on philosophers

1   The mature Nietzsche turned from being a disciple of his 'sole educator' to being his fraternal 'antipode'. The 'superman' is the direct opposite of the Schopenhauerian saint. But Nietzsche always admitted the origins of 'perspectivism' lay in *The World as Will*.

2   In that he first put the question of life's worth on the table Schopenhauer can be regarded as the first Existentialist.

3   Wittgenstein's discussion of 'ethics' in the *Tractatus* is a meditation on Schopenhauer's doctrine of 'eternal justice' and on his account of the aesthetic state. Though later on tending to minimise the significance of Schopenhauer's philosophy,

Wittgenstein's own life was one of Schopenhauerian asceticism.

4   Max Horkheimer, co-founder of the 'Frankfurt School', views Schopenhauer's demolition of Hegelian optimism as a vital deconstruction of the grounds of totalitarian Marxism and sees him as providing the necessary foundation for an ethics of solidarity.

Influence on artists

No modern philosopher has had such a strong influence on artists of the first rank: Wagner, Tolstoy, Turgenev, Proust, Hardy, Conrad, Mann, Beckett, Borges, to name but a few. The common denominator is pessimism and life-denial. If we view great artists as barometers of the mood of their age, we might regard this as telling something about the mood of desolation underlying our post-death-of-God age.

Freud

The unconscious, repression, 'Freudian slips', madness as repression and fictionalisation of the past and the centrality of sex to human life are all Freudian themes clearly anticipated by Schopenhauer. Freud seems to have been disingenuous in, while acknowledging Schopenhauer's priority with respect to these ideas, denying a direct influence.

Influence on evolutionary views of man

Schopenhauer's 'evolutionary idealism' is clearly an early exercise in what is now called 'evolutionary psychology'. And his view of the individual as driven around by 'the will of the species' – particularly in matters of sex – is clearly an anticipation of the 'selfish gene' of 'sociobiology'. He deserves to be regarded as the father, or at least the grandfather, of both disciplines.

FURTHER READING

B. Magee, The Philosophy of Schopenhauer.

ONE LIFE AND WORKS

1 *Minima Moralia*, p. 153.
2 *History of Western Philosophy*, p. 785.
3 *Metaphysics as a Guide to Morals*, pp. 57–89.
4 This is the term used by Fichte and his fellow 'German Idealists' to refer to Kant's 'thing in itself'.
5 In the chapters that follow I shall generally present Schopenhauer's philosophy in its 1844 form, without attending to differences between that and its 1818 version. The exception is chapter 4, where I specifically attend to those differences.

TWO METAPHYSICS: THE WORLD AS REPRESENTATION

1 Schopenhauer's word here is *Erscheinung*, the same word that Kant uses. E. F. J. Payne translates it as 'phenomenon', which is really somewhat too free a translation.
2 More exactly, secondary qualities characterise objects only as 'powers' to cause the experience of redness, sweetness and so on, powers they have solely in virtue of their primary qualities.
3 In the first, 'A', edition of the *Critique of Pure Reason*, Kant defines 'transcendental idealism' as the doctrine that material objects are mere, mind-dependent 'representations', not mind-independent 'things in themselves' (A 369). It is true that in the same passage he is concerned to *refute* a doctrine he *calls* idealism – 'empirical idealism'. But what Kant means by 'empirical idealism' is the doctrine which, taking the concept of an object to be the concept of a mind-independent cause of our experience, and taking it, too, to be impossible to be absolutely certain about what – if anything – causes our experience, concludes that we cannot be absolutely certain that there *are* any material objects. Kant argues that since it is ridiculous to doubt the existence of material objects, we

have to deny them mind-independent status; adopt, in other words, transcendental idealism. If we accept transcendental idealism, objects cannot be doubted since, rather than being the postulated *causes* of our experiences they are nothing more than the *contents* of those experiences. To refute 'empirical' – *epistemological* – 'idealism', he argues, we *have* to adopt 'transcendental' – *metaphysical* – idealism. (See A 366–380).

4 The entire passage discussed in the previous footnote was suppressed in the second edition.

5 As he points out, Schopenhauer persuaded J. C. F. Rosenkranz, the editor of the edition of Kant's collected works that appeared during his lifetime, to present the *Critique of Pure Reason* in the 'beauty and clarity' of the first edition, thereby 'rescuing from destruction [at its author's hand] the most important work of German literature'. Schopenhauer goes on to claim that no one who has read only the second edition can have a 'clear conception' of Kant's teaching, for he has read only a 'mutilated, spoilt, and to a certain extent ungenuine text' (WR I: 435). It is beyond the scope of this book to evaluate Schopenhauer's assessment of the relative merits of the first and second editions. Given, however, that his assessment is what it is, and given that our primary aim is to understand not Kant but rather *Schopenhauer's understanding of Kant*, the presentation of Kant's philosophy in the next few pages is based on the first rather than second edition.

6 Analytic propositions are trivially a priori: since they tell us nothing about the world we know that nothing in the world could possibly disconfirm them.

7 Schopenhauer develops, as we shall see (pp. 37–9 below) a quite elaborate theory of just how the mind goes about this business of construction.

8 This recognition of the struggle for survival was written twenty-odd years before the appearance of Darwin's *The Origin of Species*. The ways in which Schopenhauer does and does not anticipate Darwin will be discussed in the next chapter.

9 The argument leaves unanswered the question of how radical this lack of correspondence is. In the next chapter we will see Schopenhauer suggesting that, in fact, it is very radical indeed, that *material-objecthood as such* is a falsification of reality, a necessary, survival-promoting, falsehood, but a falsehood nonetheless.

10 Kant often speaks as if concepts to which no sensory experience corresponds are complete nonsense: they 'have no meaning at all', are 'entirely without meaning', a 'mere play of the understanding'. But in his ethical philosophy an important role is played by the 'ideas of reason', God, freedom and immortality, to which, he freely admits, no sensory experience corresponds. While such entities can never be objects of *knowledge* they can, he claims, be objects of *belief*,

belief which is, moreover, essential to the ethical life. Such concepts cannot, therefore, amount to nonsense. So the claim that the bounds of sense-experience are the bounds of meaning is best understood as the claim that they are the bounds of 'cognitive' – scientific – meaning, the kind of meaning that could become knowledge. The principle, in other words, is best understood, not as discriminating between meaning and nonsense, but rather between different types of meaning.

11 What this is will be explained on pp. 34–5 below.

12 Schopenhauer on women: they are 'qualified to be the nurses and governesses of our earliest childhood by the very fact that they are themselves childish, trifling and short-sighted, in a word, are all their lives grown-up children; a kind of intermediate stage between the child and the man, who is the human being in the real sense' (PP II: 614–15). Strangely enough, though, when it comes to providing examples of his ultimate hero, the mystical ascetic, Schopenhauer mentions as many women as men.

13 This represents the point of fundamental disagreement between Schopenhauer and the mature Nietzsche. In Zarathustra's parody of the Sermon on the Mount, Nietzsche says 'Blessed are the sleepy ones; for they shall soon drop off' (*Thus Spoke Zarathustra*, Part I 'On the Teachers of Virtue'). Only a philosopher suffering from life weariness, a sick philosopher, Nietzsche holds, would project peace of mind as humanity's highest goal. For him, not peace of mind but rather what he calls 'power' is the highest human goal.

14 But as we saw in discussing 'evolutionary idealism', everyday, practical perception strips things down to their bare instrumental essentials. What Schopenhauer must have in mind, here, in speaking of perception as fully determinate, is perception that has not been touched by the mechanisms of instrumentality. What this might be will be discussed in chapter 6.

15 As we will see, Schopenhauer has a tendency to picture the person of real virtue as a kind of simpleton, a holy fool, someone who *never* reflects, *always* acts intuitively. Though his critique of moral pedantry is, it seems to me, well taken, this is an exaggeration. For there are, clearly, tricky situations such as moral dilemmas (abortion, euthanasia, the distribution of limited medical funds and so on) where it would be a failure of virtue not to think carefully about what action to take.

THREE METAPHYSICS: THE WORLD AS WILL

1 Nietzsche follows him in this, demanding that we 'abjure belief in . . . "substance", in matter, in the earth-residuum and particle atom' (*Beyond Good and Evil*, section 12).

2 Since this applies to scientific as well as common-sense objects it implies that the consciousness-producing entities referred to in the argument for 'evolutionary idealism' (pp. 28–32 above) – brains, nerve fibres, eyeballs etc. – must be considered to have only provisional existence. An account of the genesis of consciousness in the language of *ultimate* science would make no reference to them.

3 A note for scholars. Schopenhauer continues the passage by saying that 'acts of will' – 'I shall *now* pull the trigger' – are not the antecedent causes of bodily action but are, rather, *identical* with them. Acts of will are actions viewed subjectively, bodily movements are the very same actions viewed objectively. It is, however, clear that acts of will are not what is meant by 'will' in the above passage (or in the corresponding passage at FR: 213–4 or at WR II: 196). For since 'will' is the 'inner mechanism' which explains the correlation of 'motives' with 'actions' – i.e. the correlation of motives with acts of will – an act of will is not that which connects motive and action but is, rather, *one of the terms that are connected*. So 'will' in the above passage cannot mean 'act of will'. Hence it cannot mean, as has sometimes been suggested, the 'non-observational' i.e. subjective awareness we have, for example, of raising an arm.

4 Notice that since character is obviously being groomed to constitute the basis of an account of the nature of natural forces Schopenhauer has a strong strategic motive for saying this. The constellation of forces, that is to say, which constitutes the nature – the reality – of a rock never changes. Once a rock always a rock. Later on, when we come to Schopenhauer's philosophy of life, we will see how this treatment of human beings as indistinguishable from other natural things (the treatment of them as 'beings-in-themselves' rather than 'beings-for-themselves' in Sartre's language) gets him into difficulties.

5 In chapter 7 we will see that Schopenhauer's position is actually more complex than this, that while the everyday self is certainly not free there is a metaphysical 'self' that is.

6 Notice that while up to now Schopenhauer has used 'motive' as a quasi-technical term to mean 'informational input', here, most confusingly, he uses it in the familiar way to refer to a desire or willing, to 'the concept of a purpose' (WR I: 533).

7 Schopenhauer treats natural forces such as gravity or electricity as natural kinds, so that to each fundamental force there corresponds an Idea.

8 Written in about 1831, the force of this qualification is to reject, I think, the ontology of traditional Christianity – world, God and devil as separate entities – in which his youthful insight is couched.

9 One can, I think, see a link between Schopenhauer's nature-pessimism and his

advocacy of animal rights. Animals suffer quite enough according to the natural order of things without having their pain increased by human beings.

10 Shortly I shall have something to say about Schopenhauer's relationship to Darwin's *Origin of Species*, which appeared in 1859, the year before Schopenhauer's death. Here, however, a decidedly un-Darwinian element is evident in Schopenhauer's philosophy. Though he seems to accept that it took aeons of time to reach its full realisation, once realised, the system of species is, for him, eternally fixed. So there is no continuous evolution of the species. As my character is innate and unalterable (see p. 66 above), so, too, is the world-will's.

11 Schopenhauer puns, here, on the title of Voltaire's parody of Leibnizian optimism, *Candide*.

12 A very similar passage occurs in Tennessee Williams's *Suddenly Last Summer*, which suggests that Williams may have read Schopenhauer.

13 'Blind' will in the sense of will that is unaccompanied by '*knowledge*' (beliefs and perceptual representations), does not, I am arguing, exist. On the other hand, Schopenhauer often talks of will as 'blind' in the sense of being *unaccompanied by consciousness*. Blind will in this sense certainly does exist – we are often unaware of our true desires – and, as we will see in the final chapter, Schopenhauer deserves great credit for noticing this phenomenon. (Notice that if will without 'knowledge' does not exist but will without consciousness does, there must be unconscious 'knowledge' as well as unconscious desire.) A still further use of 'blind' indicates purposelessness. Sometimes the 'blindness' of the world-will seems to consist in there being no (ulterior) purpose for the sake of which it wills its system of Ideas. There is nothing it wills that system *for*.

FOUR   METAPHYSICS: ULTIMATE REALITY

1 'On Schopenhauer' in *Willing and Nothingness: Schopenhauer as Nietzsche's Educator* pp. 258–65, 259. This 1868 essay, while respectful, is highly critical, particularly of Schopenhauer's claim that the will is the thing in itself. This shows that even in his youth, Nietzsche was by no means slavish in his discipleship to Schopenhauer.

2 The single possible exception here is the remark at WR I: 110 where Schopenhauer says that 'this thing in itself (we will retain the Kantian expression as a standing formula) . . . is . . . will', which might seem to inject a note of caution. Another *apparent* exception is the remark in the 'Criticism of Kantian Philosophy' published together with Volume I in 1818 that though 'will' is the solution to the 'riddle' of the world's nature, it is a solution 'only within certain limits inseparable from our finite natures', so that the metaphysics of

will lies 'midway' between the 'dogmatic' claim to knowledge of ultimate reality made by Kant's predecessors and Kant's own 'despair' of ever knowing anything beyond appearances (WR I: 428). In fact, however, this entire passage was absent from the 1818 edition of the work. It first appeared in the 1844 edition and constitutes, in my view, a highly significant reversal of the views of 1818.

3   This passage was actually published in 1836. But it is worth quoting as a particularly forceful expression of Schopenhauer's youthful view.

4   If Schopenhauer had written in English one could have looked for a linguistic origin of this confusion, noting that emotions, pains, volitions, sensations and so on are just presentations, not 're-presentations'. Unfortunately this trick will not work with the German '*Vorstellung*'.

5   In, to repeat, at least the 'A' edition of the *Critique*.

6   For example in the revisions to the 'Critique of Kantian Philosophy' mentioned in endnote 2 above.

7   Both letter's are quoted in John Atwell's *Schopenhauer on the Character of the World*, pp. 113–15. Before his untimely death John Atwell told me in private conversation that he viewed these letters as essentially confirming the reading of Schopenhauer as *not* claiming the will to be the Kantian thing in itself first proposed by me in chapter 3 of my 1987 *Willing and Unwilling*.

8   Some might prefer to say 'devious' or even 'self-deceiving'.

9   A repetition of the 1824 remark that '*to recognise* [give a name to] the *thing in itself* is a contradiction, because all cognition is [mind-processed] *representation*, whereas the thing in itself means the thing to the extent it is *not*' (see p. 12 above).

FIVE   ART

1   Nietzsche found this idea as revolting as Schopenhauer finds it impossible. He satirises it in *Thus Spoke Zarathustra* (Part I, section 5) with his portrait of 'the last man' who says 'we have invented happiness' and then blinks.

2   Schopenhauer is surely right here. From a Kantian point of view, since he believes in the historical and so temporal nature of ultimate reality, Hegel is not an idealist but a realist. Only in virtue of representing history as moving towards the 'ideal' can he be called an 'idealist', but this is a quite different sense of the word. Since Hegel is generally taken to be its leading representative, this shows how confusing the label 'German Idealism' is.

3   'Schopenhauer' in *Essays of Three Decades*, p. 394.

4   The bottom of the hierarchy, in other words, corresponds to the region of nature where Book II's 'extension' of the will was most problematic.

5 Later taken up in Wittgenstein's *Tractatus* and in P. F. Strawson's *Individuals*.

6 Note that we are speaking, here, of perceptual objects. This phrase should not be confused with the Kantian 'thing in itself'.

7 Notice Schopenhauer's admitting, here, that 'concepts', instrumental concepts, are involved in everyday perception – contrary to the earlier claim that its generation is entirely independent of concepts (see p. 37 above).

8 Note the element of autobiography here (see p. 2 above).

9 Or at least, the additions recede into the background, allowing the 'absolute essence', the being-in-itself of things to appear. In Volume II of *The World as Will*, Schopenhauer speaks of the absolute essences of things appearing 'in addition to' their relative essence (WR II: 372). By 1844 he has seen, I think, that if subjectivity disappears completely, then painters could no longer perceive or represent, for example, knives as knives. The ideal of aesthetic 'objectivity' must, surely, be importantly connected to the birth of 'abstract' and semi-abstract painting.

10 How, one might wonder, does aesthetic 'objectivity' differ from the scientific objectivity of the investigator who pretends to be 'a winged angel's head without a body' (WR I: 99) (see p. 60 above). Precisely because, I think, the latter's objectivity is a pretence. The point of science, Schopenhauer would say, is always technological and that means that its descriptions of things are ultimately subjective, even if unobviously so.

11 Compare p. 34 above.

12 Actually, since, as we will shortly see, Schopenhauer repeatedly emphasises that art is an essentially *perceptual* rather than conceptual, that the concept is, 'eternally barren and unproductive' in art (WR I: 235), had Spinoza really meant what Schopenhauer says he means he would have said 'The mind is eternal insofar as it *perceives* things from the standpoint of eternity'. Schopenhauer is not I think, making a serious effort at Spinoza scholarship but simply borrowing a phrase which he enjoys for its balanced, Latinate elegance.

13 This has a greater appearance of self-evidence in German than in English where, to distinguish them from the 'useful arts' (i.e. crafts), the fine arts are simply defined as '*die schönen Künste*', literally 'the beautiful arts'.

14 Except for the absolute equanimity that is aesthetic delight, of course. That we can experience this emotion in a state of will-lessness means Schopenhauer has to exempt it from the general thesis that emotions are 'modifications' of the will. And in fact, as we are about to see, other emotions, or rather kinds of emotions, are exempted too.

15 This is one of several passages which suggest that Schopenhauer might have made a fine career as a Gothic novelist. For another see WR II: 373–4.

16 'As nature gives the other creatures over/to the venture of their dim delight/ and in soil and branchwork grants none special cover/so too our being's pristine ground settles our plight;/we are no dearer to it; it ventures us.' Part of an unpublished poem of Rilke's discussed by Martin Heidegger in his essay 'What are Poets for?' (see *Poetry, Language, Thought*: 99).

17 Notice that since, for obvious reasons, this cannot be the evil will it must really be the *Kantian* thing in itself. Here, for the first time, is an intimation that, as well as partial idealism, radical, Kantian idealism will also play a genuine role in *The World as Will*.

18 The youthful Nietzsche, in spite of his general admiration for Schopenhauer, believes his account of lyric poetry to be seriously mistaken. In section 5 of *The Birth of Tragedy* he sets out to correct it 'in his [Schopenhauer's] spirit and in his honour.' After quoting at length from the passage in which Schopenhauer talks about the 'mingled and divided' character of the lyric state, Nietzsche says that, in Schopenhauer's account, lyric poetry turns out to be an 'incompletely attained art that arrives at its goal infrequently and only, as it were, by leaps'. Nietzsche's solution is to insist that 'the opposition between the subjective and objective . . . is altogether irrelevant in aesthetics, since the subject, the willing individual that furthers his own egoistic ends, can be conceived only as the antagonist . . . of art'. This does not mean that lyric poetry is impossible, only that Archilochus the artist and 'world-genius' is utterly distinct from 'Archilochus the passionately inflamed, loving, and hating man' who is 'but a vision' of the artist.

This really is 'in Schopenhauer's spirit'. It is a rigid application of his general theory of the aesthetic subject. It seems to me, however, that such rigidity is much inferior to Schopenhauer's own sensitive and nuanced application of the general theory. For, firstly, it misses the dialectical and redemptive quality Schopenhauer correctly perceives lyric poetry to have, misses the way in which transcendence of individuality redeems us from pain, 'deliv[ers] us from willing and its stress'. And secondly, since, on Schopenhauer's unrefined account, the aesthetic subject experiences no emotion other than absolute equanimity, it is impossible to see how, staying 'in Schopenhauer's spirit', Nietzsche can allow the emotions any proper place in art at all.

19 Of course a work intended as propaganda might, for later generations, lose its political relevance and so, as far as its reception is concerned, come to satisfy the Schopenhauerian condition of will-lessness. Moreover, though the political may be the *occasion* for the production of an atwork – Picasso's *Guernica*, for example – it does not follow that political feeling belongs to the state out of which it is actually produced.

20 As Peter Mullen's angry and powerful film *The Magdalene Sisters* (2002) shows, however, one should not exaggerate the value of this training. In the film, the sadistic nun who runs her Irish home for unwed mothers as, essentially, a concentration camp is moved to one small tear-trickle at a screening of the film *The Nun's Story*. But the next day she is driving her inmates to the point of suicide just as usual. (At the time of writing, American Catholics are attempting to have the film – which is based on fact – banned on the grounds that it is 'anti-Catholic'.)

21 It is quite possible that he took this metaphor from Schopenhauer who himself, as we shall see, comments on the 'ocean-like calmness of the spirit' (WR I: 411) of the person of true insight.

22 Nietzsche, in his later works, saw this. In a beautiful section of *Thus Spoke Zarathustra* called 'Before Sunrise', Zarathustra (Nietzsche) experiences himself as 'stand[ing]over everything as its own sky, as its round roof, its azure bell and eternal certainty'.

23 The reference of the 'my' is, to be sure, not to the empirical self. Rather, as we shall see (pp. 178–80 below), it is to the transcendent self, the unitary, supranatural thing in itself which, according to Schopenhauer, we all really are. This however, seems to me to make no relevant difference: the basic movement is to contract into the self, to own and control, rather that to expand, to flow out of the self into something vaster. The same fundamental error is, I think, also present in Kant's account of the sublime. For, like Schopenhauer, he too speaks of the feeling of the sublime as a turning of the tables, a discovering of our 'superiority to nature even in its immensity', of the hitherto vast and terrifying being rendered 'small' in comparison with our authentic selves (*Critique of Judgement*, section 28). This, of course, adds plausibility to the idea that in reading Kant as, at heart, a radical idealist, Schopenhauer was fundamentally correct.

24 The idea that a life spent in the satisfaction of the will, of physical desire, is 'vulgar' comes from Plato who, in the *Republic*, relegates the generators of wealth (the means of satisfying desire) to the 'basest' of the three social classes of his ideal state. Above them are the civil servants and above them the philosopher king. The opinion Schopenhauer implicitly expresses here that 'trade' (his father's profession, of course) is 'vulgar' represents the influence of a educational system founded on the study of Greek and Latin. Some of us still have visceral tastes that have been moulded by such an education.

25 Note the reference to the *Übermensch* ('superman' or 'overman') here, which may quite possibly have influenced Nietzsche's conception of the *Übermensch*. It has been calculated that, contrary to the picture of the Nietzschean superman

as a Nazi storm trooper, over ninety per cent of those cited by Nietzsche as approaching *übermenschlich* status are artists and writers.

SIX   ART (CONTINUED)

1 This is one of the reasons he has for regarding Hegel as a pseudo-philosopher. Whereas the object of knowledge is that which is timelessly the same, Hegel's 'philosophy of history', he thinks, by representing reality as, in its deepest nature, flux or process, denies the possibility of knowledge. Hence Hegel is a kind of sophist (WR II: 443).

2 This may look like an ad hoc device to deal with the problem of portraiture, but actually it is an integral part of Schopenhauer's conception of human character. As we will see in the final chapter, Schopenhauer launches a revolutionary attack on the familiar idea that while others are opaque and difficult to comprehend, everyone is transparent to themselves. In fact, he (correctly) argues, to know one's own character is at least as difficult as knowing the character of someone else, and requires at least as much observation and experience. One of the reasons for this (we will come to a further reason in the final chapter) is that everyone 'finds in himself the tendencies to all human aspirations and abilities, but the different degrees of these in his individuality do not become clear to him without experience' (WR I: 303). Everyone has a bit of the playboy, a bit of the saint, a bit of the artist, a bit of the sadist, and so on, in their character. Even the sadistic nun in *The Magdalene Sisters* has just a touch of compassion (see chapter 5, note 20.) But the particular weighting of all these elements, the particular 'chemistry' – in other words the 'individual idea' that makes me me – is something one has to work long and hard to find out.

3 This means that, for Schopenhauer, there are, in fact, two reasons why most of us achieve aesthetic delight more readily from art than from nature. On the one hand, that things occur within the frame of fiction means that they are placed 'outside the province of things capable of reference to the will' (WR II: 370), makes them more capable of putting us into a state of will-less bliss, makes them more *subjectively* beautiful. On the other hand, since the artist has the freedom to obscure or eliminate the irrelevant and to highlight the essential, they are also more *objectively beautiful*.

4 *The Fire and the Sun* p. 84.

5 Schopenhauer's central interests – sex, death, pain, boredom, the meaning/ meaninglessness of life, the mystical – have traditionally been on Analytic philosophy's proscribed list.

6 Notice, here, once again, Schopenhauer's treatment of the aesthetic image as a 'normal intuition' (see pp. 130–1 above).

7 Reviewing an El Greco exhibition at New York's Museum of Modern Art in 2003, the novelist John Updike observes that whereas the well-fed and well-muscled bodies in Michelangelo's religious paintings render the presence of Christian spirituality problematic, El Greco's 'brush[ing] aside' of anatomical truth, his 'wavery limbs and dwindling heads [which] have less to do with the human body than an *idea* of bodies, whose basic reality lies behind or beyond their appearance' are, in this respect, more successful. In El Greco's *Crucifixion with Two Donors* (c. 1580), Updike observes, there is 'no sense of any pain or muscular resistance, or, as in a Cellini marble sculpture . . . of sagging weight, relaxed in the surrender of death. This Christ spectacularly lives, in a transmaterial realm of blanched flesh lit from within, closely looming skies, and minimal terrestrial traces'; it lives in a 'sublime realm'. (Speaking as one brought up a Protestant, Updike goes on to record his personal dislike of this 'hyper-Catholic', Counter-Reformation spirituality.) (*The New York Review of Books*, vol. L No. 17, November 2003: 14-15.)

8 Great modern artists, of course – Matisse and Picasso, for instance – often cultivate the impression of a sketch in the finished work. But popular modern art increasingly falls into precisely the trap Schopenhauer identifies. One thinks of the Spielbergisation of film, of the way in which 'special effects' exclude the possibility of imaginative engagement on the part of the audience, render it 'gob smacked', passive, a mere *consumer* of (non-) art. And one might think, too, of A. S. Byatt's scandalous (but surely correct) remark that Harry Potter books are for people with no imagination.

9 In other words, something that is 'beyond the will' (WR II: 642).

10 I am not convinced he is right about this. Sophocles' *Antigone*, for instance, seems to me to display precisely the sublime resignation Schopenhauer takes to characterise the supreme works of tragedy.

11 As before we are talking, here, only about the 'in-itselfness' of perceptual objects, not the Kantian 'in itself'.

12 Wittgenstein, in his Schopenhauer-influenced reflections on art speaks of the object of aesthetic attention becoming 'my world' (*Notebooks 1914–16*: 83).

13 See Yuriko Saito's 'The Japanese Aesthetics of Imperfection and Insufficiency', *The Journal of Aesthetics and Art Criticism*, 55:4 Fall 1997: 377-385.

14 See Lydia Goehr's 'Schopenhauer and the musicians: an inquiry into the sounds of silence and the limits of philosophising about music' in *Schopenhauer, Philosophy, and the Arts*: 200–228.

15 The phrase seems such a perfect description of Richard Strauss's narrative tone poems, of *Til Eulenspiegel*, *Don Juan*, *Also Sprach Zarathustra* or *Ein Heldenleben*, that one has to think that, even though Strauss claimed not to have taken him seriously

(see p. 213 of the article cited in the previous note), he, too, was influenced by Schopenhauer.

16 Schopenhauer greatly admired Beethoven's symphonies (WR II: 450), which, since Beethoven would have been relatively 'modern' music for him, suggests that, in spite of his distaste for Wagner and over-valuation of Rossini, he was not a musical conservative.

17 Felix Mendelssohn said that what music expresses is 'not too indefinite to be put into words, but on the contrary too definite' (Letter to Marc-André Souchay, 1842).

18 The full title of Nietzsche's first book, the book written 'in Schopenhauer's spirit and in his honour' (see chapter 5, note 18), is *The Birth of Tragedy out of the Spirit of Music*.

19 A related point is the aforementioned poverty of language for describing the emotions, the fact that, in Mendelssohn's words, the richness of our inner life contains a great deal that is 'too definite' to be put into words.

SEVEN   ETHICS

1 'The Bourgeois Irrationalism of Schopenhauer's Metaphysics' in *Schopenhauer: his Philosophical Achievement*, pp. 183–193, p. 193.

2 Schopenhauer actually suggests that everyone must have a dim intimation that 'he is nature, the world itself', otherwise he would have 'a really lively conviction of the certainty of death', a frame of mind that would approach that of the condemned criminal. (WR I: 281). This claim, however, is vulnerable to the exhaustive detailing, in section 53 of Heidegger's *Being and Time*, of the many devices we have for dimming down the knowledge that death is annihilation, the detailing of our 'inauthentic' attitudes to death.

3 In his first book, *The Birth of Tragedy*, Nietzsche, too, speaks of the world as both a place of 'terror and horror' and as the creation of a world-will. We can, however, he suggests, become reconciled to our ultimate identity with the will by abandoning the moral point of view, by regarding it as an innocent child at play, as something, that is, 'beyond good and evil'. (For further details, see the discussion of Nietzsche in chapter 9.) Amoralism such as this, however, is something of which Schopenhauer is incapable – much, one might be inclined think, to his credit.

4 As we saw (pp. 115–20 above) transcendental idealism plays a genuine role in the discussion of the sublime in Book III. But that, as I suggested, is really a preliminary search, through art, for a consolation in the face of death.

5 Interestingly, Jean-Paul Sartre says the same thing. 'This woman whom I see coming toward me, this man who is passing by in the street, this beggar whom

I hear calling before my window' are normally, for me, mere 'objects', the reason being that their existence as people is 'purely conjectural' (*Being and Nothingness* pp: 252–3). This last remark, which repeats Schopenhauer's remark that 'theoretical egoism . . . can never be refuted by proofs' (see pp. 69–70 above), reveals the origin of both philosophers' reflections. It lies in Descartes discovery in the fourth of his *Meditations* that there is no way he can prove that those other beings 'in hats and coats' are anything more than cleverly constructed robots. There is, however, a difference between what one might come to think after philosophical reflection and 'the natural standpoint'. And concerning the latter, I think the Schopenhauer–Sartre view is extremely dubious. Although newborn babies may experience themselves in somewhat the way Schopenhauer suggests, adults, surely, do not. Compare, for example, standing naked in a room full of computers with standing naked in a room full of people. The dramatic contrast shows that in 'natural', everyday experience we actually are aware of a sharp difference between people and things.

6 A word on 'ethics' versus 'morality'. Like many philosophers, Schopenhauer often uses the words interchangeably. But sometimes he is more careful. Thus at WR II p. 589 he says that his essay *On the Basis of Morality* is concerned with 'morality in the narrower sense'. This implies, I think, that, carefully used, 'ethics' covers a broader field than 'morality'. Since, as we have just seen, the supreme principle of morality is concerned exclusively with how I should act towards others, 'ethics' is concerned with how I should act in general. It is this more careful use of 'ethics', I think, which is employed when Schopenhauer describes Book IV as an 'ethical book' (WR I: 272). For what it contains, in addition to a discussion of 'morality', is an account of personal 'salvation' (the topic of the next chapter), an account which does not have an obvious 'moral' dimension to it.

7 One would expect Schopenhauer to establish this claim by pointing out that self-interested action is not always selfish action. Eating, for example, is self-interested but usually does not harm anyone else's interests. In fact, however, what he says is that while refraining from helping others in need may well be 'cruel and diabolical' it is not 'wrong', i.e. is 'right' (WR I: 339). Since cruelty is clearly morally wrong, all 'right' can mean here is 'not the sort of thing the state should legislate against'. Schopenhauer seems, at this point, to have fallen into a confusion between moral and political theory. The confusion, however, serves to reveal the, as we would call it these days, 'neo-liberal' character of Schopenhauer's political theory. Since his view entails that the state cannot enforce taxation of the rich to alleviate the suffering of the poor, he is opposed to social welfare. It is thus consistent with his political theory that, in his will,

he left a legacy to the widows of the soldiers who had put down the workers' uprising in Frankfurt in 1848.

8 Later on, thinking of asceticism, he adds a fourth – desire for one's own 'woe' (WR II: 607 footnote).

9 The same unusual use of 'end in itself' occurs at WR I: 381–2.

10 As mentioned earlier (chapter 5, note 20), in Peter Mullen's movie *The Magdalene Sisters* even the sadistic mother superior is moved to one small tear at a screening of *The Nun's Story*.

11 This is about all Schopenhauer agrees with in Kant's ethics. Though Kant is his great hero, the Kantian identification of the good will with conscientiousness, duty for duty's sake, he rejects as completely wrong-headed, the great man's greatest error.

12 Schopenhauer's arguments for pessimism will be examined in the next chapter.

13 As we have seen, 'intuitive' or 'practical' (WR I: 104) knowledge, knowledge 'of the heart' as I called it, is the kind of knowledge that *motivates* one to act. A condition of having such knowledge is that, in appropriate circumstances, you act in the appropriate way, as it is, for example, of 'knowing how' to use a block and tackle. Schopenhauer's stress on 'intuitive' here is intended to make the point that book-learning, 'head' knowledge, is neither necessary nor sufficient for action. As I argued at the beginning of this chapter, however, Schopenhauer is wrong in taking the further step of concluding that 'philosophy *cannot* be practical', that 'virtue *cannot* be taught, that head-knowledge is just *irrelevant* to virtue.

14 'Solipsism' is the view that only I exist. So 'meta-physical' solipsism is the view that only the metaphysical 'I' exists. 'Empirical' solipsism, Schopenhauer's 'theoretical egoism' (see pp. 69–70 above), would be the view that the only 'I' that exists is the embodied, human self.

15 And, one suspects, many a neo-liberal's dream.

16 *Metaphysics as a Guide to Morals*: 63.

EIGHT SALVATION

1 Schopenhauer suggests that, even in the case of the hardened egoist, very intense personal suffering, suffering that casts a pall of pain over the totality of one's experience, can sometimes become a 'second way' in which this moment of insight can be reached (WR I: 392).

2 See M. Nicholls' 'The Influence of Eastern Thought on Schopenhauer's doctrine of the thing-in-itself' in *The Cambridge Companion to Schopenhauer*, pp. 171-212.

3 One might observe, here, that self-mortification can easily be counterproduc-
tive for the ascetic since it itself can become an obscure source of pleasure. St
Theresa of Avila, for example, was forced to ban mutual flogging sessions
among her nuns after she discovered that such sessions had become, for many,
a pleasurable sexual game.

4 Remember that the complete Schopenhauerian altruist treats *everybody* and
indeed *everything* with the same level of concern as himself. Some 'Utilitarian'
philosophers have argued that if one *really* sought to produce the 'greatest
happiness of the greatest number' one would reduce one's economic status to
that of a third-world peasant.

5 The use of this Nietzschean terminology has the advantage of showing why the
later Nietzsche, having decided that Schopenhauer is his 'antipode', spends so
much time attacking 'the ascetic ideal'.

6 Schopenhauer believes that all religions embody great metaphysical and ethical
insights expressed in mythical form. The one exception, however, is Islam. Of
the *Koran* he says (words some will find prophetic, others a cause for jihad),
'this wretched book was sufficient to start a world-religion, to satisfy the
metaphysical need of countless millions for twelve hundred years, to become
the basis of their morality and of a remarkable contempt for death, and also to
inspire them to bloody wars and the most extensive conquests. In this book we
find the saddest and poorest form of theism. Much may have been lost in
translation, but I have not been able to discover in it one single idea of value.
Such things show that the capacity for metaphysics does not go hand in hand
with the need for it' (WR II: 162).

7 Suicide, that is to say, which is a judgement on one's life's worth. Schopenhauer explicitly excludes from the sphere of his concern suicide as a religious
act, as in Hindu widow-burning (PP II: 208), and he would certainly also
exclude *hari kiri* and at least most cases of suicide bombing. He further explicitly
excludes self-starvation as the final expression of will-less asceticism (WR I:
400–1), though this, not being *intentional* self-killing (one doesn't will one's
death but simply fails to will to eat), is, strictly speaking, not a case of suicide.

8 Bluff, commonsensical Dr Johnson's stone-kicking 'realism' about empirical
objects is, remember, 'inborn' in us since it belongs to 'the original disposition
of the intellect' to serve the will (see p. 5 above).

9 This is why Schopenhauer speaks of the 'ocean-like' calmness of the mystical
ascetic (WR I: 411). The 'oceanic' feeling is one of flowing out of oneself so
that one becomes the entire ocean of Being.

10 In *The Birth of Tragedy* – written, remember, 'in Schopenhauer's spirit' –
Nietzsche spells this point out quite explicitly. 'Individuality', he says bluntly,

is 'the source of suffering' (section 10).) Notice that since, for the youthful Nietzsche, the thing in itself is a 'primal unity', and since willing requires plurality, he contradicts himself in calling the thing in itself both 'the primal unity' and 'the will'.

11 This use of image of the ladder to suggest the idea of philosophy as a process of self-transcendence reappears in Wittgenstein's *Tractatus*. 'My propositions', he writes, 'serve as elucidations in the following way: anyone who understands me eventually recognises them as nonsensical, when he has used them – as steps – to climb up beyond them. (He must, so to speak throw, away the ladder after he has climbed up it.) He must transcend these propositions, and then he will see the world aright (proposition 6.54).

12 Save for one queasy moment (see chapter 4, note 2).

13 Notice the use of the word 'theology' where one would expect to find 'metaphysics'. If philosophy *could* speak of what lies beyond the will, Schopenhauer implies, it would speak, with the mystics, of God.

14 Schopenhauer, of course, thinks of the whatness of things in terms of the Platonic Ideas, whereas I suggested (pp. 145–50 above) that, really, it should be understood as the uniquely individual being-in-itselfness of things. I shall persist with the latter understanding. But on the former, too, the apparently glaring discord between the objects of ascetic and aesthetic vision remains.

15 Martin Heidegger: *Gesamtausgabe*, vol. 4: 148; vol. 52: 193.

16 Schopenhauer uses the term 'satisfaction (*Befriedigung*)' to cover all varieties of 'pleasure (*Genuss*)' and 'happiness (*Glück*)' as these are ordinarily conceived (WR II: 575); everything we normally think of as contributing to our 'weal' (BM: 145).

17 In his depressingly titled play 'No Exit', Sartre (at least the early Sartre of *Being and Nothingness*) is actually, it seems to me, an even more thoroughgoing pessimist than Schopenhauer since, as this title indicates, there is, for him, 'no exit' from the 'hell' of human existence save suicide. Unlike Schopenhauer, Sartre (until his later conversion to Marxism) has no doctrine of 'salvation'.

18 I have been aided in my presentation of this argument by Christopher Janaway's fine essay 'Schopenhauer's Pessimism' (*The Cambridge Companion to Schopenhauer*: 318–343).

19 And quite independent of the truth or otherwise of Book II's claim that the essence of *everything* is will.

20 One might wonder, in this connection, whether the virtual disappearance of the disinterested/uninterested distinction from modern speech is a sign that we have become even less capable of just being and looking, of genuine willessness, than in the past.

21 Contemporary German sociologists speak of us as the *Erlebnis Gesellschaft;* literally the 'experience society', a society given over – in its relatively brief work-free moments – to the desperate quest for 'experiences', thrills. Bungee jumping, for example.

22 For more on Schopenhauer's account of sex see pp. 239–44 above.

23 Note how many people, asked to describe the moment of a great achievement – reaching the summit of Everest, being promoted to full professor – speak of 'relief' as the dominant feeling.

24 It is not quite clear why he does this. On pages 329–30 of PP I he speaks of the 'inexhaustible activity of ideas' which protects the thinker from boredom, from the need for trivial distractions and the craze for society – someone of great 'inner wealth' prefers solitude to society. But since there can be intellectual striving and satisfaction just as there can be material striving and satisfaction it is not true that intellectual pleasures always come 'by themselves'. What Schopenhauer must have in mind, I think, is the joy of intellectual *insight* – the joy of having *gifted* to one, rather than struggling towards, an important truth. He writes of his own experience of this gifting in his notebooks: 'What guarantees me the genuineness and hence the everlastingness of my philosophical theses is that I did not make them at all, but that they made themselves. They originated in me entirely without my participation at moments when all willing in me had, so to speak, gone soundly to sleep . . .' (MR III: 229).

25 Schopenhauer means, or at least should mean, here, the 'objective' rather than the 'subjective' form of aesthetic pleasure (see p. 113 above). The reason is that the latter, the pleasure of will-lessness, is, it seems to me, *not* exempt from the negativity thesis. For as we know Schopenhauer describes it as a (merely) 'painless state' that is 'always sought but always escaping us on [the] . . . path of willing' (WR I: 196). So the subjective side of aesthetic pleasure is merely the elimination of a (second-order) willing, the will to escape from willing.

26 There are other things, too, we might value more highly than pleasure, things, indeed, that Schopenhauer himself sometimes seems to value. One is *virtue*. Consistently, that is, he attacks 'eudaemonism' in ethics (WR I: 523, WR II: 151, 159, 443), the view held by, for example, Aristotle, that moral action is justified because, and only because, in the long run it contributes to one's happiness. Eudaemonism is, he holds, self-contradictory, since actions performed for the sake of one's own happiness can have no 'moral worth'. This suggests that for Schopenhauer himself, virtue has a higher value than personal happiness. At another place (WR II: 577) he mentions (without exploring) the idea that someone might value *life* as an 'end in itself'. Someone might, that is, value the having of experience more highly than not having experience *whatever*

the content of that experience. They might value 'being there' over not being there, no matter how much pain it might involve.

NINE   SCHOPENHAUER'S INFLUENCE AND LEGACY

1 Notice that Nietzsche is as anti-Hegelian as Schopenhauer. His affirmation of the child-god's whimsical smashing of sandcastles is a rejection of Hegel's ever-onward-and-upwards account of world history.

2 *Notebooks 1914–16*, hereafter referred to as 'NB'.

3 As earlier observed, Wittgenstein adds that if I study 'the stove' aesthetically it becomes the totality of 'my world' (NB: 83), which strongly echoes Schopenhauer's remark that in the aesthetic state, consciousness becomes 'filled and occupied by a single image of perception' (WR I: 179; see p. 111 above).

4 'Schopenhauer Today' in *Schopenhauer: His Philosophical Achievement* pp. 20–33. All further quotations from Horkheimer are taken from this work.

5 Brian Magee *The Philosophy of Schopenhauer*, pp. 389–90.

6 Quoted in *Über Arthur Schopenhauer*, the final volume of the *Zürcher Ausgabe*, p. 244.

7 *History of the Psychoanalytic Movement*, section I.

8 Quoted in *Über Arthur Schopenhauer*, the final volume in the *Zürcher Ausgabe*, p. 219. Freud is, I think, somewhat misleading in representing Schopenhauer as anticipating his account of sexuality. For as we will shortly see, Schopenhauer's account of sex, tied as it is to reproduction in a way that Freud's is not, is much closer to the sociobiological than to the Freudian view of sex.

9 I owe this point to Christopher Janaway's *Schopenhauer*, pp. 106–7.

10 *Freud: Biologist of Mind*. Sulloway also points out that the notion that children have sexual desires was, in fact, widely accepted in Viennese medical circles, and suggests that Freud greatly exaggerated the shock-horror reaction to his postulation of infant sexuality in order to exaggerate his originality. A comment I would like to add to this is that the Freudian idea of 'sublimation' – the idea that rather than being repressed, sexual desire sometimes finds its way into a diverted form of expression, namely art – is already richly developed in Nietzsche. In *The Will to Power* (section 800), Nietzsche says, for example, that 'making music is another way of making children; chastity is merely the economy of the artist', and there are many other remarks along the same lines. If Freud took repression from Schopenhauer, sublimation came from Nietzsche.

11 Schopenhauer goes on to defend the 'double standard'; adultery is more unforgivable in a woman than in a man since in her case it is 'against nature' (WR II: 542). Since nowhere else does he seek to ground ethics in the 'natural' – 'virtue', as we have seen, is precisely unnatural – this may be an obscure joke.

Bibliography

WORKS BY SCHOPENHAUER

Werke in Zehn Bänden [Zürcher Ausgabe], ed. A. Hübscher, 10 vols. Zurich: Diogenes, 1977.

Der Handschriftlicher Nachlass, ed. A Hübscher, 5 vols. Frankfurt am Main: Kramer, 1970.

Reisetagebücher aus den Jahren 1803–1804, ed. C. von Gwinner Leipzig: Brockhaus, 1923.

Gespräche/Arthur Schopenhauer, ed. A Hübscher Stuttgart: Frommann, 1971.

ENGLISH TRANSLATIONS

On the Basis of Morality, trans. E. F. J. Payne. Providence: Berghahn, 1995.

On the Freedom of the Will, trans. K. Kolenda. Oxford: Blackwell, 1985.

The Fourfold Root of the Principle of Sufficient Reason, trans. E. F. J. Payne. La Salle Ill.: Open Court, 1974.

Manuscript Remains, trans. E. F. J. Payne, 4 vols. Oxford: Berg, 1988–90.

Parerga and Paralipomena, trans. E. F. J. Payne, 2 vols. Oxford: Clarendon Press, 1974.

On the Will in Nature, trans. E. F. J. Payne. New York: Berg, 1992.

The World as Will and Representation, trans, E. F. J. Payne. New York: Dover, 1969.

OTHER WORKS

What follows is a bibliography of works I have referred to or else recommend to those interested in a more detailed study of Schopenhauer. For a comprehensive Schopenhauer bibliography see *The Cambridge Companion to Schopenhauer* ed. C. Janaway.

Adorno, Theodor, *Minima Moralia*, trans. E. F. N. Jephcott. London: Verso, 1978.

Atwell, J. E., *Schopenhauer: the Human Character*. Philadelphia: Temple University Press, 1990.

Atwell, J. E., *Schopenhauer on the Character of the World: the Metaphysics of Will*. Berkeley: University of California Press, 1995.

Bloom, A., *The Closing of the American Mind*. New York: Touchstone Books, 1988.

Camus, Albert, *The Myth of Sisyphus*, trans. J. O'Brian. London: Penguin, 2000.

Cartwright, D., *Schopenhauer: a Biography*. New York: Cambridge University Press, 2004.

Conrad, Joseph, *Joseph Conrad's Letters to R. B. Cunninghame Graham*, ed. C. T. Watts. Cambridge: Cambridge University Press, 1969.

Darwin, Charles, *On the Origin of Species*. London: Wordsworth, 1998.

Dawkins, R., *The Selfish Gene*. Oxford: Oxford Paperbacks, 1989.

Freud, Sigmund, *History of the Psychoanalytic Movement*. New York: Simon & Schuster, 1963.

Fox, M. (ed.), *Schopenhauer: His Philosophical Achievement*. Brighton: Harvester, 1980.

Gardiner, P., *Schopenhauer*. Harmondsworth: Penguin, 1967; reprinted Bristol: Thoemmes Press, 1997.

Hamlyn D. W. *Schopenhauer*. London: Routledge & Kegan Paul, 1980.

Heidegger, Martin, *Being and Time*, trans. J. Macquarrie and T. Robinson. Oxford: Blackwell, 1962.

—— *Martin Heidegger Gesamtausgabe*, ed. F.-W. von Hermann. Frankfurt am Main: Klostermann, 1977 onwards.

—— *Poetry, Language, Thought*, trans. A. Hofstadter. New York: Harper & Row, 1971.

Hume, David, *Enquiries*, ed. L. Selby-Bigge. Oxford: Clarendon Press, 1963.

Jacquette, D. (ed.), *Schopenhauer, Philosophy and the Arts*. Cambridge: Cambridge University Press, 1996.

Janaway, C. (ed.),*The Cambridge Companion to Schopenhauer*. Cambridge: Cambridge University Press, 1999.

—— *Schopenhauer*. Oxford: Oxford University Press, 1994.

—— *Self and World in Schopenhauer's Philosophy*. Oxford: Clarendon, 1989.

—— (ed.), *Willing and Nothingness: Schopenhauer as Nietzsche's Educator*. Oxford: Clarendon Press, 1989.

Kant, Immanuel, *Critique of Practical Reason and Other Writings on Moral Philosophy*, trans. L. W. Beck. Chicago: University of Chicago Press, 1949.

—— *Critique of Judgement*, trans. J. C. Meredith. Oxford: Clarendon Press, 1952.

—— *Critique of Pure Reason*, trans. N. Kemp Smith. New York: St. Martin's Press, 1965.

Locke, John, *An Essay concerning Human Understanding*, ed. J. Yolton, 2 vols. London: Dent, 1961.

Magee, B., *The Philosophy of Schopenhauer*. Oxford: Clarendon Press, 1983.

Mann, Thomas, *Essays of Three Decades*, trans. H. Lowe-Porter. New York: Knopf, 1947.

Murdoch, Iris, *Metaphysics as a Guide to Morals*. New York: Allen Lane/Penguin Press, 1992.

—— *The Fire and the Sun*. Oxford: Oxford University Press, 1977.

Nietzsche, Friedrich, *The Birth of Tragedy*, trans. W. Kaufmann. New York: Vintage Press, 1966.

—— *Beyond Good and Evil*, trans. W. Kaufmann. New York: Vintage Press, 1966.

—— *The Gay Science*, trans. W. Kaufmann. New York: Vintage Press, 1974.

—— 'Schopenhauer as Educator' in *Untimely Meditations*, trans. R. Hollingdale. Cambridge: Cambridge University Press, 1983.

—— *Twilight of the Idols* and *Thus Spoke Zarathustra* in *The Portable Nietzsche*, ed. W. Kaufmann. New York: Viking Press, 1954.

—— *The Will to Power*, trans. W. Kaufmann and R. Hollingdale. New York: Vintage Press, 1968.

Pinker, S., *How the Mind Works*. London: Penguin, 1999.

Plato, *Republic* in *The Collected Dialogues of Plato* ed. E. Hamilton and H. Cairns. New York: Pantheon, 1963.

Russell, Bertrand, *A History of Western Philosophy*. London: Allen & Unwin, 1946.

Safranski, R., *Schopenhauer and the Wild Years of Philosophy*, trans. E. Osers. London: Weidenfeld & Nicolson, 1989.

Sartre, Jean-Paul, *Being and Nothingness*, trans. H. Barnes. New York: Philosophical Library, 1956.

Strawson, P. F., *Individuals*. London; Methuen, 1959.

Sulloway, F. J., *Freud: Biologist of Mind*. New York: Basic Books, 1979.

Tanner, M. *Schopenhauer: Metaphysics and Art*. New York: Phoenix, 1998.

Wagner, Richard, *Opera and Drama*. New York: Best Books, 2001.

White, F. C. *On Schopenhauer's Fourfold Root of the Principle of Sufficient Reason*. Leiden: Brill, 1992.

Wittgenstein, Ludwig, *Tractatus Logico-Philosophicus*, trans. D. Pears and B. McGuiness. London: Routledge, 1961.

—— *Notebooks 1914–16*, eds. G. von Wright and E. Anscombe, trans., E. Anscombe. Oxford: Blackwell, 1969.

—— 'Wittgenstein's Lecture on Ethics' in *Philosophical Review*, vol. 74 (1965).

Young, J. *Willing and Unwilling: a Study in the Philosophy of Arthur Schopenhauer*. Dordrecht: Nijhoff, 1987.

Index

Adorno, Theodor 1, 233
aesthetic pleasure 105–13, 263
aesthetic state 105–13, 123, 144–7,
    196, 264; and ascetic state 204–6,
    231
altruism 67, 159, 165,178–90, 229
art 103–57; Japanese 149; and
    knowledge 133–4; and philosophy
    136–42
asceticism xvii, 7, 145, 158, 166,
    190–4, 196–9, 203–6, 226, 230–3,
    236, 246, 249, 260–3
Atwell, J. 52, 88, 102, 187, 220,
    252

beauty 30–1, 105, 110, 113–14,
    117–18, 121–2, 135–6, 144, 147,
    216, 231, 254–6
Beckett, Samuel: Schopenhauer's
    influence on 236
Beethoven, Ludwig van 139 152, 153,
    237, 258
Berkeley, George 18–19, 26, 33, 47
Bellini, Vincenzo 155
boredom 5, 152, 189, 207 209–18,
    263
Borges, Jorge Louis; Schopenhauer's
    influence on 234, 236, 246

Brahms, Johannes 150
Buddhism xvii, 10, 173, 190–1
Byatt A. S. 257

Camus, Albert 104, 194, 208, 210,
    228
Cartwright, D. 16, 187
causality 59, 62–3, 65, 163–4
Cézanne, Paul 129, 149, 204–6
character 160–8; unalterability of
    192–4
Christianity 53, 79 143, 169, 191,
    224
compassion (Mitleid) 134, 176,
    179–80, 234
concepts 8; and art 136–42, 165;
    criticism of Schopenhauer's account
    of 44–6; and ethics 165–6;
    inadequacy of 42–3; and
    instrumentality 148 253; and
    'normal intuitions' 130–1; origin
    and nature of 39–42; and
    philosophy 158, 165–6; and sense
    experience 33, 36 248–9
Conrad, Joseph: Schopenhauer's
    influence on 236
Constable, John 149
Cynics, the 36, 232

Darwin, Charles 85–7, 241, 243, 248, 251
Dawkins, Richard 243
death 80, 104, 118, 143, 168–73, 200–1, 207, 236, 257, 258, 261

egoism 173–5
El Greco (Domenikos Theotokopoulos) 138, 257
emotion 92, 152, 252–4; and art 114–25; and music 152–6
'eternal justice' 180
ethics 158–87
evolution 5, 45, 86, 216; and genius 126–7; and idealism 28–32 108–10; and perspectivism 226–7; and psychology 241–4
existentialism 227–8

Fichte, Johann 8–9
freedom 160–8
Freud, Sigmund 238–41

Gardiner, P. 52, 88, 157, 187, 220
genius 126–7
Goehr, L. 257
Goethe, Johann 9, 55, 122–4, 139

Hegel 8, 11–12, 33, 46–8, 83, 103–4, 221–2, 233, 252, 255, 256
Heidegger, Martin 24, 30, 105, 110, 166, 206, 207, 211, 220, 254, 258, 262
Hinduism 10, 173, 261
Hölderlin, Friedrich 206, 237
Horkheimer, Max: Schopenhauer's influence on 223–4
Hume, David 33, 34, 35, 174, 179

idealism 17–32; and the sublime 124–5; and immortality 171–3; and 'salvation' 197–203
illuminism 140–2
immortality 168–73
intellectual (rational) intuition 5, 8, 49–51 90–1

Jacobi, Friedrich 8, 33, 46
Jacquette. D 157
Janaway, C. 52, 88, 157, 187, 220, 264

Kant, Immanuel: 53, 86, 131, 248; on art 106–7; on concepts 36–7, 45, 184, 260; on ethics 33, 35, 43, 81 175 178; on freedom 161–2; arguments for idealism 17, 19, 21–5, 30 247–8; on intellectual intuition 49–50; on metaphysics 33, 93–4, 252; influence on Schopenhauer 4–5; on the sublime 115–16, 120, 256
knowledge: intuitive versus conceptual 42–3

Leibniz, Gottfried Wilhelm 81, 95, 151, 153, 159, 251
Liszt, Franz 150
Locke, John 18, 29, 40, 47, 48, 59
Lukács, Georg 159
lyrical, the 124–5

madness 239
Magee, B. 236, 246, 264
Mahler, Gustav 150
Magritte, René 24
Majer, F. J. 9
malice 175–7
Mann, Thomas xvi, 104, 237

matter 58–60
meaningfulness 46–51
Médon, C. 2–3
Mendelssohn, Felix 258
motives 30, 62–76, 83–5, 152, 155,
     163, 165, 175, 192–3, 211, 213,
     215, 239–46
Mozart, Wolfgang Amadeus 155
Mullen, Peter 255
Murdoch, Iris 1, 7, 15, 136, 183, 202,
     220
music 150–6
mysticism 140–2, 179, 186–7,
     197–206, 249, 261

natural forces 56–8
natural science 53–61
Nicholls, M. 102, 260
Nietzsche, Friedrich 2, 4, 15, 90, 132,
     142, 145, 153, 219; Schopenhauer's
     influence on 222–7

opera 153–6

perception 36–9
pessimism 206–19
philosophy 158–60, 165–8
Pinker, Stephen 242
Plato 75, 78; on art 133, 159, 162; cave
     simile 6; influence on Schopenhauer
     6–7; on pleasure 214, 255
Platonic Ideas 129–33
portraiture 134
postmodernism 27, 226
Prokofiev, Sergei Sergeyevitch 150

reason 32–52; and philosophy 140–2;
     practical reason 34–6; theoretical
     reason 36–52

Rembrandt (Harmenszoon van Rijn)
     135
Rilke, Reiner Maria 118, 143, 254
Rimsky-Korsakov, Nikolai Andreyevich
     150
Rossini, Gioacchino 154
Russell, Bertrand 1, 17

Safranski, R. 16
Saito, Y. 25
salvation 195–206
Sartre, Jean-Paul 67, 163, 208, 210,
     251, 258, 259, 262
Schelling, Friedrich 8
Schopenhauer, Arthur: life and
     character 1–16; philosophy of art
     103–57; practical philosophy
     158–220; theoretical philosophy
     1–102
Schopenhauer, Joanna 1
Sellars, W. xvii
sex 2, 215, 239–40, 243–4, 264
Shakespeare, William 67, 131, 139,
     144
solipsism 69–70; 'metaphysical
     solipsism' 180–6, 260
Soll, I. 157
state, the 175
Stoicism 35–6
Strauss, Richard 257–8
Strawson, P. F. 253
sublime, the 115–21, 124–5
suicide 194–5
Sulloway, F. J. 242

teleology 71–4
'thing in itself': Kantian versus
     Schopenhauerian conceptions of 89,
     102

Tolstoy, Leo: Schopenhauer's influence on 235
tragedy 142–6
Turgenev: Schopenhauer's influence on 236

Upanishads 9
Updike, John 257

van Gogh 137

Wagner, Richard 15, 150; Schopenhauer's influence on 234–5

Walter, Bruno 150
will 63–85; denial of 188–94; in inorganic nature 74–6; in organic nature 70–1
Wittgenstein, Ludwig 137; Schopenhauer's influence on 228–33

Young, J. 102

Routledge Philosophy GuideBook to Nietzsche on Morality

Brian Leiter, University of Texas at Austin, USA

'Offers one of the most comprehensive and compelling interpretations of Nietzsche's critique of morality to date. With its distinctive emphasis on naturalistic themes, it forms a very significant contribution to the study of Nietzsche, and is poised to become a work of reference in the field.' – *Notre Dame Philosophical Reviews*

198x129: 352pp
Hb: 0-415-15284-4
Pb: 0-415-15285-2

Routledge Philosophy GuideBook to Kant and the *Critique of Pure Reason*

Sebastian Gardner, Birkbeck College, UK

'This is a quite outstanding introduction to the *Critique* ... It will help students not only to study the *Critique*, but also to see why it is so worth studying ... deserves to find itself, and pretty certainly will find itself, at the very top of the reading list for any course on the *Critique*.'

– *The Philosophical Quarterly*

198x129: 392pp
Hb: 0-415-11908-1
Pb: 0-415-11909-X

Death of God and the Meaning of Life

Julian Young, University of Auckland, New Zealand

'Young is to be congratulated in producing a lively and accessible discussion of some difficult philosophical texts.' – *The London Magazine*

216x138: 248pp
Hb: 0-415-30789-9
Pb: 0-415-30790-2

Tractatus Logico-Philosophicus

Ludwig Wittgenstein

Translated by **David Pears** and **Brian McGuiness**

'Beautifully strange ... an icy, gnomic, compact work of mystical logic.' – *The Guardian*

'Among the productions of the twentieth century the *Tractatus* continues to stand out for its beauty and its power.' – *A.J. Ayer*

198x129: 144pp
Hb: 0-415-25562-7
Pb: 0-415-25408-6